Coming of Age
Around the World

Coming of Age
Around
the World

A Multicultural Anthology

EDITED BY FAITH ADIELE AND MARY FROSCH

THE NEW PRESS

NEW YORK
LONDON

Requests for permission to reproduce selections from this book
should be made through our website:
https://thenewpress.com/contact.

Published in the United States by The New Press, New York, 2007
Distributed by Two Rivers Distribution

ISBN 978-1-59558-080-1 (pbk)
CIP data available

The New Press publishes books that promote and enrich public
discussion and understanding of the issues vital to our democracy
and to a more equitable world. These books are made possible
by the enthusiasm of our readers; the support of a committed
group of donors, large and small; the collaboration of our many
partners in the independent media and the not-for-profit sector;
booksellers, who often hand-sell New Press books; librarians;
and above all by our authors.

www.thenewpress.com

Composition by Westchester Book

Printed in the United States of America

Contents

Contents

Preface

Faith:

When The New Press proposed an international version of Mary's 1994 anthology, *Coming of Age in America*, I was immediately on board. As a writer dealing with identity and global travel, I loved the idea of using fiction and nonfiction stories to explore the processes of growing up and becoming adult in a diverse array of world cultures. And as a teacher and a fan of Mary's book, I had actually designed an entire college course—well received and adopted into the core curriculum—based on it: Coming of Age in America: The Literature of Cultural Identity. Though coming of age is a popular theme in American literature and film, I knew of only one anthology chronicling the quest for identity around the globe. One was certainly not enough, I thought, particularly given our increasingly complex landscape of shifting borders, diasporic communities, national identity crises, and the cultural clash and cross-fertilization that globalization spurs.

Mary:

I was working on a revised edition of *Coming of Age in America* when The New Press contacted me and proposed that I collaborate with Faith on an international coming-of-age anthology. Ironically and coincidentally, I had already chosen a story by Faith to include in my revised *Coming of Age in America*; I was therefore excited to be teaming up with a writer whose work I already knew and admired. My own experience in the classroom had always led me to fiction or evocative memoir, rather than to edgier but sometimes, it seemed to me, dated nonfiction selections that chronicle a particular time and place. Faith had a different perspective about the value and beauty of this kind of writing, and I learned a lot from her about how to read and use selections such as Andrew Pham's imagistic account of a family escaping by boat after the fall of Saigon in *Catfish and Mandala* to teach my students less about themselves and more about lives unlike theirs that they needed to be able to imagine. I caught the Faith bug: I wanted my students to experience the unfamiliar not for the purpose of finding themselves somewhere there, but to appreciate the experience of unfamiliarity for what it is, new, strange, often frightening, and a completely compelling way of reading the way young people live across many borders and latitudes. How, then, to bring our readers with us?

Faith:

One of the worst things about anthologies is also one of the best: they tend to be carefully representative, presenting the same familiar pieces by the usual suspects. That makes them useful from a classroom standpoint and dull from every other standpoint. We knew that we wanted to tread new territory and to showcase innovative writing. First we resolved to pair writers already established in high school and college curricula with fresh voices often famous in their home countries but less familiar to American audiences. Readers will recognize literary giants such as Ben Okri, a Nigerian based in Britain, Korean American Chang-rae Lee, and Rohinton Mistry, a

Canadian émigré from India, alongside recent best-selling authors and new favorites such as Marjane Satrapi, an Iranian living in France, and Guadalupe Dueñas, from Mexico. The nontraditional structures employed by the latter pair—Satrapi's memoir done in the style of a graphic novel with stark black-and-white drawings, and Dueñas' surreal, stream-of-consciousness prose poems—provide a new twist on the *Bildungsroman*.

Another way to keep things fresh and relevant was to focus on recent writing. With some notable exceptions, such as Elisabeth Gille's piece about the Jewish Holocaust, we selected pieces written after 1975, a date we viewed as a watershed in contemporary world history. The last century has been one of rapid and staggering change around the globe, with exponential population growth, the appearance and transformation of new nations due to the decline of European colonial empires and the rise of industrialization, and the feeling that the world is becoming smaller thanks to increased international trade and technology, which are arguably leading to the creation of a single world culture. The end of World War II, with the formation of the United Nations, the creation of Israel, and independence movements across Africa, Asia, and the Middle East, signaled the first step. Next came the events of the mid-seventies that helped create the world we know today: the end of the Cultural Revolution, the death of Chiang Kai-shek in Taiwan, and the arrival of mainland China, the world's most populous country, on the world stage; the end of the Vietnam War, the triumph of Communism throughout Southeast Asia, and the flood of the boat people; the discovery of oil in Nigeria, the world's most populous black nation and Africa's largest democracy; civil war in Lebanon and the shift toward Islamic fundamentalism in the region; and the rise of the women's movement, the Supreme Court decision in *Roe v. Wade,* and the beginning of the UN Decade for Women. In the midst of this ferment, we also saw efforts to create a sense of global

community: the UN Earth Summit held in Brazil to increase international efforts to preserve the earth's natural resources, and the
Helsinki Accords, which established North American and European
standards of peacekeeping and human rights. Given all this, we
wanted stories that reflected contemporary moods and concerns, and
in many cases the narratives serve a secondary purpose of providing
readers with an insider's view into the critical events that shaped our
modern world.

A number of challenges and issues presented themselves as we
compiled this anthology. First and most practical was the issue of
language. Since, for logistical reasons, we'd decided to limit ourselves
to already-published selections, we were forced to work with authors
who either wrote in or had been translated into English. UNESCO
calculates that a mere 6 percent of world literature has been translated into English and distributed in the United States. This shock-
ing statistic guarantees that any American anthology can never claim
to be representative of the global experience. (One of our greatest re-
grets was the dearth of translated material from Brazil, the largest
country in South America.) It also raises any number of questions
that cannot be adequately addressed here, such as the politics of who
gets translated, whose stories get written in the first place, and our
ability to assess foreign literary aesthetics. As we Americans are often
charged with ethnocentrism, a criticism carrying serious political
ramifications, we wanted to produce a volume that was accessible
while still pushing the boundaries of American literary experience.
Other than the surprising surrealism of Yu Hua's Chinese countryside, the Arab- and French-influenced stream of consciousness used
by Albert Bensoussan and Patrick Chamoiseau, respectively, or the
Guyanese patois Oonya Kempadoo employs in her talk-story of
sexual and gender politics, the works we have selected will not appear alien so much in aesthetics as in cultural content. In addition

to satisfying humankind's innate hunger for narrative, stories are one of the oldest and best ways to learn about one another.

A second logistical concern was that of representation. Any anthology is automatically charged with the mission of thoroughly representing its topic, but if we wanted people to be able to lift our book, how could we hope to be comprehensive? Initially we divided the world into six regions (Middle East/North Africa, sub-Saharan Africa, Asia/Oceania, Caribbean/Latin America, Europe, and North America); however, there is still great diversity within these designations, nearly fifty countries in sub-Saharan Africa alone. And then almost all countries can be further broken down by regional identification, religion, language or ethnic group, race, gender, class, sexual orientation—the list goes on. The mobility of contemporary life and the multiplicity of social identities additionally complicate the issue of "assigning origin." For example, how to place someone such as Alexandra Fuller, born of Anglo-European parents, raised in southern Africa, and now writing from the United States? How to categorize a story written by Victor Perera, a Jew of Latin American heritage raised in Guatemala and writing from California? Do we know enough, and is it useful or misleading, to assign identity? And even if we had sought such a paint-by-numbers approach to representation—dangerous because stories then run the risk of being read as ethnographic artifacts delivering the final word on a particular culture—no matter what we did, someone was going to get left out.

Interestingly, our most significant challenge concerned the premise of the collection itself, begging the question of whether coming of age is a particularly Western concept. Initially we expected to distill those aspects of adolescence and young adulthood that are universal; however, the challenge of defining the genre to international writers revealed the cultural bias imbedded in coming-of-age literature.

The Western *Bildungsroman* follows a standard arc: the individual experiences a moment of self-realization, often precipitated by crisis or hardship, and the self is first fractured and then re-formed. Perhaps the popularity of this trope is fueled by our lack of traditional age-marking ceremonies in the West, or in the American case by the cult of individuality. Rather than going out with our agemates to kill a lion, we go on a road trip and, through encountering a wacky cast of characters, learn a little about ourselves. Whatever the allure of the *Bildungsroman*, this process is not necessarily applicable to the rest of the world.

With this in mind, we set out to explore a number of questions, some of which can only be scratched on the surface here: What does coming of age look like within traditional, communal societies where group identity, not individual identity, is valued? In these societies, is coming of age a process of self-discovery or more a matter of rites and rituals marking a public transition from child to adult? Does adolescence exist in all societies, and if not, when does coming of age occur? Globalization and the porous nature of borders and identities problematize these questions. We hope with this anthology to contribute to a broadening definition of coming of age.

In the end, we decided to organize the anthology into six themes. Three of them, Family, School Days, and Self-Discovery, are traditional categories that appeared in *Coming of Age in America*, though they manifest differently on the global stage. For example, Zimbabwe's Charles Mungoshi complicates the notion of family by exposing the politics of a polygamous household; Martinique's Patrick Chamoiseau challenges our understanding of education through a child's experience of being schooled, as much of the world is, in a foreign/colonial tongue; on self-discovery, Lebanon's Hanan al-Shaykh provides an all-too-rare poor, rural, female voice from the Arab Muslim world.

Another traditional coming-of-age category, Meeting the Other, takes on new meaning within the shifting borders of the modern world. In stories such as Albert Bensoussan's account of how gender and religion challenge the friendship between a Jewish boy and an Arab girl occupying the same contested territory in Algeria, the individual coming-of-age process is analogous to and acts as a metaphor for the coming of age of an entire community. It is our hope that later editions of the book could include the testimony from places such as Rwanda, Sudan, and Bosnia that is now just appearing. The crises in these countries, fueled in part by conflicting national narratives, make a case for the political importance of stories.

In two cases, we had to create entirely new categories. Displaced Childhood (Growing Up on Foreign Soil) and In the Shadow of War both consider the impact of history and politics on the development of the self. For example, how does migration (both voluntary and involuntary) shape the quest for identity? How do the specifics of cultural hybridity and multilingualism play out in the cohesive creation of self? How does coming of age occur—or does it?—when childhood is interrupted by survival concerns in the face of war, famine, or being orphaned? Some of our favorites in these categories include David Bezmozgis' account of social hierarchies and coping mechanisms within a Russian émigré community and Colum McCann's tale of how the long-standing conflict in occupied Ireland filters down through families.

These six categories, obviously both limited and overlapping, are but a jumping-off point for what we hope becomes an ongoing conversation about the quest for identity around the globe. We have provided introductory notes detailing the literary and historical context of each author and story. Themes and regions aside, in the end we chose stories that charmed or delighted, touched or haunted us, tales that taught us something about the human condition that transcended border and culture and whose characters and mastery of language demanded to be shared with a larger audience. With both the threat of a single world culture and the political ramifications of polarized narratives, it is now more important than ever that North Americans assume the challenge of taking literary voyages into the unknown.

Acknowledgments

Like many a good journey, this book has been a long road, with numerous folk offering direction along the way. I am deeply indebted to old friend Bennett L. Singer, my original co-editor on the project, who first brought me into The New Press fold and generously shared his research once other responsibilities demanded his attention. I am grateful for the time and intellect that my friend Geeta Kothari was able to devote before other responsibilities spirited her away as well (it's not me, really!). Not only did she find a number of our best stories, but the introduction really took shape under her innovative vision. And I am most thankful for Mary, who joined late in the race and hit the ground running, bringing with her intelligence, dedication, organizational skills, and considerable expertise. I couldn't have asked for a better partner.

Many thanks are also due Dr. David Bartholomae for encouraging me to take time off to work on the book; Hedgebrook and the Willard R. Espy Foundation for providing a room of one's own in beautiful Washington settings to do the work; our editor, Ellen Reeves, and all the staff at The New Press who produce such important books; and David Deschamps and Kristen Cosby for additional research.

Lastly, thanks always to my mother, Holly, who filled our house with books and music and art and food from around the world, and then, when the time came, let me set out to come of age.

Faith Adiele

This journey for me began with a phone call from Ellen Reeves. I am indebted, then, to Ellen and to The New Press for bringing me into this project and introducing me to Faith Adiele. Though I was familiar with Faith's work, I could not know in those early months what she would bring to my own conception of what this anthology should mean. While we didn't always agree on every selection at first, I soon began to place my trust in Faith's taste and judgment. Under her guidance, I learned to appreciate the importance of many different kinds of visions, and with Faith's unerring instinct for stories that yielded a different and important view, I expanded my own reading and teaching experience.

Nothing I do is uninformed by my colleagues in The Spence School English and World Literature Department, past and present. They are addicted to books of all kinds and to an endless stream of discussion about these books. Many thanks especially to Sandor Weiner for introducing me to David Bezmozgis' work.

The voice in my head for too many years to remember is Michele Krauthamer's. Nor can I ignore the voices of my beloved aunt, Alice Woodrow, my late mother, Jane Leighton Calvin, and my mother-in-law, Annette Frosch, the women who read.

Last, thanks are always due to my three most favorite writers in the world, Thomas, Daniel, and Jonathan Frosch. Without their inspiration, the high standards that they hold me to and model for me every day, and their abundant love, I would be nothing.

Mary Frosch

Coming of Age
Around the World

Displaced Childhood

(Growing Up on Foreign Soil)

FROM *SHADOWS*
OF A CHILDHOOD
Elisabeth Gille

TRANSLATED BY LINDA COVERDALE

*This excerpt, Chapter VI from Elisabeth Gille's autobiographi-
cal novel* Shadows of a Childhood: A Novel of War and
Friendship, *forms part of the main character's terrible discovery: that her glamorous parents, having left her three years before, will not be returning. Hidden in a Catholic boarding
school/convent in Bordeaux during the Nazi occupation of
France, Léa Lévy does not realize and cannot accept that her parents, taken to Auschwitz during a roundup of Bordeaux Jews,
will not emerge now that the war is over. The Hôtel Lutétia in
Paris, overrun by ghostly concentration camp survivors, many of
whom will last no longer than a few more weeks, does not seem a
likely place for young Léa to find her parents, but that's where,
clutching her precious box of beads and Sister Saint-Gabriel's
hand, Léa learns a horrible truth in a terrifying way.*

   *A French editor and author who died in 1996, Gille was the
daughter of Irène Némirovsky, a bourgeois Jewish Russian émigré
who arrived in Paris in 1919 to escape the Bolshevik Revolution,
the second stage of the Russian Revolution when the more radical
Bolsheviks took over from the liberal Mensheviks after they both*

had overthrown the czar in 1917. A successful author herself,
Némirovsky found acceptance in the literary salons of the extreme
Right, especially after she and her husband, Gille's father, con-
verted to Catholicism. The reality of the collaborationist Vichy
regime, the French government sympathetic to the Germans after
France's surrender to Germany in 1940, together with the be-
trayal of those Némirovsky considered her friends made her reex-
amine, too late, her Jewish identity. Némirovsky managed to
write the recently published Suite Française, *two novellas dealing*
with Nazi-occupied France, before perishing with her husband in
a Nazi concentration camp. The mystique of her parents contin-
ues to haunt Léa Lévy in Gille's novel. By opening her novel with
the word "No," Gille reclaims her heritage. As David Walton in
his New York Times *review of the book says, Gille's "theme in*
Shadows of a Childhood *is refusal—the refusal to forget or to*
cease struggling against indifference, denial, lies."

Shadows of a Childhood *follows in the tradition of the non-*
fiction novel, in the manner of Harper Lee's To Kill a Mock-
ingbird, *where the characters and events are thinly veiled*
representations of actual circumstances. You may wish to com-
pare this excerpt with the other selections in this section, espe-
cially the excerpt from The Devil That Danced on the Water:
A Daughter's Quest *by Aminatta Forna, also about a young*
girl's response to a deeply distressing separation from her parents.
It can be compared as well to "On the Road at Eighteen" by Yu
Hua, about a boy whose coming-of-age grand tour of China re-
veals a world reduced to the single truth of his own existence.

The Hôtel Lutétia wasn't far, according to a woman passing by;
they could easily walk there. On the way they passed the Lycée

Victor-Duruy. The trees in the school garden showed off their spring foliage over the surrounding wall. White flowers rained down from the tall chestnuts, their branches stirred by the occasional breeze. School was letting out, and students were pouring from the gate, flocking together in chattering groups. When they caught sight of their mothers, the girls would run off to join them, swinging their book satchels, their hair flying in the wind, dappled by sunshine and shade. The young women in their tight-waisted suits and hats with little veils would hasten forward, dainty purses waltzing in the crooks of their arms, stocking seams painted perfectly straight on the backs of their carefully stained calves. They leaned down to kiss their daughters, tenderly straightening a collar, tightening up a loose braid, flicking away a shred of tree bark, taking the heavy satchels from their hands as the girls turned around one last time to wave endless goodbyes to their classmates, as if they would never see them again. Still wearing the same worn and faded navy blue skirt that had long ago lost any trace of a pleat, her frizzy hair haphazardly pinned back by two big barrettes, Léa walked by the girls without giving them a single glance. She was too busy clutching the enormous box, which kept slipping in her grasp, and she paid no more attention to the school children than she had to the revelations of the concierge.

"My feet hurt," she grumbled after a few minutes' walk. "Is it still far away, where we're going?"

"I don't think so," replied her companion, who was afraid of getting lost and stopped at every intersection to rummage through her big black briefcase, put on her glasses, and look up at the street signs.

"What kind of hotel is it?"

"A very fancy one, it seems."

"Ah," said Léa, quickening a pace that had begun to flag. "Then my parents might be there. If that horrible concierge wouldn't let them into their apartment, they must've had to find someplace to put their things before coming to get me in Bordeaux. They really like luxury hotels. Papa took me to the Plaza one day," she added after a moment, as though struck by a distant recollection. "He picked me up and sat me down on the bar to introduce me to the bartender. He even let me have a sip of his cocktail," she added excitedly. "I remember Mama scolded him when we got home."

She fell silent and seemed lost in her memories for the rest of their walk.

After going up the Rue de Sèvres and turning onto the Boulevard Raspail, as she'd been told to do, Sister Saint-Gabriel soon realized she'd found the right place when she spotted the people massed before the hotel. It was a strange group, she saw as she drew closer: mostly old men and women, some of whom had babies in their arms. The crowd was listless, apathetic. Children slept curled up right there on the sidewalk. Almost all the adults were thin and shabbily dressed, and they held signs on which names were scrawled in big, uneven letters, next to tiny identification photos that were indecipherable from half a yard away. It was clear from their rumpled clothes and tired faces, from the way they let their clumsy, handmade signs droop toward the ground, that they had been waiting for a long while and had come there many times before. Some were all hunched over, their hands buried in their pockets, as though they felt cold despite the delightfully warm air. With Léa in tow, Sister Saint-Gabriel joined the throng. When she tried to question her neighbors, she encountered only silence and indifference.

The crowd came abruptly to life when two buses with red crosses on their sides and roofs pulled up in front of the hotel. People held their signs straight, craned their necks, closed ranks, murmured to one another. Children awoke, rubbed their eyes, scrambled to their feet. Finally, the rear doors opened. Stretcher bearers hurried into the hotel, as though trying through such haste to protect their charges from prying eyes. And yet there didn't seem to be anything beneath the brown blankets draped across their stretchers. All whispering died away. Then about fifty men in striped pajamas appeared, deathly pale, gaunt, wearing caps that could not conceal their shaven skulls. They crossed the sidewalk with infinite slowness, shielding their eyes with their hands as if to ward off the radiant sunshine. The crowd, which had parted to let the stretchers through, now shuddered violently and hurled itself forward like a wave, shrieking, calling to the newcomers, screaming out harshly resonant names that sounded like stones tumbling against one another in the rising tide. The new arrivals shrank back. A woman in a threadbare coat, too warm for the season, fell at the feet of one shuffling man, threw an arm around his knees, and with her other hand forced the little girl with her to shove a roneograph photo under her captive's nose.

"Adam Zylberstein!" she wailed in a strong foreign accent. "He's tall, a big man, with curly brown hair. He delivered bolts of cloth for a wholesale clothing manufacturer. He was picked up in Belleville, in June of '42. Do you know him, monsieur? Have you seen him anywhere?"

Thrown off balance by her attack, the man had caught hold of a comrade's shoulder to keep from falling. He freed himself with a convulsive movement of his whole body, a true gesture of repulsion, and walked on, without even looking at the leaflet the child was waving in front of his face. The woman collapsed on the sidewalk and just sat there, her arms hanging limply. Taking advantage of the dejection that had settled once more over the crowd for a moment, Sister Saint-Gabriel cut ahead of the entire line, dragging Léa along by the collar of her blouse as the child gripped her box tightly in both hands. They managed to slip through the hotel door barely an instant before it closed. As Sister Saint-Gabriel was gagging on the odor of disinfectant that immediately stung their nostrils, she received a cloud of DDT sprayed directly in her face by a uniformed nurse stationed just inside the door. Blinded by tears, half-strangled by coughing, she wiped herself off with a fold of her skirt. It was some time before she could see again.

In that huge lobby, the only things that corresponded to Sister Saint-Gabriel's idea of a deluxe hotel were the walls covered with gilt moldings and the ceiling with its tinkling chandelier. This vast space had been divided into small cubicles, each one furnished with two chairs and a wooden table at which sat people of various ages, in civilian clothes, interviewing the visitors. The partitions separating these improvised offices were completely covered with photos like those being brandished by the throng outside. Dozens, hundreds, thousands of names and faces seemed to jump out at the nun: men in suits and ties gazing solemnly into the camera, smiling women with babies on their laps, boys in their best clothes, little girls wearing starched dresses and big bows in their hair. There was even an entire class lined up on benches, sitting with their hands quietly folded, grouped around their teacher. The captions overlapped one another, as if in a desperate hurry to speak. "Have you seen, encountered, heard about . . . Can you give me any news, good or bad, regarding . . . my parents, my husband, my wife, my son, my daughter . . . picked up in Paris, Bordeaux, Marseille . . . in '42, '43, '44 . . . last seen in Drancy, Pithiviers, Beaune-la-Rolande . . . left on convoy number 10, 25, 58 . . . for Buchenwald, Ravensbrück, Auschwitz . . . Sincere thanks, large reward, eternally grateful . . ." Had half the French population disappeared, then—leaving behind only these faint traces, these fading pictures and names so full of consonants—while the other half was trying frantically to find them? Sister Saint-Gabriel was well aware that people had been shot, imprisoned, deported, but was it possible that *thousands*, and perhaps more, had been torn from their everyday lives?

She was reassured by a solitary poster tacked up on a nearby panel. It showed, from the back, two men helping a third man: they were all in striped pajamas and all walking, beneath a blue sky, toward a typically French church steeple glinting in the morning sunshine. "Political prisoners, deportees, labor conscripts," said the text. "If you have witnessed an act of cruelty during your detention, or any action contrary to the rules of war as laid down by the Geneva Convention, report it to your local police station. The guilty will be punished." So there were still laws, policemen to enforce them, victims and criminals. One had only to appeal to the responsible authorities, and order would eventually be restored. Sister Saint-Gabriel turned toward a little cubicle, one with an empty chair, but in doing so she noticed, lined up along a wall, the stretchers that had been unloaded from the bus outside only moments before. She had thought they were empty, and she had been wrong. A skull with black eye sockets, bony temples, protruding teeth, and cheeks devoured by stubble had just risen up, all by itself. The nun reached out instinctively to shield Léa from the sight, but the child simply pushed her hand away impatiently.

"Sister, what are we doing here? Let's go! I want to show my beads to Bénédicte."

"What are you talking about, Léa? You know perfectly well we're here to find your parents."

"But they're not here!"

"How can you be so sure of that?"

Putting her precious box down on the floor, setting it on edge between her calves to make sure she wouldn't lose it, Léa pointed all around her at the immense room: skulls sitting on their stretchers, cut off cleanly at the neck by brown blankets lying flat on the canvas; groups of detainees in striped pajamas, staggering, drunk with exhaustion; a nurse tending to a skeletal woman in a black dress three times too big for her, collapsed on a chair like a sack of bones; famished-looking visitors jostling one another in front of the bulletin boards, craning their necks to inspect every scrap of information; the sick, pale and drawn, returning from their X-ray examinations with envelopes tucked beneath their arms; doctors in white coats making their way through the crowd, their stethoscopes bouncing gently on their chests. And the nun was suddenly struck by the fact that despite the great press of people and activity, all this was going on in remarkable silence.

Léa gave a quick, silvery laugh, drawing a look of surprise from the elderly lady in a navy blue suit sitting at a table covered with papers in a nearby cubicle, the one with the empty chair.

"Why do you think my parents might be here?" asked Léa. "If they were back, they'd certainly have gone to get me before coming here to help all these poor people."

Sister Saint-Gabriel simply stared at her.

"But, well, Léa," she said finally, choosing her words with care, "don't you think they might themselves be among these unfortunate souls?"

This time the child burst out laughing.

"Oh, Sister, it's obvious you don't know my parents! They don't look anything at all like these people. You never believe me when I tell you that my father is very handsome, very elegant, and that my mother . . . Well, my mother would never, ever wear a dress like the one that woman over there has on."

And Léa pointed with a little wince of disgust at the shapeless black bag enveloping the pile of bones slumped on a chair.

"You always suspect me of boasting when I talk about them. I know that, but you'll see when they come back, you'll see."

So saying, she picked up her box and clutched it to her chest, pursing her lips like someone who has given up trying to get an absolute dummy to admit something that's as plain as day. Sister Saint-Gabriel shrugged and put her hand on the back of the child's neck to guide her over to the cubicle with the empty chair.

The elderly woman listened to the nun's story of the Lévys and their daughter without interrupting, as though she already knew it by heart, merely jotting a few things down in a notebook. When the nun had finished, the woman handed her a form.

"If you would just fill this out, Sister, and give us the child's identification papers, we'll be able to place her in an institution. She doesn't remember the existence of other members of her family, you say? Still, who knows whether an aunt or uncle or cousin might not turn up one day after all. Thank you, in any case, for everything you've done for her."

"But we can easily keep her in our school until her parents arrive," replied Sister Saint-Gabriel. "I only came here to try to find them more quickly and to leave you our address, so that they'll know where to find her when they do return."

The old lady sighed.

"Léa," she said, without looking up at the child, "why don't you take a little walk around the hotel? You'll find some very lovely furniture to look at. And you must be hungry, too. So just go into the dining room, over there. They'll give you something to eat. We have a few administrative problems to settle, this nun and I. If you stayed with us, you'd be bored. Come back in about fifteen minutes."

Léa, who was indeed bored, did not need to be asked twice. As soon as she had trotted off, the old lady looked up again.

"Sister," she said, "I don't think you've fully grasped the scope of the catastrophe. If the parents of this child were Jews, if they were deported to Auschwitz, on the dates you've given me—during 1942, in other words—then there is every reason to believe they will not be coming back."

"Do you think they're being held in Russia? I've heard rumors about that . . ."

"I think they're dead."

"But they were . . . I mean, they're young, healthy, there's no reason why they wouldn't have survived conditions in the camps, even if they were hard, as they claim. I've heard that several thousand Jews were deported. Really, they can't all be dead."

"As far as we know, almost eighty thousand left: men, women, and children. As of now, a few more than two thousand have returned. If the survivors' stories are to be believed, there is little chance of us seeing many more come back."

Aghast, the nun collapsed against the back of her chair, mopping her brow.

"So just fill out these forms, Sister," continued the woman, "even if you do intend to keep looking after the child. She'll be needing these papers, if only to obtain her parents' death certificate. I'll leave you to it. I'll be back for them in a few minutes."

In the meantime, still lugging around her box of beads, Léa was looking for a place where she could comfortably eat the chocolate bar and piece of bread she'd been given in the dining room. There she'd seen trays being prepared, loaded with appetizing dishes, nicely presented, and bottles of wine with old labels. This led her to think she might have been mistaken about the quality of the hotel and that if she followed one of the Lutétia's liveried staff up the imposing red-carpeted staircase she saw before her, she would find people who were different from that wretched humanity swarming in the lobby. And what she saw upstairs seemed to bear this out.

The landing gave onto a long corridor that turned several times at right angles. Big pearl-gray doors framed with moldings in a darker shade lined the walls. The man in livery pushed open one of the doors, and Léa had just enough time to notice a large, richly furnished room, although she couldn't manage to catch a glimpse of its occupant. She began by visiting the rest rooms, where the marble sinks and gilded faucets made an excellent impression on her. Yes, her parents might very well have chosen this hotel as a place where they would stay and rest after their long trip, before taking the train again for Bordeaux. Perhaps her father was here, busy tying his tie in front of the mirror, while her mother was powdering her nose, sitting on a little mahogany chair that matched the dressing table, like the ones she'd just seen a moment ago. An image—like those fleeting, incomplete scenes that would visit her briefly in the evening, in the dormitory, before vanishing as though swept away by the wind—now suddenly appeared to her, tenacious and precise. Her father was wearing a light gray suit; a fancy handkerchief of white silk gleamed in his breast pocket. From a case covered in black faille and bearing his initials inlaid with gold he withdrew a pastel-colored, gold-tipped cigarette. Her mother, a delicate brunette in a dress of sea-green muslin sprinkled with pearls, the dusky wing of her hair caressing her cheek, was bringing a tube of lipstick to her mouth with a rapt expression that Léa, standing next to her, had often imitated to amuse herself. The long necklace her mother wore looped twice around her neck clinked on the marble top of the dressing table. Next to the face-powder box, a bottle of champagne sat enthroned in an ice bucket with a white napkin wrapped around its neck.

Her heart pounding, Léa knocked on the door of the room where the hotel employee had left his tray. When there was no answer, she summoned up her courage and went in. In that sumptuous room, a skeletal man with a bald skull was stretched out on the immaculate sheets, his bony and deformed hands lying palms up, the fingers slightly curled. The pink satin bolster of his immense bed made the sagging skin of his face seem even yellower. He hadn't bothered to look up when Léa came in. The tray was sitting on a table, untouched. The silver dish covers the child had seen placed over that mouth-watering food downstairs hadn't even been removed. Suddenly afraid, Léa turned around, tiptoed out, and closed the door quietly behind her.

In all the rooms into which she peeked, after receiving no response to the polite little knock she made with one knuckle, Léa saw the same thing: men, women, alone or in couples, lying on their beds, silent, eyes closed, like wax mannequins stripped of their wigs and laid out in the showroom of a large furniture store before being piled into a truck and sent off to a factory to be melted down and re-fashioned according to the specifications of the next client. She'd read that about mannequins in the feature pages of a children's magazine. Léa had never seen any dead people, aside from the mangled and bloody bodies glimpsed at a distance after the bombing raids on Bordeaux. This was how she imagined people looked when they'd died of illness or old age. But why would anyone have turned one of the loveliest hotels in Paris into a morgue? Was it customary to bring people to a luxury hotel after they were dead, so that they could have at least one chance to enjoy the pleasures of life, if they'd never tasted them when they were alive?

Confused and upset, Léa decided to stop looking around for the moment and to continue her search in another part of the hotel. She had just happened upon an empty room and thought it would be a good place in which to eat her snack at last and open her box of beads, which she was eager to examine. Like the other rooms, this one was large and magnificently furnished. Léa didn't dare sit on the spread of quilted satin brocade hanging in perfect folds over the turned wooden feet of the bed, so she plopped down instead on the thick carpet, with her back against one of the sides of a big polished bombé chest of drawers with pulls in the shape of elaborately worked rings of gilt metal. She unwrapped her chocolate bar, stuck it into her piece of bread, and set the whole thing down on a scrap torn from the newspaper tied around her box of beads, so as not to leave any crumbs. Then she turned on a porcelain lamp with a rose-colored shade of pleated material, undid the package, and opened the box to admire her beads. There were all kinds of them, carefully sorted into compartments: large, small, round, square, oval, white, red, green—enough to make all different kinds of necklaces and bracelets with the cords provided in the set. Absorbed in the contemplation of her treasure, she reached out for her bread and chocolate. Her fingers touched another hand.

Léa started and looked up. A corpse had appeared out of nowhere and was watching her. It was the same skull as the severed heads sitting on the stretchers downstairs: ashen skin mottled with red blotches and stretched over slanting cheekbones so sharp they seemed about to slice through it; big dark circles under the eyes; yellow teeth protruding from receding gums; chapped white lips. No hair, no eyebrows, no eyelashes. No beard, either, but that wasn't surprising since the corpse, judging from its height, and if one could imagine estimating its age, was that of a boy who couldn't have been more than thirteen or fourteen years old. Léa tried to run away, but the icy hand held tight to her wrist. This exaggeratedly large hand was at the end of a knobby stick partly covered by the floppy sleeve of a gray-and-white striped pajama top just like the ones worn by the men who had gotten off the bus a little earlier. The boy was on all fours. He had probably crawled out of the space between the opposite side of the chest and the wall, where he'd been crouching in this room so neat and clean that it had seemed completely unoccupied.

He sat back on his heels and studied Léa. In the frozen face of that living corpse, the nocturnal eyes, which seemed to be all pupil, burned with a dull flame whose black light turned inward, as though a vision of hell had seared and reversed the lens, leaving only the inner surface intact and capable of sight. The corpse raised the hand holding the bread and chocolate to its mouth; the teeth in their bleeding gums began to nibble delicately, and with care. Releasing Léa's wrist, the other hand rose jerkily into the air, and a finger touched her cheek, its claw-like nail sinking into the plump rosy flesh, where it left a crescent-shaped mark. Then the hand grabbed a lock of her hair and tugged on it, as if testing its strength. Léa began quietly to cry. The finger wiped off a tear and brought it to the tongue, which licked it up. The eyes, so blind and yet so wise, grew even bigger, as though preparing to engulf the little girl in some deep well of viscous truth. Finally they looked down at the box of beads. The claw began to poke around in them. It scattered them, gathered them together, sent them rolling into one another. It picked up a handful, let them dribble back into the box, did this again, and again, ten times, more and more lazily. And all at once, as if he'd received an electric shock, the boy sat up, dropped the bread and chocolate, grabbed the box, and turned it upside down over Léa's head. The child sat stunned, at first, by the extent of the disaster. The beads had fallen all over the carpet. There was a small pile in a fold of her skirt, and she could feel the cool surface of a few inside the neckline of her blouse, while others were caught in her hair.

"I didn't mean to make you angry," she finally wailed in despair, as a rainbow-colored shower tumbled down with a tinkling noise onto the tiny glass beads piled up in her lap. "I only came in here because I'm looking for my parents. I thought they might be in one of these rooms. You see, they went away on a trip three years ago, and they haven't come back yet."

The boy had collapsed onto his heels, apparently exhausted by his fit. There was no change in his expressionless face, but the hand that had fallen back onto the striped material slowly rose again to trace a graceful spiral in the air, an arabesque uncoiling toward the window like a curl of smoke. The mouth pursed up as though in preparation for a grotesque kiss.

"Poof," it said.

The child looked at him without understanding, and searching frantically for something to say, whispered, "My name is Léa."

A rictus* twisted the cracked lips, to which a few bread crumbs

* rictus: the expanse of an open mouth

still clung, and from the withered throat, thrust forward by an enormous Adam's apple that stuck out like the barrel of a gun, another sound emerged: cackling laughter, followed by the phlegmy cough of a chain-smoker. The hand raised a striped sleeve to show, tattooed on skin that seemed glued to the bone, a series of blue numbers. Then the face became impassive once again.

Léa was silent, but something in his eyes drew her on, and she could feel a question rising from deep down inside her, rising inexorably to her mouth in spite of all her efforts to repress it, rising up until suddenly she blurted out breathlessly, "My parents—you know, right? You know where they are, don't you!"

The rictus reappeared, wider and wider, but must have proved too painful for the wounded lips and gums, because it quickly vanished. The boy leaned forward, and with the precision of an entomologist searching for rare insects in tall grass, he picked out the beads still caught in Léa's curls, one by one. Then he lifted up a lock of her hair, came so close that she could feel his feverish breath, and murmured rapidly in her ear.

"Gassed. Poisoned like rats. Burned in an oven. Turned into black smoke. Poof, your parents. Poof."

Léa reared back, shoved aside the arm still holding her hair, jumped up, and ran from the room with a strangled cry.

THE GLADE WITH
LIFE-GIVING WATER

Juozas Aputis

TRANSLATED BY ANGUS ROXBURGH

"The Glade with Life-Giving Water" reflects the Lithuanian writer Juozas Aputis' obsession with simple, timeless, country "folk" settings laced with more contemporary moral and psychological complexity certainly connected to the enormous changes that Lithuania underwent as it wrested its independence from the Soviet Union. In the story, the elder daughter's imminent departure for the city—perhaps for school, perhaps for work—brings her family to its knees. While the mother nostalgically fingers a dress her daughter long ago outgrew, the father dreams of his relinquished youthful aspirations. While the departing daughter realizes that she must draw sustenance from her soon-to-be-abandoned childhood, the younger daughter resentfully blames her sister for leaving her, even though her future will soon involve departure also. Even the dog resents this apparently inevitable, difficult change.

During the 1940–54 period of Soviet occupation and national resistance, Lithuania experienced an enormous population loss. Many residents were killed, were exiled to Siberia, or chose to emigrate. With the advent of glasnost, Mikhail Gorbachev's

*policy of openness, fifty years of Communist rule ended in
Lithuania, led by Sajudis, an anti-Communist and anti-Soviet
independence movement. Lithuania proclaimed its independence in 1990, the first Soviet republic to do so, though Soviet
forces tried unsuccessfully to block its secession until 1991.*

*Aputis, born in 1936, is one of Lithuania's most celebrated
writers; he is also a translator and editor who has served on the
staff of several periodicals. Famous for his translations of
Chekhov, whose writing is certainly a clear influence on his
own work, Aputis published his first volume of stories in 1963.
He received the National Award for Literature in 1986 for a
short allegorical novel,* An Anthill in Prussia, *but the Soviet
establishment withheld its printing until 1989. In that novel,
as in "The Glade with the Life-Giving Water," memory plays
the critical role of providing both a historical context and a
spiritual grounding for realistic problems.*

*Aputis' meticulous observations about how the individual
mind works to store memory and respond to personal loss in order to move on can be compared to David Bezmozgis' "Tapka,"
where immigrant children observe how a dog plays a pivotal
role in attempting to reestablish an old, lost connection; to
Chang-rae Lee's "Sea Urchin," a memoir of his putative attempt at fifteen to reclaim his old life in Seoul for the first time
since his departure for America twelve years before; or to Rohinton Mistry's "Of White Hairs and Cricket," where a boy
uses his perceptions about his friend's aging father to uncover
his fears about his own father's mortality.*

E ver since morning everyone had been sadly quiet and unwilling
to speak. Only the mother had occasionally asked whether her

daughter had not forgotten anything. She wouldn't be able to come home for every little thing. The father rummaged in the passage for his ax, trudged off to the woodshed, shook free the block that had embedded itself in the ground, reset it, and began chopping the young alders he had brought in the spring. A gust of wind occasionally broke through the dense green fir trees. The flowers already smelled of autumn. The sun was gleaming through the foliage of the trees, shimmering in the crowns of three oaks in the middle of the pasture. Now the father took three strokes to get through the flimsiest of the alders, while a week before he had chopped such dry saplings with a single blow. His daughter was still bending over her suitcase, checking her things, carefully turning them back with her slender fingers.

The mother, herself not quite sure why, went up to the attic, crossed over to the window, and gazed out at the rank of old fir trees; this green wall blocked almost everything from sight; all that could be seen were the branch of an oak and, farther off, at the edge of the forest, a small hill covered with trampled, blackened clover and the doleful stalks of lupins—wild strawberries grew on this knoll, and raspberries, too, some years. From this window she had often seen her two daughters there, and her heart sank with fear every time the elder girl in her short dress stooped to pick a berry, and a passerby appeared on the path. That summer she had often seen her younger daughter throw herself into the arms of her sister, who would lift her up and whirl her round for a long time, with the younger girl's sunburned legs brushing against the lilac blossoms.

The mother sighed and was about to go back to the stairs when she suddenly caught sight of an old dress hanging on a nail: her daughter had long since grown out of it. She went over and buried her face in the dress, squeezing the threadbare cloth in her hands. Down below the tiny window an overripe apple fell softly into the beetroot patch. Just under the roof ridge a speckled butterfly was fluttering in a spider's web. Father was still busy by the shed, chopping away at the logs.

Then she heard him drive his ax into the block, and she knew that he was now searching his pockets for his "Prima" and matches, and as she looked through the small window she saw him setting off toward the fir wood, along the edge of the cherry orchard, and past the three oaks. There, at the road, grew a tall fir on which, before the First World War, grandfather had erected a small shrine with a little idol carved from a birch log. Everyone who walked or drove past the tree still raised his hat, although the birch idol was no longer there: some lover of antiquity had carried it off in his shining car to a distant city.

The mother stood crumpling her daughter's dress for a long time, then took it from the nail, folded it neatly, placed it under her arm, and crossed the attic, which was strewn with flax combings, to the staircase.

The younger daughter was rolling about on the grass beside the kennel, embracing the tired mongrel, who was very fond of her. The dog had long ago grown tired of rolling with the girl on the grass and, catching a moment, cast a longing glance at the forest visible beyond the clover field, but again and again the girl tumbled him onto the grass and the old dog, not wishing to offend her, began to play with her again.

Soon the elder daughter appeared outside too. She had left her room just as her mother, hiding the threadbare dress, was coming down to the hall. The little girl abandoned the now unnecessary dog and immediately scampered toward her sister.

"Are we going? Are we going?" she asked, taking her sister's hand. But her sister said nothing, and even without a reply the little girl understood that they were already on their way.

The girls' mother paced around the room, glancing with vague apprehension at the suitcase and the lilac umbrella propped against the wall, then looked out of the window at the departing girls and at the dog complaining of its lot and of its heavy chain. The daughters turned at the hay shed toward the gurgling stream; the younger girl took hold of the branches of the small alders and kept trying to put

her arm round her sister's waist, but her sister did not feel like playing with her.

At the mill dam, which their father had built many years before,
both girls stripped bare, and the elder dived head first from the
bank, while her sister, who had not yet learned to swim well, entered
the water more gingerly.

Their mother, unable to stay any longer in the room, opened the
door, and the dog pinned his last hopes on her. She made her way
straight to the kennel, stroked the dog's coat, which was warm after a
day in the sun, glanced back and touched the part of the mongrel's
neck where his hair had long ago worn away, revealing his bluish,
pimply skin. Before the chain had rattled against the side of the kennel, the dog was already far away. He flung himself on the ground
and rolled in the grass, then darted into the front garden, sniffed at
the flowers and was about to lift his only white leg—the others were
black—but changed his mind and sped off over the clover following
the father's still-fresh tracks. The mother also left the yard, not for
the forest, however, but for the pasture, where a cow was tethered under an oak tree. Gripped in her hands was her daughter's old dress.

In various parts of this broad forest clearing there were now four
people: three adults and a child; somewhere in the forest a little dog
was bounding after the scent of a wild animal; under an oak tree
stood a cow; and in potato drills,* in the shade of the shaws,† some
hens were sitting, their dusty wings spread and beaks wide open.

The elder sister dived tirelessly into the deep water, her long wet
plaits hanging over her back, while the smaller girl tried to reach
her, asking to be taken into the middle of the pool. But the elder girl
did this only once, and even then unwillingly and without affection.
Of the grown-ups living in this forest glade she alone was not lost in

* drill: shallow furrow
† shaw: thicket

thoughts about the past. Having swum to the other bank, she sat on a large rock, letting her heavy, wet plaits hang down, and looked—with incomprehensible fear, as though for the first time—at her tanned breasts and at her legs, which were slightly scratched above the knees. Here too there was a scent of wild dahlias on the breeze; a strange, plaintively enticing presentiment enveloped her, as though someone not very frightening, but disquieting nonetheless, were stealing close. At that moment she seemed to sense a force that she would necessarily have to obey. This imperious force loomed somewhere in the distance, but the girl fearfully understood that it could already see her and was drawing toward her.

"You're bad!" said her little sister, this small, naked girl with scratched legs. "You always used to be good to me, but now you're not. Well just you go away then—I'll be good to myself!"

"What are you angry at?" said the older girl listlessly, forcing herself to remember her sister, who was sitting, her arms stretched out, in the water at the other bank. "I *am* good. You know I am . . ."

She spoke tenderly, but the vague feeling of yearning did not leave her. She could not stay here any longer. Touching the things of her infancy and childhood, the constantly coursing and seething water and the rocks covered with slime, she sensed that she was pushing herself away from them, breaking natural links forever, yet at the same time she was engraving these things in her memory, so that many years later she might find strength in them in a moment of weariness.

Her father, however, was young again, like many years before, and was sitting under a large fir tree. He was a strong man, he knew his own strength and realized that at a time like this, on the brink of separation, it was not for a man to absorb himself in the past—but he could not help it. Perhaps this hour would become the foothold for a new unrealizable dream, for new forest clearings—yet, who knows, he smiled, who knows. There used to be dense forest here, in the middle of which he had cleared a spacious, square glade and used the logs for buildings, leaving only four oaks in the middle of the clover field; he had dammed up the stream and begun to build a mill and a bathhouse, such as no one in the neighborhood had built, on stout oak posts, where the weary traveler could look forward to hot water. For many years the posts intended for the bathhouse jutted out of the water; something happened to the owner—one spring day all his endeavors appeared petty and absurd to him and he grew restless, and finally with a crash the drifting ice demolished the posts of his strange construction and bore them off. That same spring he could not resist the call of life, and heeding the cry of the trees and the grass and the birds he rode on horseback from the glade that he had cleared himself in the black forest and in the evening he returned with the young woman who now, supporting her chin with one hand and crumpling her daughter's old dress with the other, was standing under one of the oaks, looking into the eyes of a chewing cow. The animal's tranquility calmed her. The woman was also immersed in the past; she was wondering whether after this day she would have new dreams, or that foothold that had brought a smile to her husband's lips as he sat bareheaded under the tall fir. The mother saw only her own flesh and blood and the dress that her daughter had outgrown, and heard the words the girl had said a few days before. She had come inside, having been sitting under the oak tree, holding a linen shawl that her mother had woven, and sat down on a bench under an embroidered towel.

"You didn't stay long!"

The daughter looked out of the kitchen window.

"Wasn't it nice under the oak tree?"

"It was lovely under the oak tree, Mother. Only frightening. When the leaves rustle I can feel time passing. Right through me I can feel what time is and how it is passing."

The girl's mother started; she had experienced the same sad sensation long ago, but had not been able to express it so clearly in words. She went up to her daughter and placed her hand on her head.

The passing time rustled in the leaves of the oaks.

Now the mother squeezed her daughter's dress in her hand; the girl had outgrown it long ago. Time was passing with terrifying speed.

But her elder daughter was still sitting in the water and could not understand what was going on in this forest clearing. Trying to dispel her thoughts about the distant force that was spying on her and weighing on her, she got up from the rock, swam over to her little sister, and lifted her up in her arms, showering her with kisses. The child hurriedly blurted out words that her sister had no desire to hear: "Don't you start crying, though. We're the ones that should be crying, because you're going away."

Panting loudly, the dog came running up to the millpond, slid down the bank, and sank down greedily at the water's edge. The little girl forced him to take a swim too.

Presently, from three directions, the father, the mother, and both girls returned to the cottage. The wet dog was again rolling about on the grass, and the younger girl asked her sister: "Will you come home often? Study a bit, and then come and bathe in our pond!"

The dog was listening, and perhaps even understood a thing or two—water does refresh the brain!

The elder sister answered: "Yes, of course I'll come."

It was a joyless reply. Probably she already understood a thing or two herself: it is impossible, after all, to go away and to return just like that; never again would she be the person she used to be, neither on the knoll where strawberries grow, and sometimes raspberries, nor in the refreshing water of the pond, though this quiet glade would surely entice her more and more as the years went by, and each homecoming would be a return only to the past, to the violet clover, to the rock in the millpond and to the three oaks, because there would no longer be such things in her life.

The first to stride along the path, as was fitting, was the father, carrying his daughter's suitcase. He was followed by his elder daughter, her mother, the child, and the dog. On reaching the three oaks, the mother ran back, treading barefoot along the grass-covered path, hung her daughter's old dress on the fence, and plucked a flower from below the window; the daughter took the flower and gave her mother her umbrella. Now and again the dog would dart ahead, showing off that he also knew the way.

"There once was a secular oak here as well, but it was struck by lightning and dried up. I made a table out of it, and a footbridge across the stream. Only three remained."

"You told us about it, Father . . ."

"Over there where the clover is now, our dog was once gored by a wild boar."

"You told us, Mother . . ."

"It's all right for you, you're going away. But I've got to stay here," said the younger girl, overtaking her mother and clasping her sister's hand.

"You'll be leaving soon, too."

"Huh, that won't be for a long time."

"The time will fly—you won't even notice it."

"It just seems like that to you because you're going."

The people from the forest clearing reached the scorching road quickly. They did not have to wait long for the bus, which stopped at the curb grunting and snorting like an enormous wild boar. The father helped to carry the suitcase in, the mother gave the umbrella to her daughter and saw how the young driver stared at the girl, while her sister remained on the other side of the ditch, facing the other way and no longer looking at the bus. The bus moved off, blowing sand, which looked blue in the exhaust fumes, from the asphalt, and those who were left behind could see the girl smiling to them and holding in front of her the flower her mother had picked. The dog evidently agreed at heart with the younger sister: he leapt onto the road and, yelping angrily, tried to catch up with the bus and bite its wheel.

FROM *DON'T LET'S GO TO THE DOGS TONIGHT: AN AFRICAN CHILDHOOD*

GETTING THERE: ZAMBIA, 1987

Alexandra Fuller

In this chapter from the bestselling memoir Don't Let's Go to the Dogs Tonight, *the end of apartheid precipitates an identity crisis for Alexandra Fuller, a white girl raised in southern Africa. Both countries referenced here, Northern and Southern Rhodesia, were named for Cecil Rhodes, whose plunder of natural resources and use of force to seize the land (through his British South Africa Company) helped the British colonize the region. Southern Rhodesia became a settlement colony for Scots, white South Africans, and Afrikaners. This white minority ruled until 1980, when after a long armed struggle known as the Second Chimurenga ("rebellion" in Shona), the nation won independence as the Republic of Zimbabwe. Northern Rhodesia, just across the Zambezi River, had become the independent Republic of Zambia in 1964. As the family drives from their farm in Zambia to Fuller's newly integrated boarding school in Zimbabwe, Bobo (Fuller's childhood nickname) witnesses the racism—and humor—of her alcoholic parents, especially her manic-depressive mother.*

Nonfiction writer Alexandra Fuller was born in England

in 1969 and moved with her family to Rhodesia when she was two years old. In the 1980s, civil conflict in the area led them to relocate first to Malawi, then to Zambia. Fuller graduated from Acadia University in Nova Scotia, Canada, and moved to Wyoming in 1994. After writing a number of unpublished novels, she achieved international success with Don't Let's Go to the Dogs Tonight *(2001), a* New York Times *Notable Book, finalist for the Guardian First Award, and BookSense Best Nonfiction Book of the Year, followed by* Scribbling the Cat *(2004). Fuller, her husband, and their children divide their time between Wyoming, Idaho, Zambia, and Tanzania.*

One of the best recent memoirs by Anglo-Africans, Don't Let's Go *has a lively, humorous take on a childhood with dysfunctional parents struggling on a succession of poor bush farms against a backdrop of civil strife. Fuller's writing style is deceptively simple. As she explains, "I wanted to show [that] if you're a kid in war you have no idea what's going on. You try to make sense of it . . . but . . . you don't have the vocabulary." Her desire to honor the native voices that influenced her ("I want sometimes to sound as if English is my second language") creates an elliptical childhood language of hyphenated adjectives and evocative sound: "I was really trying to capture the staccato of the sound when you're there, this constant rat-a-tat-tat of the birds and the voices of the Africans." You may wish to compare Fuller's perspective to Charles Mungoshi's, whose "Shadows on the Wall" obliquely references black life under white minority rule in Rhodesia, and to the excerpt from Aminatta Forna's* The Devil That Danced on the Water *and Faith Adiele's "Black Men," both memoirs written by women struggling with their African/Anglo identities in exile.*

To begin with, before Independence, I am at school with white children only. "A" schools, they are called: superior schools with the best teachers and facilities. The black children go to "C" schools. In-between children who are neither black nor white (Indian or a mixture of races) go to "B" schools.

The Indians and coloureds (who are neither completely this nor completely that) and blacks are allowed into my school the year I turn eleven, when the war is over. The blacks laugh at me when they see me stripped naked after swimming or tennis, when my shoulders and arms are angry sunburnt red.

"Argh! I smell roasting pork!" they shriek.

"Who fried the bacon?"

"Burning piggy!"

My God, I am the *wrong* color. The way I am burned by the sun, scorched by flinging sand, prickled by heat. The way my skin erupts in miniature volcanoes of protest in the presence of tsetse flies, mosquitoes, ticks. The way I stand out against the khaki bush like a large marshmallow to a gook with a gun. White. African. White-African.

"But what are you?" I am asked over and over again.

"Where are you from *originally?*"

I began then, embarking from a hot, dry boat.

Blinking bewildered from the sausage-gut of a train.

Arriving in Rhodesia, Africa. From Derbyshire, England. I was two years old, startled and speaking toddler English. Lungs shocked by thick, hot, humid air. Senses crushed under the weight of so many stimuli.

I say, "I'm African." But not black.

And I say, "I was born in England," by mistake.

But, "I have lived in Rhodesia (which is now Zimbabwe) and in Malawi (which used to be Nyasaland) and in Zambia (which used to be Northern Rhodesia)."

And I add, "Now I live in America," through marriage.

And (full disclosure), "But my parents were born of Scottish and English parents."

What does that make me?

Mum doesn't know who she is, either.

She stayed up all night once listening to Scottish music and crying.

"This music"—her nose twitches—"is so beautiful. It makes me homesick."

Mum has lived in Africa all but three years of her life.

"But this *is* your home."

"But my heart"—Mum attempts to thump her chest—"is Scottish."

Oh, *fergodsake*. "You hated England," I point out.

Mum nods, her head swinging, like a chicken with a broken neck. "You're right," she says. "But I love Scotland."

"What," I ask, challenging, "do you love about Scotland?"

"Oh the . . . the . . ." Mum frowns at me, checks to see if I'm tricking her. "The music," she says at last, and starts to weep again. Mum hates Scotland. She hates drunk-driving laws and the cold. The cold makes her cry, and then she comes down with malaria.

Her eyes are half-mast. That's what my sister and I call it when Mum is drunk and her eyelids droop. Half-mast eyes. Like the flag at the post office whenever someone important dies, which in Zambia, with one thing and another, is every other week. Mum stares out at the home paddocks where the cattle are coming in for their evening water to the trough near the stables. The sun is full and heavy over the hills that describe the Zambia-Zaire border. "Have a drink with me, Bobo," she offers. She tries to pat the chair next to hers, misses, and feebly slaps the air, her arm like a broken wing.

I shake my head. Ordinarily I don't mind getting softly drunk next to the slowly collapsing heap that is Mum, but I have to go back to boarding school the next day, nine hours by pickup across the border to Zimbabwe. "I need to pack, Mum."

That afternoon Mum had spent hours wrapping thirty feet of electric wire around the trees in the garden so that she could pick up the World Service of the BBC. The signature tune crackled over the syrup-yellow four o'clock light just as the sun was starting to hang above the top of the msasa trees. " 'Lillibulero,' " Mum said. "That's Irish."

"You're not Irish," I pointed out.

She said, "Never said I was." And then, follow-on thought, "Where's the whisky?"

We must have heard "Lillibulero" thousand of times. Maybe millions. Before and after every news broadcast. At the top of every hour. Spluttering with static over the garden at home; incongruous from the branches of acacia trees in campsites we have set up in the bush across the countryside; singing from the bathroom in the evening.

But you never know what will set Mum off. Maybe it was "Lillibulero" coinciding with the end of the afternoon, which is a rich, sweet, cooling, melancholy time of day.

"Your Dad was English originally," I tell her, not liking the way this is going.

She said, "It doesn't count. Scottish blood cancels English blood."

By the time she has drunk a quarter of a bottle of whisky, we have lost reception from Bush House in London and the radio hisses to itself from under its fringe of bougainvillea. Mum has pulled out her old Scottish records. There are three of them. Three records of men in kilts playing bagpipes. The photographs show them marching blindly (how do they see under those dead-bear hats?) down misty Scottish cobbled streets, their faces completely blocked by their massive instruments. Mum turns the music up as loud as it will go, takes the whisky out to the veranda, and sits cross-legged on a picnic chair, humming and staring out at the night-blanketed farm.

This cross-leggedness is a hangover from the brief period in Mum's life when she took up yoga from a book. Which was better than the brief period in her life in which she explored the possibility of converting to the Jehovah's Witnesses. And better than the time she bought a book on belly-dancing at a rummage sale and tried out her techniques on every bar north of the Limpopo River and south of the equator.

The horses shuffle restlessly in their stables. The night apes scream from the tops of the shimmering-leafed msasa trees. The dogs set up in a chorus of barking and will not stop until we put them inside, all except Mum's faithful spaniel, who will not leave her side even when she's throwing what Dad calls a wobbly. Which is what this is: a wobbly. The radio hisses and occasionally, drunkenly, bursts into snatches of song (Spanish or Portuguese) or chatters in German, in Afrikaans, or in an exaggerated American accent. "This is the Voice of America." And then it swoops, "Beee-ooooeee!"

Dad and I go to bed with half the dogs. The other half of the pack set themselves up on the chairs in the sitting room. Dad's half deaf, from when he blew his eardrums out in the war eight years ago in what was then Rhodesia. Now Zimbabwe. I put a pillow over my head. I can hear Mum's voice, high and inexact, trembling on the high notes: "Speed, bonny boat, / Like a bird on the wing, / Over the sea to Skye," and then she runs out of words and starts to sing, loudly to make up for the loss of words, "La, la la laaaa!" In the other room, at the end of the hall, Dad is snoring.

In the morning, Mum is still on the veranda. The records are silent. The housegirl sweeps the floor around her. The radio is in the tree and has sobered up, with a film of shining dew over its silver face, and is telling us the news in clipped English tones. "This is London," it says with a straight face, as the milking cows are brought in to the dairy and the night apes curl up overhead to sleep and the Cape turtledoves begin to call, "Work-hard-er, work-hard-er." An all-day call, which I nevertheless associate with morning and which makes me long for a cup of tea. The bells of Big Ben sound from distant, steely-gray-dawn London, where commuters will soon be spilling sensibly out of Underground stations or red double-decker buses. It is five o'clock Greenwich Mean Time.

When I was younger I used to believe it was called "Mean" time because it was English time. I used to believe that African time was "Kind" time.

The dogs are lying in exhausted heaps on the furniture in the sitting room, with their paws over their ears. They look up at Dad and me as we come through for our early morning cup of tea, which we usually take on the veranda but which the cook has set in the sitting room on account of the fact that Mum is lying with her forehead on the picnic table where he would usually put the tray. Still cross-legged. Still singing. I bet hardly anyone in yoga can do *that*.

We wedge Mum into the back of the pickup along with my suitcase and satchel and books and the spare tires, next to the half-built generator we are taking into Lusaka to be fixed. She is humming "Flower of Scotland." And then Dad and I climb into the front of the pickup and set off down the farm road. I am going to start crying. There go the horses, two white faces and one black peering over the stable doors, waiting for Banda to bring them their breakfasts. And here come the dogs running, ear-flapping hopeful after the pickup, willing us to stop and let them ride along in the back. And there goes the old cook, hunched and massive, his bony shoulders poking out of the top of his threadworn khaki uniform. He is almost seventy and has just sired another baby; he looks exhausted. He's sitting in the kitchen doorway with a joint the size of a sausage hanging from his bottom lip; a fragrant pillow of blue marijuana smoke hangs above his head. Marijuana grows well behind the stables, where it thrives on horseshit, cow dung, pilfered fertilizer intended for Dad's soybean crop. Adamson raises one old hand in salute. The gardener stands to attention on his bush-broom, with which he is sweeping leaves from the dusty driveway. "Miss Bobo," he mouths, and raises his fist in a black power salute.

Mum leans over the rim of the pickup briefly, precariously, to blow the dogs a kiss. She waves at the staff for a moment, royally, and then collapses back into the folds of the tarpaulin.

Dad offers me a cigarette. "Better have one while you still can," he says.

"Thanks." We smoke together for a while.

Dad says, "It's tough when you can't smoke."

I nod.

"Don't smoke at school."

"I won't."

"They won't like it."

"They don't."

It's past seven in the morning by the time we leave the farm. I have to be at school by five-thirty that evening to make it in time for sign-in and supper. That leaves us half an hour for business and lunch in Lusaka and an hour to get through the border between Zimbabwe and Zambia.

I say, "Better be polite to the blokes at the border today. We don't have time for silly buggers."

"Bloody baboons," mutters Dad.

When we get to Lusaka, Dad and I drop off the generator at the Indian's workshop on Ben Bella Road.

"Hello, Mr. Fuller," says the Indian, head bobbing like a bobbin of thread on a sewing machine. "Come in, come in, for tea? Coffee? I have something for you to look at."

"Not today," says Dad, waving the man away. "Big hurry with my daughter, you see." He talks between clenched teeth.

He gets in the pickup. Lights a cigarette. "Bloody Indians," he mutters as he reverses out of the yard, "always up to something."

We buy boiled eggs and slabs of white cornbread from a kiosk on the side of Cha Cha Cha Road, near the roundabout that leads to Kafue, the Gymkhana Club, or home, depending on where you get off. We wave some food at Mum, but she isn't moving. She has some oil on her face from the generator, which has been leaking thick, black engine blood. Otherwise she is very white, bordering on pale green.

We stop before Chirundu, the small hot nothing town on the Zambezi River which marks the border crossing into Zimbabwe, to make sure she is still alive. Dad says, "We'll get into trouble if we try and take a dead body over the border."

Mum has undone the tarpaulin which was meant to keep the dust out of my school clothes, and has wrapped herself up in it. She is asleep with a small smile on her lips.

Dad puts his forefinger under her nose to feel for breath. "Still alive," Dad announces, "although she looks nothing like her passport photo now."

From the back, as we ease into the melting hot, tarmac-shining car park in front of the customs building (broken windows like thin ice in the white sun), we can hear Mum shuffling back into life. She eases herself into a sitting position, the vast tarpaulin over her shoulders like a voluminous plastic operatic cloak in spite of the oven-breath heat. She is singing "Olé, I Am a Bandit."

"Christ," mutters Dad.

Mum has sung "Olé, I Am a Bandit" at every bar under the southern African sun in which she has ever stepped.

"Shut your mother up, will you?" says Dad, climbing out of the pickup with a fistful of passports and papers, "eh?"

I go around the back. "Shhhh! Mum! Hey, Mum, we're at the border now. Shhh!"

She emerges blearily from the folds of the tarpaulin. "I'm the quickest on the trigger," she sings loudly.

"Oh, great." I ease back into the front of the pickup and light a cigarette. I've been shot at before because of Mum and her singing. She made me drive her to our neighbor's once at two in the morning to sing them "Olé, I Am a Bandit," and he pulled a rifle on us and fired. He's Yugoslav.

The customs official comes out to inspect our vehicle. I grin rabidly at him.

He circles the car, stiff-legged like a dog wondering which tire to pee on. He swings his AK-47 around like a tennis racket.

"Get out," he tells me.

I get out.

Dad gets uneasy. He says, "Steady on with the stick, hey?"

"What?"

Dad shrugs, lights a cigarette. "Can't you keep your bloody gun still?"

The official lets his barrel fall into line with Dad's heart.

Mum appears from under the drapes of the tarpaulin again. Her half-mast eyes light up.

"Muli bwanje?" she says elaborately: How are you?

The customs official blinks at her in surprise. He lets his gun relax against his hip. A smile plays around his lips. "Your wife?" he asks Dad.

Dad nods, smokes. I crush out my cigarette. We're both hoping Mum doesn't say anything to get us shot.

But her mouth splits into an exaggerated smile, rows of teeth. She nods toward Dad and me: *"Kodi ndipite ndi taxi?"* she asks: Should I take a taxi?

The customs official leans against his gun for support (hand over the top of the barrel) and laughs, throwing back his head.

Mum laughs, too. Like a small hyena, "Hee-hee," wheezing a bit from all the dust she has inhaled today. She has a dust mustache, dust rings around her eyes, dust where forehead joins hairline.

"Look," says Dad to the customs official, "can we get going? I have to get my daughter to school today."

The customs official turns suddenly businesslike. "Ah," he says, his voice threatening hours of delay, if he likes, "where is my gift?" He turns to me. "Little sister? What have you brought for me today?"

Mum says, "You can have her, if you like," and disappears under her tarpaulin. "Hee, hee."

"Cigarettes?" I offer.

Dad mutters, "Bloody—" and swallows the rest of his words. He climbs into the pickup and lights a cigarette, staring fixedly ahead.

The customs official eventually opens the gate when he is in possession of one box of Peter Stuyvesant cigarettes (mine, intended for school), a bar of Palmolive soap (also intended for school), three hundred kwacha, and a bottle of Coke.

As we bump onto the bridge that spans the Zambezi River, Dad and I hang out of our windows, scanning the water for hippo.

Mum has reemerged from the tarpaulin to sing, "Happy, happy Africa."

If I weren't going back to school, I would be in heaven.

FROM *THE DEVIL THAT DANCED ON THE WATER: A DAUGHTER'S QUEST*

Aminatta Forna

In this chapter from her memoir, The Devil That Danced on the Water, *Aminatta Forna, the daughter of a Scottish mother and a Sierra Leonean father, struggles at British boarding school while her father—unbeknownst to school officials—is held as a political prisoner back in Sierra Leone. Like neighboring Liberia, Sierra Leone was settled by freed slaves, in this case under the auspices of the British Crown. Soon after independence in 1961, Forna's father, a Scottish-educated doctor, returned home with his wife and children and was named minister of finance. When he resigned and formed an opposition party, he was arrested. Forna would later learn that he was hanged on charges of treason a year later. "Allergic" to England, she lives for weekends with her stepmother, called Mum (as opposed to Real Mum, her biological mother, who, according to African tradition, surrendered custody during the divorce), and relates to only two schoolmates: a girl who's been traumatized by her father's treatment of Africans, and another biracial girl whose white mother and stepfather don't want her around.*

Born in Aberdeen, Scotland, in 1964, journalist and doc-
umentary filmmaker Aminatta Forna spent her first ten years
in Sierra Leone. Twenty-five years after her father's execution,
she returned to investigate his death. The Devil That Danced
on the Water: A Daughter's Quest *(2002), runner-up for the*
Samuel Johnson Prize, was serialized as Book of the Week on
BBC Radio and excerpted in the Sunday Times. *In the*
United States, it was selected for the Barnes and Noble Dis-
cover Great New Writers Series. Forna lives in London, where
she works for the BBC and contributes to such newspapers as
the Independent, *the* Observer, *the* Sunday Times, *and the*
Evening Standard. *She is the author of* Mother of All Myths:
How Society Molds and Constrains Mothers *(1998) and*
the novel The Ancestor Stones (2006).

In what has been called a "memoir–cum–detective story" that
involved reviewing transcripts from her father's trial for treason,
interviewing witnesses, and negotiating Sierra Leone's brutal civil
war, Forna reconstructs her own history, that of her family, and
that of postcolonial Africa to explore, as she puts it, "a past in
Africa . . . and . . . a child's innocence that [were both] gone."
Memoirs by African women are rare. You may wish to compare
this one to the excerpt from Alexandra Fuller's Don't Let's Go to
the Dogs Tonight, *by an Anglo-African girl similarly confused*
about her identity in boarding school, and Faith Adiele's "Black
Men," also written by a biracial woman with a white mother
and absent African politico father; or to "Last-Gamble" by
Andrew X. Pham, whose father was also a political prisoner.

The pale-blue aerogramme arrived on 6 July 1971. On the right-
hand side, above the address, was a red eagle, with the words:

"Sierra Leone, Land of Iron & Diamonds, 9 Cents." It was addressed to "Sheka, Memuna and Aminatta Forna" and arrived at Grenbeck Court a few months before we moved to our new place. It was from our father. Inside, at the top of the page, was the oval stamp of the prison office in purple ink and our father's prisoner number: D 6/70. I looked at the address at the top of the letter, the signature of the prison censor, and I thought about my father being in prison and what that meant.

At Minister's Quarters a group of prisoners had come to clear the garden. We had watched them from the upstairs bedroom window as they scythed the overgrown grass. They wore ill-fitting, buttoned cotton jackets and trousers that had once been white. They were barefoot and worked silently, uncomplaining, before they were herded back into the unmarked prison Land Rover. They did not look awesome or frightening as I thought criminals should, but rather small and skinny and old. Nonetheless we did not venture out to play until they were gone. We went to the garden where they had been working, looking for I don't know what—some evidence of their criminality left behind on the lawn, perhaps—then we saw the enormous pile of cuttings and we jumped into it, laughing, and rolled about there for the remainder of the day. Next morning we were back: we leapt straight in to begin again, only to find the cuttings were now alive with thousands of red and green caterpillars.

On our way to and from town I had seen gangs of prisoners by the side of the roads. Their legs were chained and they worked clearing ditches and mending potholes. After my stepmother had finished reading the letter from our father I asked her: "Does Daddy have to mend the roads and work in people's gardens now he's in prison?"

"What do you mean?" she asked. And I told her what I remembered seeing: men stripped to the waist; they had looked like moving shadows beneath the glare of the sun.

"No," she said. "Don't worry. He doesn't have to do that."

"Why doesn't he?"

"Because he's not that kind of prisoner."

"He's not *what* kind of prisoner?"

"The kind that has to mend roads." She meant he wasn't a criminal, although the *Daily Mail* in Freetown did its best to portray him as one. All the same the idea of my father being forced to labour in front of crowds of onlookers chafed at my imagination. I could not let go of the terrible image.

At school on Sundays we wrote to our parents after we had been to church and eaten our lunch of grey meat and colourless vegetables. We filed into the unheated classrooms for letter-writing, sat at our desks and filled our fountain pens with ink, while a teacher handed out puper: plain white, ruled paper for everyone except the overseas pupils, who were issued with floating leaves of onion skin.

My father slept in a cell no more than six foot by eight foot. It had no natural light, except for a small opening protected by steel bars high up by the ceiling, but the electric bulb hanging in the middle of the room glowed day and night so that there was never a time when it was dark. After years under the bright light many detainees left prison with their eyesight permanently ruined. In the centre of the door was a peephole which allowed the guards to see in, but my father could not see out. The cell contained nothing except a blanket and a chamber pot, which was emptied once a day. On the first day he was stripped naked and issued with prison clothes. He was held in solitary confinement and fed a plate of rice and stew twice a day for two weeks, after which he was allowed out for a single hour of exercise in the evening. A whole month elapsed before he was taken to the shower block and given a bucket of water to wash. In time, through lawyers, he was able to request books, which he sometimes received: novels by Morris West, Edwin Fadiman and Solzhenitsyn's five-hundred-page volume *Cancer Ward*, which parallels a prisoner's life on a ward for the dying in a Soviet labour camp, and the cancer at the heart of the police state. After the first few months he was given writing paper.

In his letters my father urged me to work hard at school, praised me on my grades when they were good, and asked me if I had stopped sucking my thumb. I told everyone I had, but secretly I continued to suck it at night. He asked about the goldfish Goldie and Orangie, and remembered the names of the girls with whom I was currently friends at school. I wrote back in turn begging him to allow us home. I was allergic to England—my skin was dry and ashy, my lips were cracked and I couldn't help licking them, which only made the problem worse; my hair had turned frizzy and my fingers were tattered with bleeding rag nails. I hated being stuck at boarding school and I hated being in England, and in my mind one was synonymous with the other.

Our father placed an unshakeable faith in the British education system—as did many Africans in those days. They believed the key to success lay in a British education, of which by far the most superior was one acquired at boarding school. Going to Bo School had changed his life immeasurably. My father wanted me to become a lawyer (I got as far as completing my degree before I gave up law for journalism) and Memuna, who was the brightest of us, to become a doctor, as he had been. I can't remember what ambitions he had for my brother—something equally elevated, certainly. As an adult, when I spoke to other friends of mine—other children of the empire growing up in Commonwealth countries after independence— I found we often shared similar experiences. Most of our parents did not own their own homes; foreign holidays were rare or unheard of; the bulk of our parents' income went on their children's schooling— this was the price of securing our future. Many years later I finally began to understand the sacrifices our parents had made to give us our education and why they cherished this particular dream. But at the time I felt as if I were being punished.

I must have gone on begging and pleading with him, and Mum must have described in her letters how I clung to her legs on the platform at Victoria Station at the start of every term and the end of each exeat, forcing her to prise me off and hand me over to the teacher escorting the Horley train. Three months into our second year apart, my father wrote to me at length: "The Fornas, men as well as women, boys as well as girls, are brave people and they never cry. So you should not cry. Okay? The Fornas face everything bravely." He promised, when the time was right, we would be a family again one day. But not just yet. Never just yet.

One Sunday at High Trees a new teacher came in to supervise our letter-writing session. His name was Mr. Newman; he had a fat grey moustache and silver spectacles. At the end of the session we lined up as usual while Mr. Newman wrote out our parents' addresses neatly on the front of our envelopes. When it was my turn I gave him our address in London. Mr. Newman asked why, if I lived in London, my letter was written on airmail paper.

"My father lives in Sierra Leone." I gave the most minimal and discouraging reply I could.

"And what's your father's address in Sierra Leone?"

"I don't know. My mum has it. We send our letters to her and she sends them to him. That's the way she likes to do it."

"Well that's a bit of a silly waste of time, not to mention stamps. Why on earth don't you just post the letters from here, you daft girl?" I quite liked Mr. Newman, really. He was very funny and when he called you daft he didn't really mean it. It was just his way. But I still couldn't tell him the reason my letters weren't posted directly to Freetown was because no one at school, neither teachers nor pupils, knew our father was in jail.

I left the old Nissen hut that served as a classroom with Caroline, one of my closest friends. I had spent a weekend at her home near Winchester and, in return, I asked her home to Philbeach Gardens.

Caroline was clever, small and neatly turned out, with matching clothes and the kind of grown-up manners English children have.

"How do you do, Mrs. Forna?" Caroline extended her hand confidently, formally. A beat passed before Mum took her hand. She greeted her pleasantly, but there was an expression upon Mum's face I couldn't quite read.

At Caroline's house I had slept in the spare bedroom, where everything matched the sprigged yellow paper on the walls: curtains, eiderdown, valance, dressing-table cloth, cushion covers. In the corner was a washbasin and a bowl of miniature, scented soaps. When I invited Caroline to stay with us I imagined showing her to a room just like the one I had stayed in. But we didn't have a spare room and I shared the same bedroom under the eaves of the building with Mum and Memuna. At bed time it occurred to me for the first time there was nowhere for Caroline to sleep. I had spent the night on the divan in the sitting room, while Caroline took my bed. It made no difference to our friendship, but I hadn't invited anyone home since.

"Why is your dad in Africa when you're all here?" Caroline asked me. "And how come you never go home to see him?"

It was the first time anyone had ever enquired directly. I suppose I could have made an excuse, but I didn't. A few minutes later, sitting on the damp grass of the lower playing fields, I asked Caroline if she could keep a secret. I told her my father was in prison and though I didn't understand all the details myself, I gave her the best account I could.

When I had finished speaking, Caroline regarded me gravely and at length. "I've a secret about my father, too," she said presently in a low tone which spoke of confidences about to be shared.

"What kind of secret?" I was a bit worried I had said too much and now I was eager to be reassured in any way.

"My father's a murderer."

I looked her straight in the face. I certainly hadn't been expecting that. "Who did he murder?"

This is the story Caroline told me that day on the playing fields, while we watched the rest of the boarders playing a game of Stuck in the Mud: Caroline and her family had lived in the Cameroons, where her father was an executive with an oil company. They lived outside the capital, close to the rain forest in an area then being surveyed and scouted for drilling opportunities. In due course new reserves of oil were indeed discovered, the land was cleared and work began.

"One day," Caroline recounted, "some Africans came up to our house, lots, a whole crowd of them. They asked to speak to my father. They were villagers and they said they used to live on the land. Now the land was gone they had nowhere to go and nothing to eat. They were so poor. They begged my father to help them, to give them something to eat."

"Why did they come to your house?"

"Because my father was head of the company. They thought he would be able to help them. They didn't know where else to go. They were just asking, begging.

"They stood there for ages. My mother didn't like it at all. She said they were treading on the flower beds and so in the end my father went out, but he wouldn't speak to them. He told them to go away. He said they must get off our land. So they all went away. There were old people and women and children." Caroline stopped speaking.

When she began the story I had fancied maybe he'd pushed her mother down the stairs or put a poisonous snake into her bed. "But that doesn't make your dad a murderer."

"The people went away and they never came back. I asked my father what would happen to them and he said he didn't know. But one of the Africans who worked for us told me they'd all died. They didn't have anything to eat and they died of hunger . . . all of them, even the children." Caroline had tears in her eyes. "So you see, your dad might be in prison. But mine's a murderer and that's worse. He killed all those people . . . he didn't care what happened to them."

I wondered if Caroline was right. After all, nobody had sent her father to prison for what he had done. Caroline called him a murderer. We were children guarding our parents' shame, hiding from the world adult secrets we barely understood ourselves. Caroline never betrayed my confidence, nor I hers, although our friendship ebbed and flowed as the affections of small girls are inclined to do. But even so, at some level we always remained close until the day we both left the school in 1975.

After the first letter, our father wrote to each of us separately and we came to expect his letters at the beginning of every month. Every now and again there would be an unexplained gap, and once for four consecutive months none of his letters reached us and none of ours reached him. When the airmails arrived at the flat in London Mum kept them until we came home at weekends and often I would ask her to read mine. I pretended I had difficulty with his doctor's script, but really it was an excuse for me to curl up and just listen.

Since the day we parted we had not heard once from my mother. After she married our stepfather and returned from Mexico our father had written to her to say the Mexican divorce was not recognised in Sierra Leone. He went to court in Freetown and obtained a divorce himself, and then applied through the Nigerian courts for custody. It was under this authority that he arrived in Lagos to claim us back; our mother saw no alternative but to hand us over. Since then, throughout all the upheavals, there had been no word from her.

Finally a letter did come: Christmas cards arrived at Grenbeck Court, posted from East Africa. There were three of them. The illustrations on the front cover were all by the same artist, coloured drawings of Masai people. Sheka's had a warrior carrying a spear,

Memuna's showed a woman with a baby on her back. My own, the most striking in my opinion, was of a woman wearing dozens of coloured rings about her swan-like neck. Our stepmother had called us together one day and handed the cards to each of us. Afterwards she asked me: "Do you remember your mother?"

"Sure," I said, although I wasn't. I had stopped thinking of her so much lately. Sometimes, and for a few days after the cards arrived, the three of us talked about her together in secret. We called her "Real Mum" now and if anyone had ever overheard us they would have been confused. Mum was what we called our stepmother, and then there was Real Mum or Other Mum. Sometimes we called them both Mum and Mummy interchangeably—we always knew who we meant. When we talked about Real Mum we talked about her hair, mostly her hair. Or we rehearsed certain memories over and over, like the time Memuna found cockroaches in her Wellington boots. Once at school we had sung "Lord of the Dance" in assembly. It was the first time I had heard the song since our days in Koidu and I didn't understand why the words and the tune were so familiar, or why I knew them by heart. I suddenly felt overwhelmed by the memory of my mother and instead of singing along with the others I began to cry, cross-legged on the floor in the middle of two hundred other children. My form teacher picked her way across to me and led me out of the hall, assuming it was a case of homesickness. I asked Mum: "Are we going to see Mummy again?"

Mum answered slowly: "I don't think so, Am. I think she has a new family of her own now."

"You mean she has other children?" This thought had simply never crossed my mind and it shocked me. "How many other children does she have?"

"I don't know. One? Maybe two? I don't really know."

Later I thought about what Mum had said and I wondered who they could be, these other children who had my mother now.

In my dormitory I had a friend called Helen, the only other person at the school, apart from Memuna, whose skin was the same shade as mine. Soon after I began at High Trees Helen had told me her mother was white and her parents were divorced. Helen lived with her mother, her new stepfather, who was white as well, and two half sisters. But Helen and her brother were the only ones sent away to boarding school; she said it was because her parents didn't want them around.

"Is that why you're here, too?" she had asked. We'd been sitting on our beds in the Pink Room. Helen was picking at a scab on her arm—it made me wince to watch.

"No." At the time I had explained how really I lived with my dad, although he was in Africa, so we couldn't actually be together. Helen looked at me and shrugged.

Poor Helen. I did not want to be like her. She had such an air of dejection about her that she attracted few friends. She spent most of her time alone, sitting on the swings or walking down to the main school. As the term strung out, long after the rest of us overcame our homesickness, I would hear Helen at night crying. I could see the outline of her body, her face turned to the wall, and though I leant out of my bed and whispered to her, she never answered me.

In the Shadow
of War

IN THE SHADOW OF WAR

Ben Okri

*In Ben Okri's short, powerful tale, a young village boy follows a
supposed witch into the Nigerian forest only to discover that she
is in fact all too human and sneaking aid to war victims. There
he witnesses soldiers committing atrocities but is unable to tell his
father what he's seen. Nigeria's civil war, or Biafran War
(1967–70), made international headlines due to the government's infamous use of starvation as a weapon against the
breakaway republic of Biafra and to Nigeria's prominence since re-
gaining its independence from Britain in 1960. In addition to
vast oil reserves and a highly educated populace, Nigeria can
claim one in five Africans and one in ten blacks in the world.*

*Poet, novelist, and short-story writer Ben Okri was born in
1959 in Lagos. He was influenced by his boyhood experience of
the war and by the African, classical, and European mythology
he encountered in his father's library. Despite not gaining entrance to a Nigerian university, he had his work published as a
teenager and completed his first novel by age eighteen. He traveled to England to attend the University of Essex and soon won
international acclaim, eventually receiving the Commonwealth*

Writers Prize and the Booker Prize. He currently lives and writes in London.

Nigerians, ranging from bestselling Chinua Achebe, the father of the African novel in English, to Nobel laureate Wole Soyinka and pioneering female novelist Buchi Emecheta, are the most prolific and prominent Anglophone authors on the continent. Okri leads the second wave of writers following the giants associated with the independence struggle; he addresses postcolonial themes such as the tension between Western and native traditions, and the poverty, corruption, and violence of urban centers. According to Robert Bennett,* Okri's work falls into three phases, each "marked by radical shifts in genre, style, and narrative strategy." The first blends the Bildungsroman, *or Western coming-of-age novel, with Nigerian dialects and concerns. The second, including* Stars of the New Curfew *(1988), in which "In the Shadow of War" appears, marks a shift to short stories and experimentation with African narrative strategies. The final phase, including the Booker-winning* The Famished Road *(1991), combines Western and African traditions into new hybrid forms. You may wish to compare the story to "Everything in This Country Must," Colum McCann's tale about a girl witnessing her father's humiliation at the hands of soldiers, or Charles Mungoshi's "Shadows on the Wall," from the viewpoint of an African village boy similarly unable to communicate with his father.*

T hat afternoon three soldiers came to the village. They scattered the goats and chickens. They went to the palm-frond

---

* Robert Bennett, "Ben Okri," in *Postcolonial African Writers: A Bio-Bibliographical Critical Sourcebook*, ed. Puspa Naidu Parekh and Siga Fatima Jagne (Westport, CT: Greenwood Press, 1998), 364–73.

bar and ordered a calabash of palm-wine. They drank amidst the flies.

Omovo watched them from the window as he waited for his father to go out. They both listened to the radio. His father had bought the old Grundig cheaply from a family that had to escape the city when the war broke out. He had covered the radio with a white cloth and made it look like a household fetish.* They listened to the news of bombings and air raids in the interior of the country. His father combed his hair, parted it carefully, and slapped some aftershave on his unshaven face. Then he struggled into the shabby coat that he had long outgrown.

Omovo stared out of the window, irritated with his father. At that hour, for the past seven days, a strange woman with a black veil over her head had been going past the house. She went up the village paths, crossed the Express road, and disappeared into the forest. Omovo waited for her to appear.

The main news was over. The radio announcer said an eclipse of the moon was expected that night. Omovo's father wiped the sweat off his face with his palm and said, with some bitterness:

"As if an eclipse will stop this war."

"What is an eclipse?" Omovo asked.

"That's when the world goes dark and strange things happen."

"Like what?"

His father lit a cigarette.

"The dead start to walk about and sing. So don't stay out late, eh."

Omovo nodded.

"Eclipses hate children. They eat them."

Omovo didn't believe him. His father smiled, gave Omovo his ten kobo allowance, and said:

---

* household fetish: an object revered for its magical properties or association with a spirit

"Turn off the radio. It's bad for a child to listen to news of war."

Omovo turned it off. His father poured a libation* at the doorway and then prayed to his ancestors. When he had finished he picked up his briefcase and strutted out briskly. Omovo watched him as he threaded his way up the path to the bus-stop at the main road. When a danfo† bus came, and his father went with it, Omovo turned the radio back on. He sat on the window-sill and waited for the woman. The last time he saw her she had glided past with agitated flutters of her yellow smock. The children stopped what they were doing and stared at her. They had said that she had no shadow. They had said that her feet never touched the ground. As she went past, the children began to throw things at her. She didn't flinch, didn't quicken her pace, and didn't look back.

The heat was stupefying. Noises dimmed and lost their edges. The villagers stumbled about their various tasks as if they were sleep-walking. The three soldiers drank palm-wine and played draughts†† beneath the sun's oppressive glare. Omovo noticed that whenever children went past the bar the soldiers called them, talked to them, and gave them some money. Omovo ran down the stairs and slowly walked past the bar. The soldiers stared at him. On his way back one of them called him.

"What's your name?" he asked.

Omovo hesitated, smiled mischievously, and said:

"Heclipse."

The soldier laughed, spraying Omovo's face with spit. He had a face crowded with veins. His companions seemed uninterested. They swiped flies and concentrated on their game. Their guns were on the table. Omovo noticed that they had numbers on them. The man said:

---

*libation: liquid poured as a sacrifice in honor of a dead person
† *danfo* bus: a Volkswagen taxi-van that seats seven passengers
†† played draughts: British version of checkers

"Did your father give you that name because you have big lips?"

His companions looked at Omovo and laughed. Omovo nodded.

"You are a good boy," the man said. He paused. Then he asked, in a different voice:

"Have you seen that woman who covers her face with a black cloth?"

"No."

The man gave Omovo ten kobo and said:

"She is a spy. She helps our enemies. If you see her come and tell us at once, you hear?"

Omovo refused the money and went back upstairs. He repositioned himself on the window-sill. The soldiers occasionally looked at him. The heat got to him and soon he fell asleep in a sitting position. The cocks, crowing dispiritedly, woke him up. He could feel the afternoon softening into evening. The soldiers dozed in the bar. The hourly news came on. Omovo listened without comprehension to the day's casualties. The announcer succumbed to the stupor, yawned, apologized, and gave further details of the fighting.

Omovo looked up and saw that the woman had already gone past. The men had left the bar. He saw them weaving between the eaves of the thatch houses, stumbling through the heat-mists. The woman was further up the path. Omovo ran downstairs and followed the men. One of them had taken off his uniform top. The soldier behind had buttocks so big they had begun to split his pants. Omovo followed them across the Express road. When they got into the forest the men stopped following the woman, and took a different route. They seemed to know what they were doing. Omovo hurried to keep the woman in view.

He followed her through the dense vegetation. She wore faded wrappers* and a grey shawl, with the black veil covering her face.

---

* wrappers: a length of cloth worn around the bodies as a skirt; also called *wrappa*

She had a red basket on her head. He completely forgot to deter-mine if she had a shadow, or whether her feet touched the ground.

He passed unfinished estates, with their flaking ostentatious signboards and their collapsing fences. He passed an empty cement factory: blocks lay crumbled in heaps and the workers' sheds were deserted. He passed a baobab tree, under which was the intact skeleton of a large animal. A snake dropped from a branch and slithered through the undergrowth. In the distance, over the cliff edge, he heard loud music and people singing war slogans above the noise.

He followed the woman till they came to a rough camp on the plain below. Shadowy figures moved about in the half-light of the cave. The woman went to them. The figures surrounded her and touched her and led her into the cave. He heard their weary voices thanking her. When the woman reappeared she was without the basket. Children with kwashiorkor stomachs* and women wearing rags led her half-way up the hill. Then, reluctantly, touching her as if they might not see her again, they went back.

He followed her till they came to a muddied river. She moved as if an invisible force were trying to blow her away. Omovo saw cap-sized canoes and trailing waterlogged clothes on the dark water. He saw floating items of sacrifice: loaves of bread in polythene wrap-pings, gourds of food, Coca-Cola cans. When he looked at the ca-noes again they had changed into the shapes of swollen dead animals. He saw outdated currencies on the riverbank. He noticed the terri-ble smell in the air. Then he heard the sound of heavy breathing from behind him, then someone coughing and spitting. He recog-nized the voice of one of the soldiers urging the others to move faster. Omovo crouched in the shadow of a tree. The soldiers strode

---

* kwashiorkor stomachs: the swollen bellies associated with a type of malnutrition caused by protein deficiency

past. Not long afterwards he heard a scream. The men had caught up with the woman. They crowded round her.

"Where are the others?" shouted one of them.

The woman was silent.

"You dis witch! You want to die, eh? Where are they?"*

She stayed silent. Her head was bowed. One of the soldiers coughed and spat towards the river.

"Talk! Talk!" he said, slapping her.

The fat soldier tore off her veil and threw it to the ground. She bent down to pick it up and stopped in the attitude of kneeling, her head still bowed. Her head was bald, and disfigured with a deep corrugation. There was a livid gash along the side of her face. The bare-chested soldier pushed her. She fell on her face and lay still. The lights changed over the forest and for the first time Omovo saw that the dead animals on the river were in fact the corpses of grown men. Their bodies were tangled with river-weed and their eyes were bloated. Before he could react, he heard another scream. The woman was getting up, with the veil in her hand. She turned to the fat soldier, drew herself to her fullest height, and spat in his face. Waving the veil in the air, she began to howl dementedly. The two other soldiers backed away. The fat soldier wiped his face and lifted the gun to the level of her stomach. A moment before Omovo heard the shot a violent beating of wings just above him scared him from his hiding place. He ran through the forest screaming. The soldiers tramped after him. He ran through a mist which seemed to have risen from the rocks. As he ran he saw an owl staring at him from a canopy of leaves. He tripped over the roots of a tree and blacked out when his head hit the ground.

When he woke up it was very dark. He waved his fingers in front

*You dis witch! You want to die, eh?: Nigerian pidgin for "You are this witch! What, you want to die?"

of his face and saw nothing. Mistaking the darkness for blindness he screamed, thrashed around, and ran into a door. When he recovered from his shock he heard voices outside and the radio crackling on about the war. He found his way to the balcony, full of wonder that his sight had returned. But when he got there he was surprised to find his father sitting on the sunken cane chair, drinking palm-wine with the three soldiers. Omovo rushed to his father and pointed frantically at the three men.

"You must thank them," his father said. "They brought you back from the forest."

Omovo, overcome with delirium, began to tell his father what he had seen. But his father, smiling apologetically at the soldiers, picked up his son and carried him off to bed.

FROM *NOTES FROM THE HYENA'S BELLY: AN ETHIOPIAN BOYHOOD*

A RELUCTANT GUERRILLA

Nega Mezlekia

"A Reluctant Guerrilla" is taken from Notes from the Hyena's Belly: An Ethiopian Boyhood, *Nega Mezlekia's first-person account of a childhood interwoven with his country's history. One of the few African countries to avoid colonization, Ethiopia (originally Abyssinia) has one of the most richly documented histories in the world, with Christian kingdoms dating back to the fourth century* A.D., *a centuries-old Jewish population, and a Muslim presence as old as Islam itself. In 1974, revered emperor Haile Selassie, whose interest in modernization had ignored widespread poverty and drought crises, was deposed by a military junta, the Derg. Nega and his best friend Wondwossen initially support the Derg, believing Communists can solve the problem of feudalism. While still in school, they run away to join Somali rebels fighting for a homeland and learn how to survive in the desert, witness the refugee problem, and do battle armed with unreliable old Soviet weapons. Nega is soon disillusioned, and over the next few years, the Derg executes one hundred thousand people, mainly youths, in the Red Terror.*

Writer and structural engineer Nega Mezlekia was born in

1958 in Jijiga, a desert mountain town split between Amhara
Christians (his group) and Somali Muslims. In 1983, after his
experience fighting and in jail, he left for the Netherlands on an
engineering fellowship. Later he applied for political asylum in
Canada, where he lives and practices engineering today. Though
his mother tongue is Amharic, an ancient language with an al-
phabet of two hundred letters, Notes from the Hyena's Belly
(2000) received the Governor General's Award for English Lan-
guage Nonfiction, Canada's highest literary honor. Controversy
later erupted when his editor alleged that she ghost-wrote the
memoir. Mezlekia has since published a novel, also concerned
with Ethiopian myth, folklore, and political history.

    The African oral tradition is evident in Notes from the
Hyena's Belly, *which the* New York Times *lauded for "skill-*
fully interweaving personal history, politics and Amhara fa-
bles." As Mezlekia puts it, "I've always wanted storytelling to be
very much like a fable or an anecdote," adding, however, that
"writing shouldn't be entertaining only. It should be informa-
tive as well. [I have] an obligation." You may wish to compare
this to the excerpt from Catfish and Mandala, *Andrew Pham's*
account of becoming war refugees with his Vietnamese family,
and "On the Road at Eighteen," Yu Hua's surreal tale of a boy
whose quest to see what he's made of turns sour.

H ussain led us through our first weeks. Like children, we had to
be taught all over again how to sleep, how to wash our faces,
how to relieve ourselves, and many other things that one takes for
granted.

    I received my first shock in field etiquette when I went out to
wash my face. Hussain gathered us all together that first morning,

and led us down a hill, towards some grazing cattle. He asked us to pick our wash basins. He knew we were confused, and he had already begun to cry with laughter, his gold tooth flashing with each rib-cracking laugh. When he finally composed himself, he offered to show us how it was done. Hussain carefully surveyed the docile herd, finding an animal that suited him. He circumspectly approached the cow and gently began to rub its hindquarters. The animal appeared to relax, raised its tail and let out a fountain of urine. Hussain immediately bent down, and splashed handfuls of the yellow liquid over his face. Still grinning, he invited us to do likewise. I was revolted, and refused. The rest, some hesitating briefly, others for longer, all with an eye on the cows' hooves, followed suit.

Wondwossen decided to prove that prudence did not mean avoiding risks altogether, but minimizing them. He attempted to draw his wash water from a camel, thereby advancing the breakthrough, while minimizing the risk to himself. While we stood by, curious, he stroked the camel's hindquarters, accidentally brushing the animal's knee in the process. All camels have an aversion to this kind of knee-touching intimacy. This camel reacted swiftly and violently, kicking Wondwossen in the stomach and knocking him a full six feet away. As we laughed ourselves silly, Wondwossen brushed the dust from his clothes and stood up uncertainly. All that was hurt was his pride.

A couple of days later, five of us were sent to fetch water. There were no rivers, lakes or wells within twenty kilometres of the base. During the rainy season, water had collected on various surfaces, but most of the local ponds were already running low—holding more in the way of tadpoles than water. It took us the better part of the day to find a fresh watering hole. The hole itself was easy to spot; we just had to look for the cattle, donkeys, camels and nomads who gathered en masse around the precious water-filled basin. Though we were all sweaty, and in desperate need of a drink, the guerrillas did not rush for the water. Binoculars were trained, strategic positions held and the area carefully studied for a full hour before it was declared safe.

The nomads were not in the least surprised to see us. They must have crossed paths with the rebels too often to consider them intruders. The nomadic men came over to greet us, extending both hands, and touching their chests to indicate that their welcome was heartfelt. We did likewise. The women and children continued at their tasks, washing themselves in the pond alongside animals that were drinking, rolling and urinating in the water. These were people who had never heard of disease-causing bacteria and viruses. They sickened and died only after they had learned about the existence of dangerous micro-organisms. Until then, they neither filtered their water nor thought of boiling it, and they lived long enough to be killed by drought.

After we had filled our containers with water filtered using some contraption the Somalis had obtained from their Soviet suppliers, we rushed back to the base and informed the front of our discovery. There wasn't even time for a bath, as it was growing dark. When we arrived, a large group of men was sent, with donkeys and camels bearing huge receptacles, to collect more water.

Food was something I had worried about long before leaving home. It wasn't that I had a special liking for anything, so much as I tend to be particular about all things I eat. I had broken bread with Somali friends numerous times, and knew that our foods were, for the most part, similar. But I didn't know what to expect in the field. In Jijiga, when a dish is called Christian or Muslim, it refers to the meat that is used in the stew. Muslims, like Christians, offer prayers over the animal before slaughtering it. These few ritualistic words, uttered more out of tradition than conviction, are the most divisive.

Christians and Muslims maintain separate abattoirs,* butchers, meat-caterers, restaurants and kitchens, at a respectable distance from one another. The majority of the Somalis of Jijiga, like their Christian counterparts, are not fervent in their beliefs, observing the major religious events like Ramadan the way that even lukewarm Christians will observe Christmas. Even at these times Christians and Muslims commingle, sharing food (except meat) and festivities alike.

I had often wondered why such rituals were significant only when they involved meat, and not other foods, like festival bread, which is also prayed over before being broken. When I asked Mam, she replied that the meat, owing to the simple prayers uttered before slaughter, changed in texture, taste and delectable qualities. She had never touched Muslim meat, but was certain that it had an earthy, flat flavour to it. Mam claimed that she could tell a piece of Muslim meat from three metres, though I did not put her to the test.

Mam did not mind that I ate Muslim meat. She only warned me never to bring it home to her, and to scrub my hands cleaner than the cat before returning from such a meal. When I invited my Muslim friends home to lunch or dinner, Mother never alluded to our religious differences; she simply treated my friends as she would her own children.

The main diet among the rebels was sorghum grain, soaked in raw milk, with, if you were lucky, a touch of unclarified butter and a dash of sugar. Occasionally, there was a piece of barbecued camel meat to share. Most of the foodstuffs were either bought from, or donated by, the nomads. It was the rebels' policy not to rob their own people.

Sorghum and maize are the two grains cultivated in Ogaden. Even by Ethiopia's standards, the farming is primitive. There are no yoked

* abattoirs: slaughter houses

bulls or horses to open the earth before planting the seed; no weeding; no tilling the soil to aerate the ground once the seed has germinated. In Ogaden, farming is typically a one-man venture.

Shortly before the rainy season commences, the nomads begin to stake out their territory. Caravans of camels laden with all the worldly possessions of each nomad arrive at their staked lot. The women unload the camels and in a matter of minutes assemble their huts— slender wooden domes covered over with leather. Within a fortnight, the dusty fields of Ogaden, once barren and utterly desolate, teem with life. The landscape, once a dusty plain with nothing to relieve the eye, is dotted with intricately crafted "nomad helmets."

After the first rain, the clay dust settles, the ground cracks and breathes, and life begins to press up into the sun. These grounds are among the most fertile in Africa, and a mere twenty-four hours after the first drop of precious rain touches the earth, the land is felted over with green. The nomads emerge from their helmet-shaped huts, pointed stick in one hand, bag of seeds in the other. They walk their parcel of land, end to end, stabbing the earth with the stick, dropping a single seed and, in a barely perceptible motion, covering the seed over with their heel. For the next few days each nomad-turned-farmer repeats this unvarying routine from dawn to dusk. For as far as the eye can see, this strange halting dance is performed simultaneously by hundreds of stoop-backed men, peering earthwards, stabbing and scattering without pause. To the casual observer, it looks like the fields of Ogaden have been overrun by a colony of lunatics, all under the delirious influence of an identical disease.

The nomads remain with their crops until they are two feet high, keeping them safe from winged predators. Then, as suddenly as they appeared, they disappear from sight, domed frames neatly bound to the backs of camels. No trace is left of their residence save for the green fields. During the coming months, the domesticated plants will fight the persistent weeds and survive the occasional rolling

assault of wild animals on their own. Shortly before harvest, the nomads return.

There is no communal effort involved in the harvesting of the
plants either. Each nomad prepares his own storage bin, carefully
digging a hole in the ground—a single small opening at the surface,
and a deep protected belly in the earth. The bin is lined with wet
ash, to protect the seed from insects. Then, after deducting a few
sacks of grain for the market and his own consumption, the nomad
stores the rest in this bulb-shaped recess, sealing the mouth with a
lid and covering it over with dirt.

Once again, the camps are gone, and the landscape reverts to its
original condition. There is no trace of the previous occupants to be
found. Dust quickly settles over the small mounds of earth marking
the scattered bins that lie just under the surface, making them indis-
tinguishable from the numerous molehills that ravage the land. A
few months later, the nomad will return to dig up his stored grains.
He will use his pointed stick and a couple of distant landmarks to
establish the location of his bin, triangulating between them. After
removing the first few inches of dirt, he verifies that he is not breaking into another's property; then he bails out the recess and fills his
sacks with grain, leaving a scattering of seeds for the coming rainy
season. For the remainder of the year, the nomad will live off his
cattle, fervently reminding his God to bring rain.

After we had lived among the rebels for two weeks, a decision was
reached by the leaders as to the status of the newcomers. The numbers of male and female refugees of all ages who were coming to the
front had been growing at an exponential rate. The situation was already critical; normal activities had been halted, security had been
compromised, and an urgent solution was needed if the rebel army
was going to continue.

The organization tentatively picked some of the newcomers as potential members, and allowed others to remain with them while they secured a safe passage to Somalia, where they would remain as refugees. Whether or not someone was awarded a firearm depended on how well he spoke the Somali language, and how well he could recite passages from the Holy Koran.

Wondwossen and I had joined up with four other boys, natives of Jijiga. Three were local Somalis; one was from the Adere ethnic group; and Wondwossen was Amhara, like me. The others, excepting Wondwossen and myself, were all Muslims, though none of us practised religion. All of the group, except for me, spoke excellent Somali, and so our group was accepted by the rebels.

Each of us was issued a carbine rifle and two rounds of ammunition. The guns were very old and often jammed when they were fired successively, leaving us with a general sense of anxiety. Hussain had promised to get us replacements, but they had never materialized. Perhaps the matter was out of his hands.

The first three months of our existence at the front were filled with excitement and anticipation. We were constantly on the move and took part in a number of dramatic and daring actions involving army convoys heading south. We were not able to claim a major military victory, but that didn't matter much at the time. We were satisfied that we were able to settle some old scores with the junta.

Wondwossen and I were separated about four months after we joined the front. He was sent to the eastern highlands.

Approximately a month later, my group mounted an impressive mission against an Ethiopian Army training camp in Chinaksen. A week before D-day, the activities in our camp had reached a fever pitch. We had been told of the imminence of a mission, and knew it was serious, but only the top commanders were privy to the actual target and date of attack.

Chinaksen was an eight-hour walk from the recent rebel base. Before reaching the target, we had to cross several mountains and pass through dangerously open terrain. The day before the attack, many of the Somali rebels smuggled themselves and their rifles into town, unbeknownst to the Ethiopian Army. It is not unusual for nomads travelling in twos and threes to pass into any city in Ogaden, and the disguised rebels had hidden their armaments under a pile of firewood carried on the back of a camel, where no one would think to look.

On D-day, at about 3 A.M., the big guns were drawn closer to the army barracks, mines were dug into the road leading out of town, and we took up our strategic positions and waited for the signal. At the first sound of machine-gun fire and mortar explosions, the alarm bell in the training camp was sounded. Conscripts, dressed only in their underwear, ran from the dormitories in panic. Many held their clothes in their hands, dragging them across the dusty ground, as they ran about the compound to escape the fire. The guns were locked away in the depot each night, and those unarmed boys were massacred by the dozens. If a boy raised his hands in submission, this sad gesture was the last he would make. The guerrillas took no prisoners.

After the training camp was bombed, machine-gunned and burned, we walked downtown, shooting our guns in the air, at village houses and at the church. Then the Somalis among us began to hunt for dogs. They were still smiling from the pleasure of victory as they killed the animals. Not angry or twisted smiles, as one might expect, but smiles that would be appropriate during some festivity, smiles I had taken pleasure in on long afternoons, when Hussain told his fantastic stories. The faces of these men conveyed no hint of the brutality of their hands.

Within a matter of hours, a village that had once been considered an island of peace had been devastated. When we left Chinaksen, a terrible silence hung over the remains of the camp and the
streets of the town.

My friends and I were silent on the way to the rebel camp. We
reminded ourselves that these boys had been training to be soldiers
who would one day be at war with us. But it was impossible to rec-
oncile a future possibility with the terror marking faces that still
bore the vestiges of childhood. We had watched them run for cover,
terrified and half-dressed, only to be slaughtered. What had occurred defied all logic, defied our comprehension.

The dogs had become eerily quiet the moment machine guns and
mortar fire broke the night, and remained silent even as the rebels
hunted them with the same determination that had strewn the training compound with the bodies of the dead. Somalis, perhaps because of their faith, have always abhorred dogs. They refer to these
animals as *Haram* (cursed) and do not own them as pets. Street dogs
are not treated well anywhere, but in the Muslim quarter they are
stoned, starved, and forced, through adversity, into showing their
true animal nature.

After burning down the Chinaksen training camp, we retreated to
the base. There was not a single casualty in the troop, and the success was considered a godsend. Once we had passed through the flat
terrain, we relaxed and rested. I was very tired, and rested my head
against a rock. Within a matter of seconds I was sound asleep.

What happened next sounded like a bad dream. I could hear tor-
rents of machine-gun fire. People around me were running for cover,
and someone was tugging my shirt. I tried to turn over and sleep on
my other side when I felt a sharp jab in my ribs. It was Hussain, trying desperately to wake me. Suddenly reality hit me: we were at war.

The rebels panicked. We had been tracked by an elite Ethiopian Army unit stationed some thirty kilometres away, and it was our turn, disoriented and half asleep, to scramble barefoot for cover. But there was not much chance. Mortars, high-calibre machine guns and grenades ploughed the field. Before we could make out where the enemy was and where the shots were coming from, the heavens opened fire on us. Out of the blue horizon, four fighter jets headed our way; they dipped down, spread us with machine-gun fire, and on their way up dropped bombs on us that shattered the rocks and multiplied the shrapnel. I discovered to my horror that when someone you don't know fires a .50-calibre anti-aircraft gun at you, he actually means to kill you.

I attempted to run for cover but I tripped over my shadow* and fell into a hole in the ground. Fine dust got into my eyes, ears and nose, and I could barely make out my surroundings. When I finally managed to find my legs, I discovered that the sky had fallen. It was now supported by the tip of the mountain, and hung down so low over my head that I could easily have reached up and torn a piece from the blue canvas.

The mountains shrank. Everything around me—the trees, the people and the boulders—shrank, gaining in width what they lost in height. It looked to me as though the Earth was slowly being drawn through the two huge rollers of a heavenly extruder.

I tried to move but the air had tangibly thickened. It had solidified around me into a thick gelatinous ocean, and I was unable to move. I tried to slice at that jelly with my arms and legs and managed a few painful steps, but quickly ran out of breath. I opened my mouth wide and bit a piece of that jelly, but it got stuck in my throat. I reached down for my canteen to wash it down with water, but I found my rifle instead.

---

* I tripped over my shadow: refers to an Amhara belief in the spirit world

When I looked up again, I was relieved to see that the sky had receded, the mountains had regained their reassuring majesty, and the
wind was once more blowing weightlessly past me. I noticed some
fellow rebels dashing for the impregnable cover of the mountain and
followed their lead. Many did not make it. I was one of the fortu-
nate few to find safety in a cave. The camp below was smouldering;
human limbs were scattered over a wide range. I paused in the dark
belly of the mountain to see if I had sustained any injuries. There
were tiny nicks all over my body and a gash under my right knee,
looking up at me, wondering whether or not to bleed. I grabbed
some fine dust and sprinkled it on.

Those of us who survived did not wait to witness the end. After
collecting our units and gathering our strength, we ran for the only
place we knew, the current rebel base, some twenty kilometres
away. That night, when the casualties were counted, over one hundred and forty were dead, more than fifty seriously wounded, and
the remaining three hundred psychologically crippled. Hussain was
among the dead.

Darkness shrouded the base. The next few days were spent in
mourning; the easy confidence that had permeated the rebels had
been shaken to the core. Some members defected, heading for the
relative safety of Somalia. I was undecided—until I heard what had
happened to my friend Wondwossen. He had been killed while
fighting to take over the town of Gursum.

I was told of his death, casually, by the group commander as
he was making the morning rounds. I was not sure that I had heard
the commander right, so I asked him to repeat what he had said, but he
just patted me on the shoulder, adding a few comforting words before resuming his daily duties. Hundreds of fighters were dying in
those perilous days. To him, Wondwossen was just another soldier.

———

I was stunned. Unable to carry my weight, I sought a solitary corner at the far end of the camp and collapsed on the thorny ground. My mind was racing. My eyes blurred. I felt such a terrible heat in my guts that it seemed to me that I might melt down unless I removed my skin. I searched for my battered canteen and dumped what little water it held over my head.

When my vision finally cleared, I found myself staring into pictures of my childhood as they rolled across the blue screen of the heavens. I saw myself in Memerae's shed with baby oil all over my face; I saw myself with Wondwossen hunting birds with slings as they returned to town at night; building toy planes from scrap metal; injecting Mr. Alula's cows with the avenging fluid. Soon the blue sky flickered with a scene from my childhood in which the mistress of a mansion drenched me with dirty laundry water, tossed over the fence of the compound. I could hear myself being regaled with all sorts of names, but when I looked around I was all by myself in the midst of a desert. The mansion leaped from the sky and lumbered after me. There was nowhere to hide, no one to comfort me. With each step I took, I sank deeper and deeper into the scorching desert sand. When I was about to give up and let the building press me down into the sand, I heard a voice say, "Never give up."

I leaped up with a start, but there was no one around except a large lizard who lay sunning himself on top of an immense rock, staring at me with unabashed confidence. I said a few words of prayer for Wondwossen, then got up to join the group.

I took a few tentative steps towards camp when I heard what was unmistakably Wondwossen's voice repeat the phrase I had heard before: "Never give up." I turned around as though I had just been slapped. All that remained of my vision was an empty field. The light morning wind tossed a tumbleweed across the expanse. The lizard and the bare rock it had been perched on were gone.

FROM *CATFISH AND MANDALA:*
A TWO-WHEELED VOYAGE
THROUGH THE LANDSCAPE AND
MEMORY OF VIETNAM

LAST-GAMBLE

Andrew X. Pham

This chapter from Andrew X. Pham's memoir, Catfish and Mandala, *takes place during the family's preparations to flee Vietnam after his father's escape from a reeducation camp (i.e., labor camp for political prisoners). After winning its independence from France, Vietnam was partitioned into north (allied with Communist superpowers) and south (allied with the United States). In 1965 American troops stepped up efforts to quash the Vietcong, the Communist insurgency in the south. Public sentiment against heavy military and civilian casualties led to American withdrawal in 1973. Fighting continued another two years until the South fell. After reunification under North Vietnam, sympathizers of the old government were sent to "reeducation camps" and "new economic zones." These purges, coupled with widespread poverty, caused millions to take to the seas as Boat People. Despite this, nine-year-old An and his siblings enjoy a beach idyll with their sister Chi and indulgent grandmother. An's first crush accompanies a growing awareness that his middle-class family is better off than the hungry peasants around them. The chapter ends with their departure for "beautiful free America," unaware of the dangers that await them on the open seas and beyond.*

Andrew X. Pham was born in Vietnam in 1967 and moved to San Jose, California, with his family in 1977. After the suicide of his transgendered sibling Chi—to whom the book is dedicated—Pham sold his possessions, left his job as an engineer, and embarked on a year-long bicycle journey, culminating in a return to Vietnam. Catfish and Mandala: A Two-Wheeled Voyage Through the Landscape and Memory of Vietnam *(1999), a* New York Times *Notable Book of the Year, won the Kiriyama Pacific Rim Book Prize. The recipient of a Whiting Writers Award, Pham lives in Portland, Oregon.*

The large body of Vietnam War literature comes primarily from American soldiers and journalists; now that the Boat People are coming of age, however, memoirs by Vietnamese Americans, called derogatorily Viet-kieu *("foreign Vietnamese") in Vietnam, are beginning to emerge. With its lyrical, imagistic prose and complex weave of stories (his parents' histories, coupled with the family's life in the United States and Pham's return/investigation into identity), Pham's account is much more than a war tale, the* New Yorker *crediting it with "the universality of a* Bildungsroman." *You may wish to compare "Last-Gamble" to the excerpts from Aminatta Forna's* The Devil That Danced on the Water *or Nega Mezlekia's* Notes from the Hyena's Belly. *Both are memoirs of childhoods interwoven with tumultuous national history, Forna sharing a political prisoner father and Mezlekia a witness to refugees. Or compare it to "Sea Urchin," Chang-rae*

Lee's attempt to return to and reclaim Korea twelve years after his departure for America.

On the highway downwind, the Saigon bus driver, at the first whiff of fish, announced, "Phan Thiet, the Fishsauce Capital—two more klics."

I was nine, traveling with Uncle Long back to the town of my birth. The trip initiated my family's second escape attempt from Communist Vietnam. The plan had been hatched half a year before, on the very night my father stumbled home, barefoot and bedraggled, from Minh Luong Prison. For months he paced the attic, fearful of recapture, poring over books and maps, ironing out every detail with my mother's help. This morning, he guided me out the back door saying, "Don't be afraid, son. It'll be fine. You're going home."

The bus rolled into Phan Thiet. It was one of those odd Vietnamese coastal towns steeped in one trade and indecisive about the cloak it wore. In the rainy season, rich red clay swamped the province, pasty on thatched walls, runny on children's faces. In the hot season, blistering shards of wind blasted sand into every crevice so thoroughly that old women complained it gritted their joints. This was the narrow season of transition. It had the air of paradise despite a briny tinge of decomposing fish that haunted the streets and alleys year-round. This town, after all, was famous for its fishsauce.

My step-grandfather Grandpa Le was a fishsauce baron, born into a sea-heritage that dated back before the Japanese and the French occupation. He used to claim that his ancestors invented fishsauce. The whole town was built on this industry. Everyone knew how it was made and at one time most people in town, when they weren't dragging the ocean for fish, were putting fresh fish, unwashed and ungutted, into salt barrels to ferment. While they waited on the decomposition process, all they ever talked about was fishsauce. Which fish produced the best-tasting extract? How to mix various types of fish to make a balanced bouquet. Indeed, there were many varieties of fishsauce, each suitable for a certain style of cooking. The finest batches were flavorful enough to be savored directly from the bottle. In a few weeks, a smelly black ooze seeped out the bottom of the barrel. Fisherfolk diluted and bottled this black gold and sold it all over the country. Blend masters—like Grandpa Le—guarded their secrets zealously and made fortunes. In the old days, the village folk prized bottles of fishsauce concentrate as great gifts, the equivalent of fine wine and cash.

Uncle Long said these days people treated it like an illicit narcotic, hiding their production from the tax collectors, squirreling bottles of it away for bartering. Liberated into Communism or not, Vietnamese needed fishsauce the way we needed air. For us, it was salt and a thousand other spices, the very marrow of the sea to a country of coastal people. It was a good thing Grandpa left us a stockpile of fishsauce when he died.

Grandma Le's house and sundry shop sat five yards from the main road, the national highway. The bus dropped us at the front door. Grandma, Auntie Dung, and all my siblings—Chi, Huy, Tien, and Hien—came out to greet us. Grandma took me into her shop and said I could eat as much candy from her store as I could swallow on account that she hadn't had chance to spoil me as she had my siblings. They had been living with Grandma when we came back from prison. While I was locked up in Saigon, they were running wild with the local kids.

Auntie Dung took all of us out for milkshakes. We walked down the shady avenue, holding hands, singing, our sandals scrunching on sand—this a beach town—to a kiosk that had been in the same spot under a tamarind tree since I could remember. The vendor, whose laughs were as fresh as the sweet fruits she served, hand-shaved ice for us until her arms ached. Huy and Chi had durian milkshakes made with shaved ice and condensed milk. Tien had his favorite, a bread-fruit milkshake. I had soursop.

The feasting started then and lasted until the moment we left. Grandma didn't think she would see us again so she made us our favorite dishes. Grandma and Great-Grandaunt, who was so old and stooped I could touch the top of her head, roasted chickens for Huy and Chi, stewed hams for Tien and Hien, and fried mountains of delicious egg rolls for me. Grandma's little house was full of laughter; the stove in her kitchen, which was separate from the main quarters, never cooled off. They were constantly making treats for us. There was so much to eat, we forgot the rest of the country was beginning to starve.

I could tell people were hungry because I often watched the store for Grandma. It was a mom-and-pop operation, hardly bigger than an average bedroom, carrying a variety of goods: a dozen bolts of cloth, kitchen knives, flour, candles, several shelves of canned foods, spices, dried edibles, and the occasional baked goods from a local baker. Neighbors came in and bought ingredients, one meal at a time: a grab of dried shrimp, a cup of fishsauce, a few spoons of sugar, a scoop of lard. The bin of white rice stayed full. I sold it by the cup to be offered to portraits of dead ancestors. People ate the red rice, a dry, tasteless wild variety that farmers once fed to chickens and pigs.

One afternoon while I was snouting through a jar of candy, the cute girl who lived next door came in. She smiled and gave me a nickel-bill and two chipped teacups.

"My mom needs a tablespoon of cooking oil and half a cup of fishsauce," she said.

"What is she making?" I mumbled, trying to swallow a mouthful of sesame caramel and grinning like a moron. My parents had enrolled me in an expensive boys' prep school. I didn't know any girls except my friend who used to live in the alley behind our house in Saigon.

"Stir-fried spinach and onion omelet."

"Oh." I filled one teacup with cooking oil, the other with fish-sauce. "You want some peppermint candy?" I handed her a fistful.

She shook her head, hesitating.

"It's free!" I said, grinning so wide my face nearly split.

"Really?"

"Yes, it's all mine." I exaggerated, pointing at the row of candy jars.

"Thanks."

"My name is An. What's yours?"

"Hoa."

"What else would you like, Hoa?" I gestured magnanimously at the entire inventory.

Grandma knew I was pilfering her store for a few smiles from Hoa, but she looked the other way, kindly going inside for a nap when Hoa came around. She was letting me grow up the way she had let Chi find her footing.

I could tell Chi was different. She smiled a lot, a lopsided grin brought on by growing up among the coconut palms and basking in Grandma's affection. This place had seeped into her, filled her out, made her a part of it. She was tall and strong. She swam, climbed trees, chopped wood, and practiced martial arts. She bullied the bullies and fasted with Grandma, who was a devout Buddhist. Chi owned the village the way it owned her and she shared it generously with me, something I, the spoiled first son, never expected.

Early every morning, Chi took Huy, Tien, and me down to the bay to teach us to swim. Grandma sent us off with steamed rice cakes filled with peppered pork and sweet beans. We walked down to the beach, our breakfasts warm in our pockets. These were to be saved for after our swim, but we ate them on the road, knowing there was a meal waiting on the beach. In the water, Chi held each of us up by our stomachs and we learned to dog-paddle. We swam, waded, and built sand castles. Entire clans of fisherfolk, from grandfathers to toddlers, gathered on the shore to bring in the morning catch. When they hauled in the nets, we pitched in, digging our feet into the sand, heaving the lines to their rhythm in a tug-of-war with the sea. The net made a great big U in the water, taking a bite of the ocean as we brought it in. Silvery fish came out of the water like coins pouring, bouncing, hopping out of a slot machine. The fisherfolk went mad with laughter, dashing about, scooping up the jackpot into hand-woven baskets, screeching to each other to grab this one or that one before it flopped back into the water. We worked with them, laughing, competing to see who bagged the most. In return, they gave us a couple of fish and lent us a pan and oil. Chi built a driftwood fire on the beach and fried the fish. We pinched the meat from the bones, and ate it off banana leaves with salt and lime, sitting on the sand, watching the sun come up out of the water. It felt as though Chi had never gone to live with Grandma. I never thought we could be so happy again, Chi and me playing as though it had never happened. Like I'd never betrayed her and Leper-boy, three years before.

The village leper didn't have a name. People called him Leper-boy although he was at least a young man. Perhaps that was because he was short, very small-boned—"hardly more than a lame chicken," Grandma used to say. I was in kindergarten then, and he didn't seem all that much bigger than me. He walked on one leg and crutches. His other foot had withered around the ankle like a bad squash. But he was a great traveler, getting around the village more than most two-legged folks. They said he even made it out to the countryside a couple of times a week. It was how he ate.

From house to house, he begged with his one gift, singing in a voice so pure the older folks grieved over his tragedy. That misshapen face, they said, cheated him of a professional career in the opera. But really, it was their way of overlooking his malady. Sad, sad, they hushed, his ancestors must have done something horrible to cause him such misfortune.

An observer of courtesy, Leper-boy made himself scarce in the morning when merchants went to market. Begging from the sellers before they could sell, people believe, brought bad commercial luck. Leper-boy let the vendors returning from market find him in the afternoon sitting by the side of the road, serenading them a cappella. Kind souls gave him bits of what they could not sell. Snack girls, walking with rounds of rice crackers, as big as trays, stacked three feet high on their heads, would stop. They often gave him a little of what they had left. He thanked them and put their gifts into a bag he slung over his shoulder, the bag a gift from some Buddhist monks, who were also, in their fashion, great beggars.

Leper-boy didn't like sesame crackers and shrimp paste as much as he liked tobacco, and he found, in my sister Chi, a suitable trading partner. He exchanged his tidbits with her for cigarette butts she had salvaged from the family's ashtrays. It was a transaction which my father had forbid. Dad said Leper-boy might be contagious and none of us could talk to him or touch anything he touched. But as children, we were not allowed to have money, and sesame rice crackers and shrimp paste were my sister's favorite snack.

Dad came home after work and found Chi snacking. He asked her how she got the food. He knew that without money she couldn't have bought it. Chi said a friend gave it to her. He asked me and I don't know why I said it. Maybe I was angry at Chi. Or, simply, I was just spoiled. Full of a first-son righteousness, I told on her. Dad raged through the house, furious at Chi. *You dare disobey me! I'll teach you how to be respectful in this house!* He laid her out on the living room divan and broke bamboo canes on her, exacting the Vietnamese punishment in a cloud of blind wrath. Neighbors crowded the

front door, begging him to stop. Men shook their heads, women be-
seeched him for mercy. Yet no one crossed the threshold. It was a
man's right to beat his child. The police weren't summoned because
they wouldn't have intervened. Mom cried, kneeling beside the divan. Dad rose above them, his visage terrible to behold, an angry god,
vengeful and unyielding. Thwack! Thwack! Thwack! Chi screamed.
Thwack! Thwack! Thwack! Thwack! Thwack! Thwack! Thwack!
Thwack! People clamored for mercy. I cried, cowering in the hallway
terrified, for I had brought these blows on her. Like striking vipers,
the canes blurred through the air, swishing, biting into Chi, one
after another. Thwack! Thwack! Thwack! She howled. I cringed,
covering my ears, knowing well the taste of bamboo, the way it licks
out at flesh, first a jolt like electricity, then sharp like a fang, then hot
like a burn. The canes broke over her back. The neighborhood
women, wringing their shirttails, muttered that Dad's cruelty was a
curse upon our house. The last cane splintered into bits, and Dad
stormed away to find another. Mom dragged Chi up and put Chi's
hand in mine. Take her to Grandma's, Mom told me. Chi and I fled
the house. I returned home that evening, but Chi never wholly came
back into our lives again.

Mom came out to Grandma's a week before Dad. When she finally
sent word for him that things were ready, he sneaked out of Saigon
and arrived in Phan Thiet by hiding on a cargo train. Dad came into
Grandma's house like a rat crossing a dark street. We were sitting on
straw floor mats in the living room eating dinner. He stepped into
the pumpkin warmth of our oil lamp and I, familiar with the care-
free beach days, saw him as though I hadn't seen him in months. He
was a thin bag of shallow breaths and sweaty skin. Fear had bled
away his commanding air. His cheekbones poked out while his eyes

sank deeper into his head. His new stoop and rain-sloped shoulders made him small.

In one step, he reunited the whole family for the first time in over a year. And suddenly, I felt Chi withdrawing to the side. She started lurking on the edge of us, constantly on one errand or another when Dad was around. She developed an eerie knack for sensing him around corners, and she had this ability to melt into the furniture when he came into the room. She never looked him in the eye. Fourteen summers old now, she was too young to have fallen permanently from grace with Dad. There was a wedge between them driven, perhaps, deeper by the fact that she lived with Grandma, who was never fond of Dad in the first place.

Our last night in Phan Thiet, Chi and I monkeyed up the starfruit tree and onto the tin roof of the kitchen shack. We picked star fruits and, dipping the wedges in chili-spiced salt, ate them sitting below a glittering sky. The fruit tasted sun-baked, for in full ripeness it was golden, the color of cloud underbellies tickled by a slanting sun. It had a flowery texture halfway between a melon and an apple, though it was less substantial than either. Its juice was sharp, indecisive between sour and sweet, resulting in a dizzied tanginess that made me think of being out in the sun too long. Chi said it was how sunlight tasted.

I told her a secret game I played when Mom and Dad left me at home alone overnight. I talked to space aliens with my flashlight, flickering photons to the reaches of darkness. Spaceships would come if I ever really needed them, I told her.

"What would you do if a spaceship came?" Chi asked.

"I'd ask them to take us to America. Here, your turn."

Chi beamed her message into the sky.

"What did you say to the spaceships?"

"I sent my wish to the angels."

"Angels? They're up there with space aliens?"

Chi nodded solemnly.

"What did you wish for?"

"I want them to watch over Grandma when we're gone."

Chi wasn't as excited about going to America as I was. She felt at home in Phan Thiet and she loved Grandma. Chi said she'd asked Mom to let her stay with Grandma, but both Mom and Dad wouldn't hear of it. We babbled late into the night, waiting to eavesdrop on the adults discussing the escape inside the kitchen shack. Everyone was there, including the fishermen who would be taking us out onto the ocean. Some of them were angry about Uncle Hung's last-minute decision to stay with Grandma. He said she was too old and needed someone to take care of her. He was convinced that with the continuing food shortages burglars would break into the house and rob her.

"You're a turtle!" Mom mocked her brother. "You never stick your neck out to take a chance. A little noise and—fffthhh—in goes your head, scared of everything." She looked around the room for emphasis and threw up her hands. "There's nothing for you here. We have relatives who will take care of Mother."

Everyone, including Grandma, urged him to go, but nothing could sway him into risking the open sea in a fishing boat. Aunt Dung, his sister, on the other hand, was all for it. She was twenty, and full of fire. A repressed little town with neither opportunity nor food was not for her. Neither were its cowardly men.

"I'll take care of Mother better than any relatives," Uncle Hung said doggedly. "Besides, maybe I'll go back to Saigon and watch your house so that it'll be there if you come back."

At this, joy bled from Mom's face. The house was her greatest treasure, their milestone in life, their monumental accomplishment. Banks didn't make home loans. The house meant security, a departure from their difficult past. They couldn't sell it because that would look suspicious. They had started out with nothing and now they were about to lose everything.

"No." Dad shook his head. "Let it go. The government will confiscate it. I don't want you implicated in our escape. We won't be back. If we return, we are as good as dead." Dad knew if we waited till next spring, he stood a fair chance of being discovered and executed. The cops swept through the neighborhood regularly and dragged people off to labor camps. Properties were "seized" and "redistributed." If they took Dad, they would send us to live in jungle hamlets.

Mom nodded, saying over and over that he was right. She was a smart and resourceful woman who had bribed the prison guards to keep her husband alive, making sure he had the little food and medicine he needed to survive the jungle. Besides rescuing him, she had worked with her brother to find seven fishermen with a boat willing to risk the high seas with us. The crew were young men from Phan Thiet, the oldest twenty-five, the youngest seventeen. Phan Thiet was my mother's hometown so it was the safest place to recruit, but it was also my father's former government station, the place where he was most likely to be recognized. They had been planning for months. The men had been stashing government-rationed diesel by the pint and hoarding spare engine parts. At first, Dad worried it was a trap, for there were many fishermen-turned-pirates who took passengers out to sea to rob and murder. Then he suspected that it was a military sting to capture would-be escapees.

"Tai, the skipper, is Mr. Tang's son," said Uncle Long, introducing his handpicked crew one by one. When he finished, he vouched for them: "I've known every man here since they were kids. All these men are safe. They have as much riding on this escape as you do, Brother Thong. If they're caught, their families can lose their boats and all fishing privileges. They will become beggars."

They began to discuss rations and details of our escape, slated for the next day.

"Oy! An." It was Hoa standing in a tree in her backyard, calling me over the fence.

"Hi, Hoa. You want some star fruit?" I whispered, hoping the adults below couldn't hear me.

"Yes. Meet me out front?"

Chi giggled. My face burned. She said loud enough for Hoa to hear, "Take some chili-salt for your girlfriend."

Too embarrassed to say anything, I stuffed my shirttail into my pants, put some star fruit down my shirt, and ran out. Hoa sat on the front porch with me. Other kids were playing Knock the Can in the street.

"I know what your family is doing," Hoa said, nibbling the point of a star fruit.

I pretended I wasn't listening. Dad had said it was supposed to be a big secret.

"All those men going into the store, then sneaking behind into the house. They don't leave until really late at night. They're fishermen, aren't they? Your family is going to cross the border, aren't you?"

I shook my head, almost feeling my father's cane on my backside. It was my fault she was hanging around the house every day.

"Everybody knows. You can tell me. We're friends, aren't we?" she insisted, calling our friendship into question, which was more than I could bear.

"Yes, we're leaving," I admitted.

We sat quietly. She picked up pebbles with her toes. The kids in the street were laughing, having a good time at their game. I wished I had brought some of my toys from Saigon to give her.

"You'll come back and visit?"

"Sure, I have to visit my grandma, don't I?"

I gave her my flashlight and she let me hold her hand. My palm turned sweaty, but she didn't let go. I liked the feel of her hand. It was soft and it made me dizzy. All my blood was dammed up in my ears.

Early in the morning, Mom ordered us into tattered clothes. The lot of us were going to pass as peasants. She had bought each of us a pair of sandals, known as Viet Cong sandals because they were made out of used tires, the cheapest footwear available. Mom and Aunt Dung hired two rickshaws to take us out of town. Going to visit relatives out in the countryside to have a picnic, Mom explained to the drivers. After they dropped us well beyond the fisherfolk's shanties that ringed the town, we walked for several hours on back roads and trails. The sandals retained their tire curvature and rubbed our feet raw. Huy and Tien began to bawl about the blisters on their toes, but I was too frightened about having told Hoa about our escape to care. If she'd told anyone, we were all going to jail again.

We threw away the sandals and went barefoot. Chi held up bravely, carrying Hien on her back for miles when he was too tired to walk. We were supposed to meet up with Dad sometime late that night, then halfway to dawn our fishermen would come for us. I was frightened that I wouldn't be able to make the swim to the boat. Yet as we walked deeper into the trees, I found myself becoming entranced by the coconut forest. The palms swayed gently in the evening breeze, their naked trunks sweeping into the sky, their splaying leaves, bright green oranging in the sunset, arcing out and down like frozen fireworks. Not a soul traveled the road.

It seemed, then, that we could simply walk out of Vietnam and right into America, beautiful free America, somewhere at the end of this wondrous road. It seemed so easy I didn't think about the thousands of boat people who died trying to escape Vietnam, or about the Vietnamese navy shooting at boats on sight. I almost forgot that this truly was our last gamble.

EVERYTHING IN THIS
COUNTRY MUST

Colum McCann

*In "Everything in This Country Must," political conflicts dev-
astating Northern Ireland in the 1980s take an intensely personal turn when a Catholic father, already suffering from the
loss of his wife and son, stands to lose both his only remaining
child, a "slow" teenage daughter, and his favorite draft horse to
the "enemy," British soldiers.*

    *Northern Ireland's diverse history dates back to Irish resis-
tance toward the English plantations of Queen Elizabeth I.
The all-island Kingdom of Ireland (1541–1800) merged into
the United Kingdom of Great Britain and Ireland in 1801
under the terms of the Act of Union. The Protestant Unionists
were a minority on the island of Ireland as a whole but were a
majority in the northern province of Ulster. Civil war contin-
ually threatened to tear the country in two over whether Ireland should be governed by the British government, based in
London, or by its own Parliament. This conflict eventually
resulted in a partition of Ireland, with six of nine Ulster coun-
ties forming Northern Ireland, and the remaining three joining three other provinces to form the largely Catholic Southern*

Ireland, later called the Republic of Ireland. In the 1980s, many families on both sides died in the "Troubles," the victims of bombings and assassinations.

Told from the perspective of Katie, the daughter, we experience her father's diminishing control over the everyday difficulties of his rural life, here centered on the imminent drowning of his horse in an unexpected flood and the horse's rescue by British soldiers who happen by. While Katie finds herself attracted to the kindness of the soldiers, her father discovers that he can no longer even determine who, what, or when those around him get to die—his life and the lives of those he loves are not under his jurisdiction.

Colum McCann, an Irish expatriate, was born in Dublin in 1965 and has lived and worked in America, Japan, and Ireland. Though he currently lives in New York City with his American wife and children, he considers himself an Irish writer. He has published two short-story collections and several novels, notably his recent biographical novel based on Rudolf Nureyev, Dancer. "Everything in This Country Must" forms part of a short-story collection of the same name; in it, McCann comments on the often violent civil unrest caused by nationalists who opposed Northern Ireland's alliance with Britain. Their sense of helplessness in the face of the hostile and repressive British rule is portrayed in the title story through the father's fury over the successful rescue of his horse and his daughter's innocent attempt to show the rescuers the warmth and dignity of her gratitude. McCann helped to turn this story into a short film in 2004.

The influence of divisive politics and cultures on personal lives can also be observed in Albert Bensoussan's "The Lost Child," in which a Jewish boy and an Arab girl must abandon their friendship once they reach a certain age, and in the *excerpt from Patrick Chamoiseau's* School Days, *in which learning the language of the oppressor becomes the battle a small boy must win.*

I t was a summer flood when our draft horse was caught in the river and the river smashed against stones. The sound of it to me was like the turning of locks. It was silage time, and the water smelled of grass. The draft horse, Father's favorite, had stepped in the river for a sniff maybe, and she was caught, couldn't move, her foreleg trapped between rocks. Father found her and called, *Katie!* above the wailing of the rain. I was in the barn, waiting for drips on my tongue from the ceiling hole. I ran out past the farmhouse into the field. At the river the horse stared wild through the rain; maybe she remembered me. Father moved slow and scared, like someone traveling deep in snow except there was no snow, just flood, and Father was frightened of water, always frightened. Father told me, *Out on the rock there, girl.* He gave me the length of rope with the harness clip, and I knew what to do. I am taller than Father since my last birthday, fifteen. I stretched wide like love and put one foot on the rock in the river middle and one hand on the tree branch above it and swung out over the river flood.

Behind me Father said, *Careful now hai.* The water ran warm and fast, like girl blood, and I held the tree branch, still able to lean down from the rock and put the rope to the halter of the lovely draft horse.

The trees went down to the river in a whispering, and they hung their long branches over the water, and the horse jerked quick and sudden, and I felt there would be a dying, but I pulled the rope up to keep her neck above water.

Father was shouting, *Hold it, girl!* and I could see his teeth clenched and his eyes wide and all the traveling of veins in his neck, the same as when he walks the ditches of our farm, many cows, hedgerows, fences. Father is always full of ditches and fright for the losing of Mammy and Fiachra and now his horse, his favorite, a big Belgian mare that cut fields once in the peaceful dark soil of long ago.

The river split at the rock and jumped fast into sprays coming up above my feet into my dress. But I held tight to the rope, held it like Father sometimes holds his last Sweet Afton cigarette at mealtime before prayers. Father was shouting, *Keep it there, girl, good!* He was looking at the water as if Mammy was there, as if Fiachra was there, and he gulped air and down he went in the water and he was gone so long he made me wail to the sky for being alone. He kept a strong hold of one tree root but all the rest of his body went away under the quick brown water.

The night had started stars. They were up through the branches. The river was spraying in them.

Father came up splutter spluttering for air with his eyes all horse-wild and his cap lost down the river. The rope was jumping in my hands and burning like oven rings, and he was shouting, *Hold it, girl, hold it, for the love of God hold it, please!*

Father went down in the water again but came up early, no longer enough in his lungs to keep down. He stayed in the river holding the root, and the water was hitting his shoulders and he was sad watching the draft horse die like everything does, but still I pulled on the halter rope so it would not, because Molly in the sweet shop told me it is not always so.

One more try, Father said in a sad voice like his voice over Mammy and Fiachra's coffins long ago.

Father dipped under and he stayed down as long as yesterday's yesterday, and then some headlights came sweeping up the town road.

The lights made a painting of the rain way up high and they put shadows on the hedgerows and ditches. Father's head popped out of the water and he was breathing heavy, so he didn't see the light. His chest was wide and jumping. He looked at the draft horse and then at me. I pointed up the road and he turned in the flood and stared. Father smiled, maybe thinking it was Mack Devlin with his milk truck or Molly coming home from the sweet shop or someone come to help save his favorite horse. He dragged on the tree root and out-struggled from the river and stood on the bank, and his arms went up in the air like he was waving, shouting, *Over here over here hai!*

Father's shirt was wet under his overalls and it was very white when the headlights hit it. The lights got close close closer, and in the brightening we heard shouts and then the voices came clear. They sounded like they had swallowed things I never swallowed. I looked at Father and he looked at me all of a sudden with the strangest of faces, like he was lost, like he was punched, like he was the river cap floating, like he was a big alone tree desperate for forest. Someone shouted out. *Hey, mate, what's goin' on?* in a strange strange way, and Father said, *Nothing,* and his head dropped to his chest and he looked across the river at me and I think what he was telling me was *Drop the rope, girl,* but I didn't. I kept it tight, holding the draft horse's neck above the water, and all the time Father was saying but not saying, *Drop it, please, Katie, drop it, let her drown.*

They came right quick through the hedge, with no regard for the uniforms that hide them. One took off his helmet while he was running, and his hair was the color of winter ice. One had a moustache that looked like long grasses, and one had a scar on his cheek like the bottom end of Father's barn hay knife.

HayKnife was first to the edge of the river, and his rifle banged against his hip when he jumped out to the rock where I was halter-holding. *Okay, love, you're all right now*, he said to me, and his hand was rain-wet at my back, and he took the halter and shouted things to the other soldiers, what to do, where to stand. He kept ahold of the halter and passed me back to LongGrasses, who caught my hand and brought me safely to the riverbank. There were six of them now, all guns and helmets. Father didn't move. His eyes were steady looking at the river, maybe seeing Mammy and Fiachra in each eye of the draft horse, staring back.

One soldier was talking to him loud and fast, but Father was like a Derry shop-window dummy, and the soldier threw up his arms and turned away through the rain and spat a big spit into the wind.

HayKnife was all balance on the rock with the halter, and he didn't even hold the branch above his head. IceHair was taking off his boots and gun and shirt and he looked not like boys from town who come to the barn for love, he looked not like Father when Father cuts hay without his shirt, no, he looked not like anybody; he was very skinny and strong with ribs like sometimes a horse has after a long day in the field. He didn't dive like I think now I would have liked him to, he just stepped into the water very slow and not show-offy and began making his way across, arms high in the air getting lower. But the river got too deep and HayKnife shouted from the rock, saying, *Stay high, Stevie, stay high side, mate.*

And Stevie gave a thumb up to HayKnife and then he was down under the water and the last thing was the kick of the feet.

LongGrasses was standing beside me and he put Stevie's jacket on my shoulders to warm me, but then Father came over and pushed LongGrasses away. Father pushed hard. He was smaller than Long-Grasses, but LongGrasses bashed against the trunk of the tree. Long-Grasses took a big breath and stared hard at him. Father said, *Leave her alone, can't you see she's just a child?* I covered my face for shame, like in school when they put me in class at a special desk bigger than the rest,

not the wooden ones with lifting lids, except I don't go to school anymore since Mammy and Fiachra died. I felt shame like the shame of
that day, and I covered my face and peeped through my fingers.

Father was giving a bad look to LongGrasses. LongGrasses stared
at Father for a long time too and then shook his head and walked
away to the riverbank where Stevie was still down in the water.

Father's hands were on my shoulders, keeping me warm, and he
said, *It'll be all right now, love*, but I was only thinking about Stevie
and how long he was under water. HayKnife was shouting at the
top of his voice and staring down into the water, and I looked up
and saw the big army truck coming through the hedgerow fence
and the hedge was broken open with a big hole and Father screamed
No! The extra lights of the truck were on and they were lighting up
all the river. Father screamed again. *No!* but stopped when one of
the soldiers stared at him. *Your horse or your bloody hedge, mate.*

Father sat down on the riverbank and said, *Sit down, Katie*, and I
could hear in Father's voice more sadness than when he was over
Mammy's and Fiachra's coffins, more sadness than the day after
they were bit by the army truck down near the Glen, more sadness
than the day the judge said, *Nobody is guilty, it's just a tragedy*, more
sadness than even that day and all the other days that follow.

Bastards, Father said in a whisper, *bastards*, and he put his arm
around me and sat watching until Stevie came up from the water
swimming against the current to stay in one place. He shouted up at
HayKnife, *Her leg's trapped*, and then, *I'm gonna try and get the hoof
out*. Stevie took four big gulps of air and HayKnife was pulling on
the halter rope and the draft horse was screaming like I never heard
a horse before or after. Father was quiet and I wanted to be back in
the barn alone, waiting for drips on my tongue. I was wearing Stevie's jacket but I was shivering and wet and cold and scared, because
Stevie and the draft horse were going to die, since everything in this
country must.

Father likes his tea without bags, like Mammy used to make, and so there is a special way for me to make it. Put cold cold water in the kettle, and only cold, and boil it, and then put a little boiling water in the teapot and swish it around until the bottom of the teapot is warm. Then put in tea leaves, not bags, and then the boiling water, and stir it all very slowly and put on the tea cozy and let it stew on the stove for five minutes, making sure the flame is not too high so the tea cozy doesn't catch flame and burn. Then pour milk into the cups and then the tea, followed at last by the sugar all spooned around into a careful mixture.

My tea fuss made the soldiers smile, even Stevie, who had a head full of blood pouring down from where the draft horse kicked him above his eye. Father's face went white when Stevie smiled, but Stevie was very polite. He took a towel from me because he said he didn't want to get blood on the chair. He smiled at me two times when I put my head around the kitchen door, and held up one finger, meaning *One sugar, please*, and a big O from fingers for *No milk, please*. Some blood was drying in his hair, and his eyes were bright like the sky should be, and I could feel my belly sink way down until it was there like love in the barn, and he smiled at me number three.

Everyone felt good for saving a life, even a horse life, maybe even Father, but Father was silent in the corner. He was angry at me for asking the soldiers to tea, and his chin was long to his chest and there was a puddle at his feet. Everybody was towel-drying except Father and me, because we had not enough towels.

LongGrasses sat in the armchair and said, *Good thing ya had heat lamps, guvnor.*

Father just nodded.

How was it under the water, Stevie? LongGrasses said.

Wet, Stevie said, and everybody laughed but not Father. He stared at Stevie and then looked away.

The living room is always dark with Father grim, but it was brighter now. I liked the green of the uniforms and even the red of Stevie's blood. But Stevie's head from the horse kick must have been very sore. The other soldiers were talking about how maybe the army truck should take Stevie straight off to hospital and not get dry, just get stitches, and not get tea, just come back later to see about the draft horse if she survives under the heat lamps. But Stevie said, *I'm okay, guys, it's just a scrape. I'd kill for a cuppa.*

The tea was good-tasting from long brewing, and we had biscuits for special visitors. I fetched them from the pantry. I tasted one to make sure they were fresh-tasting and I carried out the tray.

I was sneezing but I was very careful to sneeze away from the tray so as to have politeness like Stevie. Stevie said, *God bless you* in his funny funny way, and we were all quiet as we sipped on the tea, but I sneezed again three four five times, and HayKnife said, *You should change out of them wet clothes, love.*

Father put down his teacup very heavy on the saucer and it was very quiet.

Everyone, even the soldiers, looked at the floor, and the mantelpiece clock was ticking and Mammy's picture was staring down from the wall, and Fiachra when he was playing football, and the soldiers didn't see them but Father did. The long silence was longer and longer until Father called me over, *Come here, Katie,* and he stood me by the window and he took the long curtain in his hands. He turned me around and wrapped the curtain around me and he took my hair and started rubbing not tender but hard. Father is good; he was just wanting to dry my hair because I was shivering even in Stevie's jacket. From under the curtain I could see the soldiers and I could see most of all Stevie. He sipped from his tea and smiled at me, and Father coughed real loud and the clock ticked some more until HayKnife said, *Here, guv, why don't you use my towel for her?*

Father said, *No, thanks.*

HayKnife said, *Go on, guv,* and he put the towel in a ball and made about to throw it.

Father said, *No!*

Stevie said, *Take it easy.*

Take it easy? HayKnife said.

Maybe you should all leave, Father said.

HayKnife changed his face and threw the towel on the ground at Father's feet, and HayKnife's cheeks were outpuffing and he was breathing hard and he was saying, *Fat lot of fuckin thanks we get from your sort, mister.*

HayKnife was up on his feet now and pointing at Father, and the light shone off his boots well polished, and his face was twitching so the scar looked like it was cutting his face. LongGrasses and Stevie stood up from the chairs and were holding HayKnife back, but HayKnife was saying. *Risk our fuckin lives and save your fuckin horse and that's all the thanks we get, eh?*

Father held me very tight with the curtain wrapped around me, and he seemed scared and small and trembly. HayKnife was shouting lots and his face was red and scrunched. Stevie kept him back. Stevie's face was long and sad and I knew he knew because he kept looking at Mammy and Fiachra on the mantelpiece beside the ticking clock. Stevie dragged HayKnife out from the living room and at the kitchen door he let go. HayKnife turned over Stevie's shoulder one last time and looked at Father with his face all twisted, but Stevie grabbed him again and said, *Forget it, mate.*

Stevie took HayKnife out through the kitchen door and into the yard toward the army truck, and still the rain was coming down outside, and then the living room was quiet except for the clock.

I heard the engine of the army truck start.

Father stood away from me and put his head on the mantelpiece near the photos. I stayed at the window still in Stevie's jacket, which Stevie forgot and hasn't come back for yet.

I watched the truck as it went down the laneway, and the red lights on the green gate as it stopped and then turned into the road past where the draft horse was lifted from the river. I didn't hear anything then, just Father starting low noises in his throat, and I didn't turn from the window because I knew he would be angry for me to see him. Father was sniff sniffling. Maybe he forgot I was there. It was going right down into him and it came in big gulps like I never heard before. I stayed still, but Father was trembling big and fast. He took out a handkerchief and moved away from the mantelpiece. I didn't watch him because I knew he would be shamed for his crying.

The army truck was near out of sight, red lights on the hedgerows.

I heard the living room door shut, then the kitchen door, then the pantry door where Father keeps his hunting rifle, then the front door, and I heard the sounds of the clicker on the rifle and him still crying going farther and farther away until they were gone, and he must have been in the courtyard standing in the rain.

The clock on the mantelpiece sounded very loud, so did the rain, so did my breathing, and I looked out the window.

It was all near empty on the outside road, and the soldiers were going around the corner when I heard the sounds, not like bullets, more like pops one two three and the echo of them came loud to me.

The clock still ticked.

It ticked and ticked and ticked.

The curtain was wet around me, but I pulled it tight. I was scared, I couldn't move. I waited it seemed like forever.

When Father came in from outside I knew what it was. His face was like it was cut from a stone and he was not crying anymore and he didn't even look at me, just went to sit in the chair. He picked up his teacup and it rattled in his fingers, so he put it down again and put his face in his hands and stayed like that. The ticking was gone from my mind, and all was quiet everywhere in the world, and I held the curtain like I held the sound of the bullets going into the draft horse's head, his favorite, in the barn, one two three, and I stood at the window in Stevie's jacket and looked and waited and still the rain kept coming down outside one two three one two three one two three and I was thinking oh, what a small sky for so much rain.

Meeting the Other

TAPKA

David Bezmozgis

*"Tapka," David Bezmozgis' story about Latvian Jewish immi-
grant children responding to the difficulties of cultural adaptation
in Toronto, focuses on six-year-old Mark and his cousin as they
dog-sit a neighbor couple's beloved Lhasa Apso, with near-tragic
consequences. Though the cousins start off assuming this responsibility with pride in their ability to put Tapka through her walking and playing routines, things do not go well. Mark's mother
feels nothing but contempt for the couple's devotion to their dog,
an obvious surrogate child; Mark and his cousin soon become
bored with their duties and resort to spicing them up by distracting themselves with newly acquired English-language repartee
picked up from their school playground. While they have already
shown signs of assimilating, none of these characters will ever tri-
umph over the dislocation described in Mark's assessment of this
moment in their lives that takes place at the end of the story.*

*David Bezmozgis, like the story's narrator, Mark Berman,
came to Canada from Latvia when he was six, in 1980, during
the exodus of Soviet Jews. Educated at McGill University in
Montreal and later at the University of Southern California's*

film school, Bezmozgis has written screenplays and directed documentaries. "Tapka" became part of the seven linked stories in his debut short-story collection, entitled Natasha and Other Stories; *these stories about the Berman family, who, like his own family, arrive in Canada from Latvia and struggle to adapt as best they can to a strange new life, are prime examples of autobiographical fiction—the Bermans have the same address as the Bezmozgis family once did, and Mark Berman goes to the same elementary school that David Bezmozgis attended. Part of the common refugee experience is played out when the Bermans, former Baltic aristocrats, mingle with an older, childless, socially inferior couple from Minsk, the Nahumovskys. The Nahumovskys are the proud owners of Tapka, the remaining link to their former lives and the focus of Rita Nahumovsky's devotion.*

This story's emphasis on estrangement and otherness can be compared to the excerpt from Elisabeth Gille's autobiographical novel Shadows of a Childhood, *in which the only significant difference separating Léa Lévy's hard discovery from Mark Berman's is Bezmozgis' use of humor to convey the sense of sadness and loss. Using humor as a way of simultaneously emphasizing and undercutting sadness and loss can also be found in the excerpt from Patrick Chamoiseau's* School Days *and in Tiffany Midge's short story "Beets," where both narrators suffer social alienation created by discrimination within their own native culture.*

Goldfinch was flapping clotheslines, a tenement delirious with striving. 6030 Bathurst: insomniac scheming Odessa. Cedarcroft: reeking borscht in the hallways. My parents, Baltic aristocrats, took an apartment at 715 Finch fronting a ravine and across from an elementary school—one respectable block away from the Russian swarm. We lived on the fifth floor, my cousin, aunt, and uncle directly below us on the fourth. Except for the Nahumovskys, a couple in their fifties, there were no other Russians in the building. For this privilege, my parents paid twenty extra dollars a month in rent.

In March of 1980, near the end of the school year but only three weeks after our arrival in Toronto, I was enrolled in Charles H. Best elementary. Each morning, with our house key hanging from a brown shoelace around my neck, I kissed my parents goodbye and, along with my cousin Jana, tramped across the ravine—I to the first grade, she to the second. At three o'clock, bearing the germs of a new vocabulary, we tramped back home. Together, we then waited until six for our parents to return from George Brown City College, where they were taking their obligatory classes in English.

In the evenings we assembled and compiled our linguistic bounty.
Hello, havaryew?
Red, yellow, green, blue.
May I please go to the washroom?
Seventeen, eighteen, nineteen, twenny.

Joining us most nights were the Nahumovskys. They attended the same English classes and traveled with my parents on the same bus. Rita Nahumovsky was a beautician, her face spackled with makeup, and Misha Nahumovsky was a tool and die maker. They came from Minsk and didn't know a soul in Canada. With abounding enthusiasm, they incorporated themselves into our family. My parents were glad to have them. Our life was tough, we had it hard—but the Nahumovskys had it harder. They were alone, they were older, they were stupefied by the demands of language. Being essentially helpless themselves, my parents found it gratifying to help the more helpless Nahumovskys.

After dinner, as we gathered on cheap stools around our table, my mother repeated the day's lessons for the benefit of the Nahumovskys and, to a slightly lesser degree, for the benefit of my father. My mother had always been a dedicated student and she extended this dedication to George Brown City College. My father and the Nahumovskys came to rely on her detailed notes and her understanding of the curriculum. For as long as they could, they listened attentively and groped toward comprehension. When this became too frustrating, my father put on the kettle, Rita painted my mother's nails, and Misha told Soviet jokes.

In a first-grade classroom a teacher calls on her students and inquires after their nationality. "Sasha," she says. Sasha says, "Russian." "Very good," says the teacher. "Arnan," she says. Arnan says, "Armenian." "Very good," says the teacher. "Lubka," she says. Lubka says, "Ukrainian." "Very good," says the teacher. And then she asks Dima. Dima says, "Jewish." "What a shame," says the teacher, "so young and already a Jew."

The Nahumovskys had no children, only a white Lhasa-apso named Tapka. The dog had lived with them for years before they emigrated and then traveled with them from Minsk to Vienna, from Vienna to Rome, and from Rome to Toronto. During our first month in the building, Tapka was in quarantine and I saw her only in photographs. Rita had dedicated an entire album to the dog, and to dampen the pangs of separation, she consulted the album daily. There were shots of Tapka in the Nahumovskys' old Minsk apartment, seated on the cushions of faux Louis XIV furniture; there was Tapka on the steps of a famous Viennese palace; Tapka at the Vatican; in front of the Coliseum; at the Sistine Chapel; and under the Leaning Tower of Pisa. My mother—despite having grown up with goats and chickens in her yard—didn't like animals and found it impossible to feign interest in Rita's dog. Shown a picture of Tapka, my mother wrinkled her nose and said "foo." My father also couldn't be bothered. With no English, no money, no job, and only a murky conception of what the future held, he wasn't equipped to admire Tapka on the Italian Riviera. Only I cared. Through the photographs I became attached to Tapka and projected upon her the ideal traits of the dog I did not have. Like Rita, I counted the days until Tapka's liberation.

The day Tapka was to be released from quarantine Rita prepared an elaborate dinner. My family was invited to celebrate the dog's arrival. While Rita cooked, Misha was banished from their apartment. For distraction, he seated himself at our table with a deck of cards. As my mother reviewed sentence construction, Misha played hand after hand of Durak* with me.

—The woman loves this dog more than me. A taxi to the customs facility is going to cost us ten, maybe fifteen dollars. But what can I do? The dog is truly a sweet little dog.

When it came time to collect the dog, my mother went with Misha and Rita to act as their interpreter. With my nose to the window, I watched the taxi take them away. Every few minutes, I reapplied my nose to the window. Three hours later the taxi pulled into our parking lot and Rita emerged from the back seat cradling animated fur. She set the fur down on the pavement, where it assumed the shape of a dog. The length of its coat concealed its legs, and as it hovered around Rita's ankles, it appeared to have either a thousand tiny legs or none at all. My head ringing "Tapka, Tapka, Tapka," I raced into the hallway to meet the elevator.

That evening Misha toasted the dog:

—This last month, for the first time in years, I have enjoyed my wife's undivided attention. But I believe no man, not even one as perfect as me, can survive so much attention from his wife. So I say, with all my heart, thank God our Tapka is back home with us. Another day and I fear I may have requested a divorce.

---

* *Durak:* the most popular card game in Russia; "Durak" means a fool or loser—the player left with cards after everyone else has run out

Before he drank, Misha dipped his pinkie finger into his vodka glass and offered it to the dog. Obediently, Tapka gave Misha's finger a thorough licking. Duly impressed, my uncle declared her a good Russian dog. He also gave her a lick of his vodka. I gave her a piece of my chicken. Jana rolled her a pellet of bread. Misha taught us how to dangle food just out of Tapka's reach and thereby induce her to perform a charming little dance. Rita also produced "Clonchik," a red and yellow rag clown. She tossed Clonchik under the table, onto the couch, down the hallway, and into the kitchen; over and over Rita called, "Tapka get Clonchik," and, without fail, Tapka got Clonchik. Everyone delighted in Tapka's antics except for my mother, who sat stiffly in her chair, her feet slightly off the ground, as though preparing herself for a mild electric shock.

After the dinner, when we returned home, my mother announced that she would no longer set foot in the Nahumovskys' apartment. She liked Rita, she liked Misha, but she couldn't sympathize with their attachment to the dog. She understood that the attachment was a consequence of their lack of sophistication and also their childlessness. They were simple people. Rita had never attended university. She could derive contentment from talking to a dog, brushing its coat, putting ribbons in its hair, and repeatedly throwing a rag clown across the apartment. And Misha, although very lively and a genius with his hands, was also not an intellectual. They were good people, but a dog ruled their lives.

Rita and Misha were sensitive to my mother's attitude toward Tapka. As a result, and to the detriment of her progress with English, Rita stopped visiting our apartment. Nightly, Misha would arrive alone while Rita attended to the dog. Tapka never set foot in our home. This meant that, in order to see her, I spent more and more time at the Nahumovskys'. Each evening, after I had finished my homework, I went to play with Tapka. My heart soared every time Rita opened the door and Tapka raced to greet me. The dog knew no hierarchy of affection. Her excitement was infectious. In Tapka's presence I resonated with doglike glee.

Because of my devotion to the dog and their lack of an alternative, Misha and Rita added their house key to the shoelace hanging around my neck. Every day, during our lunch break and again after school, Jana and I were charged with caring for Tapka. Our task was simple: put Tapka on her leash, walk her to the ravine, release her to chase Clonchik, and then bring her home.

Every day, sitting in my classroom, understanding little, effectively friendless, I counted down the minutes to lunchtime. When the bell rang I met Jana on the playground and we sprinted across the grass toward our building. In the hall, our approaching footsteps elicited panting and scratching. When I inserted the key into the lock I felt emanations of love through the door. And once the door was open, Tapka hurled herself at us, her entire body consumed with an ecstasy of wagging. Jana and I took turns embracing her, petting her, covertly vying for her favor. Free of Rita's scrutiny, we also satisfied certain anatomical curiosities. We examined Tapka's ears, her paws, her teeth, the roots of her fur, and her doggy genitals. We poked and prodded her, we threw her up in the air, rolled her over and over, and swung her by her front legs. I felt such overwhelming love for Tapka that sometimes when hugging her, I had to restrain myself from squeezing too hard and crushing her little bones.

It was April when we began to care for Tapka. Snow melted in the ravine; sometimes it rained. April became May. Grass absorbed the thaw, turned green; dandelions and wildflowers sprouted yellow and blue; birds and insects flew, crawled, and made their characteristic noises. Faithfully and reliably, Jana and I attended to Tapka. We walked her across the parking lot and down into the ravine. We threw Clonchik and said "Tapka get Clonchik." Tapka always got

Clonchik. Everyone was proud of us. My mother and my aunt wiped tears from their eyes while talking about how responsible we were. Rita and Misha rewarded us with praise and chocolates. Jana was seven and I was six; much had been asked of us, but we had risen to the challenge.

Inspired by everyone's confidence, we grew confident. Whereas at first we made sure to walk thirty paces into the ravine before releasing Tapka, we gradually reduced that requirement to ten paces, then five paces, until finally we released her at the grassy border between the parking lot and ravine. We did this not out of laziness or recklessness but because we wanted proof of Tapka's love. That she came when we called was evidence of her love, that she didn't piss in the elevator was evidence of her love, that she offered up her belly for scratching was evidence of her love, all of this was evidence, but it wasn't proof. Proof could come only in one form. We had intuited an elemental truth: love needs no leash.

That first spring, even though most of what was said around me remained a mystery, a thin rivulet of meaning trickled into my cerebral catch basin and collected into a little pool of knowledge. By the end of May I could sing the ABC song. Television taught me to say "What's up, Doc?" and "super-duper." The playground introduced me to "shithead," "mental case," and "gaylord," and I sought every opportunity to apply my new knowledge.

One afternoon, after spending nearly an hour in the ravine throwing Clonchik in a thousand different directions, Jana and I lolled in the sunlit pollen. I called her "shithead," "mental case," and "gaylord," and she responded by calling me "gaylord," "shithead," and "mental case."

—Shithead.

—Gaylord.

—Mental case.

—Tapka, get Clonchik.

—Shithead.

—Gaylord.

—Come, Tapka-lapka.

—Mental case.

We went on like this, over and over, until Jana threw the clown and said, "Shithead, get Clonchik." Initially, I couldn't tell if she had said this on purpose or if it had merely been a blip in her rhythm. But when I looked at Jana, her smile was triumphant.

—Mental case, get Clonchik.

For the first time, as I watched Tapka bounding happily after Clonchik, the profanity sounded profane.

—Don't say that to the dog.

—Why not?

—It's not right.

—But she doesn't understand.

—You shouldn't say it.

—Don't be a baby. Come, shithead, come, my dear one.

Her tail wagging with accomplishment, Tapka dropped Clonchik at my feet.

—You see, she likes it.

I held Clonchik as Tapka pawed frantically at my shins.

—Call her shithead. Throw the clown.

—I'm not calling her shithead.

—What are you afraid of, shithead?

I aimed the clown at Jana's head and missed.

—Shithead, get Clonchik.

As the clown left my hand, Tapka, a white shining blur, oblivious to insult, was already cutting through the grass. I wanted to believe that I had intended the "shithead" exclusively for Jana, but I knew it wasn't true.

—I told you, gaylord, she doesn't care.

I couldn't help thinking, "Poor Tapka," and looked around for some sign of recrimination. The day, however, persisted in unimpeachable brilliance: sparrows winged overhead; bumblebees levitated above flowers; beside a lilac shrub, Tapka clamped down on Clonchik. I was amazed at the absence of consequences.

Jana said, "I'm going home."

As she started for home I saw that she was still holding Tapka's leash. It swung insouciantly from her hand. I called after her just as, once again, Tapka deposited Clonchik at my feet.

—I need the leash.

—Why?

—Don't be stupid. I need the leash.

—No you don't. She comes when we call her. Even shithead. She won't run away.

Jana turned her back on me and proceeded toward our building. I called her again but she refused to turn around. Her receding back was a blatant provocation. Guided more by anger than by logic, I decided that if Tapka was closer to Jana, then the onus of responsibility would become hers. I picked up the doll and threw it as far as I could into the parking lot.

—Tapka, get Clonchik.

Clonchik tumbled through the air. I had put everything in my six-year-old arm behind the throw, which still meant that the doll wasn't going very far. Its trajectory promised a drop no more than twenty feet from the edge of the ravine. Running, her head arched to the sky, Tapka tracked the flying clown. As the doll reached its apex it crossed paths with a sparrow. The bird veered off toward Finch Avenue and the clown plummeted to the asphalt. When the doll hit the ground, Tapka raced past it after the bird.

A thousand times we had thrown Clonchik and a thousand times Tapka had retrieved him. But who knows what passes for a thought in the mind of a dog? One moment a Clonchik is a Clonchik and the next moment a sparrow is a Clonchik.

I shouted at Jana to catch Tapka and then watched as the dog, her attention fixed on the sparrow, skirted past Jana and into traffic. From the slope of the ravine I couldn't see what had happened. I saw only that Jana had broken into a sprint and I heard the caterwauling of tires followed by a shrill fractured yip.

By the time I reached the street a line of cars was already stretched a block beyond Goldfinch. At the front of the line were a brown station wagon and a pale blue sedan blistered with rust. As I neared, I noted the chrome letters on the back of the sedan: D-U-S-T-E-R. In front of the sedan Jana kneeled in a tight semicircle with a pimply young man and an older woman wearing very large sunglasses. Tapka lay panting on her side at the center of their circle. She stared at me, at Jana. Except for a hind leg twitching at the sky at an impossible angle, she looked much as she did when she rested on the rug at the Nahumovskys' apartment after a romp in the ravine.

Seeing her this way, barely mangled, I started to convince myself that things weren't as bad as I had feared and I edged forward to pet her. The woman in the sunglasses said something in a restrictive tone that I neither understood nor heeded. I placed my hand on Tapka's head and she responded by turning her face and allowing a trickle of blood to escape onto the asphalt. This was the first time I had ever seen dog blood and I was struck by the depth of its color. I hadn't expected it to be red, although I also hadn't expected it to be not-red. Set against the gray asphalt and her white coat, Tapka's blood was the red I envisioned when I closed my eyes and thought: red.

I sat with Tapka until several dozen car horns demanded that we clear the way. The woman with the large sunglasses ran to her station wagon, returned with a blanket, and scooped Tapka off the street. The pimply young man stammered a few sentences of which

I understood nothing except the word "sorry." Then we were in the back seat of the station wagon with Tapka in Jana's lap. The woman kept talking until she realized that we couldn't understand her at all. As we started to drive, Jana remembered something. I motioned for the woman to stop the car and scrambled out. Above the atonal chorus of car horns I heard:

—Mark, get Clonchik.

I ran and got Clonchik.

For two hours Jana and I sat in the reception area of a small veterinary clinic in an unfamiliar part of town. In another room, with a menagerie of various afflicted creatures, Tapka lay in traction, connected to a blinking machine by a series of tubes. Jana and I had been allowed to see her once but were rushed out when we both burst into tears. Tapka's doctor, a woman in a white coat and furry slippers resembling bear paws, tried to calm us down. Again, we could neither explain ourselves nor understand what she was saying. We managed only to establish that Tapka was not our dog. The doctor gave us coloring books, stickers, and access to the phone. Every fifteen minutes we called home. Between phone calls we absently flipped pages and sniffled for Tapka and for ourselves. We had no idea what would happen to Tapka, all we knew was that she wasn't dead. As for ourselves, we already felt punished and knew only that more punishment was to come.

—Why did you throw Clonchik?

—Why didn't you give me the leash?

—You could have held on to her collar.

—You shouldn't have called her shithead.

At six-thirty my mother picked up the phone. I could hear the agitation in her voice. The ten minutes she had spent at home not knowing where I was had taken their toll. For ten minutes she had been the mother of a dead child. I explained to her about the dog and felt a twinge of resentment when she said "So it's just the dog?" Behind her I heard other voices. It sounded as though everyone was speaking at once, pursuing personal agendas, translating the phone conversation from Russian to Russian until one anguished voice separated itself: "My God, what happened?" Rita.

After getting the address from the veterinarian my mother hung up and ordered another expensive taxi. Within a half hour my parents, my aunt, and Misha and Rita pulled up at the clinic. Jana and I waited for them on the sidewalk. As soon as the taxi doors opened we began to sob. Partly out of relief but mainly in the hope of eliciting sympathy. As I ran to my mother I caught sight of Rita's face. Her face made me regret that I also hadn't been hit by a car.

As we clung to our mothers, Rita descended upon us.

—Children, what oh what have you done?

She pinched compulsively at the loose skin of her neck, raising a cluster of pink marks.

While Misha methodically counted individual bills for the taxi driver, we swore on our lives that Tapka had simply gotten away from us. That we had minded her as always, but, inexplicably, she had seen a bird and bolted from the ravine and into the road. We had done everything in our power to catch her, but she had surprised us, eluded us, been too fast.

Rita considered our story.

—You are liars. Liars!

She uttered the words with such hatred that we again burst into sobs.

My father spoke in our defense.

—Rita Borisovna, how can you say this? They are children.

—They are liars. I know my Tapka. Tapka never chased birds. Tapka never ran from the ravine.

—Maybe today she did?

—Liars.

Having delivered her verdict, she had nothing more to say. She waited anxiously for Misha to finish paying the driver.

—Misha, enough already. Count it a hundred times, it will still be the same.

Inside the clinic there was no longer anyone at the reception desk. During our time there, Jana and I had watched a procession of dyspeptic cats and lethargic parakeets disappear into the back rooms for examination and diagnosis. One after another they had come and gone until, by the time of our parents' arrival, the waiting area was entirely empty and the clinic officially closed. The only people remaining were a night nurse and the doctor in the bear paw slippers who had stayed expressly for our sake.

Looking desperately around the room, Rita screamed: "Doctor! Doctor!" But when the doctor appeared she was incapable of making herself understood. Haltingly, with my mother's help, it was communicated to the doctor that Rita wanted to see her dog.

Pointing vigorously at herself, Rita asserted: "Tapka. Mine dog."

The doctor led Rita and Misha into the veterinary version of an intensive care ward. Tapka lay on her little bed, Clonchik resting directly beside her. At the sight of Rita and Misha, Tapka weakly wagged her tail. Little more than an hour had elapsed since I had seen her last, but somehow over the course of that time, Tapka had shrunk considerably. She had always been a small dog, but now she looked desiccated. Rita started to cry, grotesquely smearing her mascara. With trembling hands, and with sublime tenderness, she stroked Tapka's head.

—My God, my God, what has happened to you, my Tapkachka?

Through my mother, and with the aid of pen and paper, the doctor provided the answer. Tapka required two operations. One for her leg. Another to stop internal bleeding. An organ had been damaged. For now, a machine was helping her, but without the machine she would die. On the paper the doctor drew a picture of a scalpel, of a dog, of a leg, of an organ. She made an arrow pointing at the organ and drew a teardrop and colored it in to represent "blood." She also wrote down a number preceded by a dollar sign. The number was 1,500.

At the sight of the number Rita let out a low animal moan and steadied herself against Tapka's little bed. My parents exchanged a glance. I looked at the floor. Misha said, "My dear God." The Nahumovskys and my parents each took in less than five hundred dollars a month. We had arrived in Canada with almost nothing, a few hundred dollars, but that had all but disappeared on furniture. There were no savings. Fifteen hundred dollars. The doctor could just as well have written a million.

In the middle of the intensive care ward, Rita slid down to the floor. Her head thrown back, she appealed to the fluorescent lights: "Nu,* Tapkachka, what is going to become of us?"

I looked up from my feet and saw horror and bewilderment on the doctor's face. She tried to put a hand on Rita's shoulder but Rita violently shrugged it off.

My father attempted to intercede.

—Nu, Rita Borisovna, I understand that it is painful, but it is not the end of the world.

—And what do you know about it?

—I know that it must be hard, but soon you will see . . . Even tomorrow we could go and help you find a new one.

My father looked to my mother for approval, to ensure that he had not promised too much.

—A new one? What do you mean a new one? I don't want a new one. Why don't you get yourself a new son? A new little liar? How about that? New. Everything we have now is new.

* *nu*: Yiddish from the Russian, meaning "well now," or "so"

On the linoleum floor, Rita keened, rocking back and forth. She hiccuped, as though hyperventilating. Pausing for a moment, she looked up at my mother and told her to translate to the doctor. To tell her that she would not let Tapka die.

—I will sit here on this floor forever. And if the police come to drag me out I will bite them.

—Ritachka, this is crazy.

—Why is it crazy? My Tapka's life is worth more than fifteen hundred dollars. Because we don't have the money she should die here? It's not her fault.

Seeking rationality, my mother turned to Misha. Misha, who had said nothing all this time except "My dear God."

—Misha, do you want me to tell the doctor what Rita said?

Misha shrugged philosophically.

—Tell her or don't tell her, you see my wife has made up her mind. The doctor will figure it out soon enough.

—And you think this is reasonable?

—Sure. Why not? I'll sit on the floor too. The police can take us both to jail. Besides Tapka, what else do we have?

Misha sat on the floor beside his wife.

I watched as my mother struggled to explain to the doctor what was happening. With a mixture of words and gesticulations she got the point across. The doctor, after considering her options, sat down on the floor beside Rita and Misha. Once again she tried to put her hand on Rita's shoulder. This time, Rita, who was still rocking back and forth, allowed it. Misha rocked in time to his wife's rhythm. So did the doctor. The three of them sat in a line, swaying together like campers at a campfire. Nobody said anything. We looked at each other. I watched Rita, Misha, and the doctor swaying and swaying. I became mesmerized by the swaying. I wanted to know what would happen to Tapka; the swaying answered me.

The swaying said: Listen, shithead, Tapka will live. The doctor will perform the operation. Either money will be found or money will not be necessary.

I said to the swaying: This is very good. I love Tapka. I meant her no harm. I want to be forgiven.

The swaying replied: There is reality and then there is truth. The reality is that Tapka will live. But let's be honest, the truth is you killed Tapka. Look at Rita; look at Misha. You see, who are you kidding? You killed Tapka and you will never be forgiven.

FROM *BUXTON SPICE*

Oonya Kempadoo

In this excerpt from Buxton Spice, *Oonya Kempadoo's lush, semi-autobiographical novel, the ten-year-old tomboy narrator Lula voices her ambivalence about growing up and accepting the fate that awaits her as a woman (her "she-self "). Instead she studies the boys in her neighborhood to see how each manages his "man-self " and to learn the "man-self language." Lula's world is as overwhelming as her burgeoning sexuality. She lives with her* dougla, *or mixed-race, family in rural Guyana in a lively neighborhood as diverse as the nation. Guyana of the 1970s reels from the racial and political conflicts that accompanied independence, and Lula's Indian father is constantly at odds with the current regime. Her sexual awakening is accompanied by a political one.*

Of mixed Indian, African, Scottish, and Amerindian heritage, novelist Oonya Kempadoo was born in Sussex, England, in 1966, the year Guyana regained its independence from England. The family returned to Guyana when she was five years old, and she has lived most of her life in the Caribbean, in St. Lucia, Trinidad and Tobago, and currently Grenada. She has worked designing costumes for Carnival, run a textile design business, and done computer graphics. She began writing in 1997, achieving almost instantaneous success with Buxton Spice *(1998) and* Tide Running *(2001).*

Though situated on the northern coast of South America, Guyana is considered part of the Caribbean, having shared what Antonio Benítez Rojo calls a common history of genocide, slavery, im/migration, and plantation economies. Language and colonial history, however, have resulted in distinct differences between the Anglophone, Francophone, and Hispanophone parts of the Caribbean. Kempadoo's use of creole (or Guyanese patois) throughout the novel continues a literary shift away from colonial influence and toward African traditions. The oral folktales brought by African slaves evolved into the popular "talk-story," an informal community event that is now becoming a recognized literary form. You may wish to compare Buxton Spice *to Patricia Grace's "Kura," a Maori talking-tale about girls under colonialism, and the excerpt from Patrick Chamoiseau's* School Days, *about a boy in the Francophone Caribbean struggling to negotiate French.*

I watched Iggy's spriggy-hair hefty man-self. He had an ease with it. Some other boys did too. Not like the hard black-black Rastas silhouetted in the streetlight. They were slinky cats moving into the night, their bodies liquid, rolling on to one foot and then the other, cool. They held their man-self tighter inside them, coiled, ready to spring. I gauged how much of that cool I could really get right, practised the walk. But all that really came off was the stance—legs apart, bounce-me-nuh look. All the nights I studied their movements from the upstairs window—the way they pulled on the bright cigarette stub and then swung down the hand, grab the crotch, shift to the other leg. That stance was all I could honestly imitate. But I could do it anytime I wanted to, even in a dress, and feel my man-self standing like that. Didn't matter that I didn't have a lolo muscle. Didn't have things that girls have either—small feet and smooth hands. My bunge bone looked like it was about to grow a muscle anyway. I could climb trees as high as any boy. Had corns across my palms from swinging on branches. Judy had a man-self too. Could climb good. She could hang on for longer with her strong arms and pull herself back up. When we played Dungs War and one of her dungs hit you, it stung hard, like was one of the boys pelt it. Rachel and Sammy, with their eye-blinking selves, always howled when she pelted them.

Some of them big men's man-self was sloppy. It just hung around in the flab round they waist. Jiggled in their shaking thighs and big bellies. Came out in a belch or a too-loud laugh or a slap on a woman's arse rolling by. Others held it stiff in their muscles, like Night Helicopter the watchman at Enmore Estate. When he walked down the road to work he strapped in some of his man-self with a big broad leather belt over his khaki shirt. The thing was pulled in so tight, looked like he wasn't going to breathe till he got there, two miles down the road. He'd roll from leg to leg, an aluminium saucepan of food in one hand and his baton in the other. And if you couldn't see his man-self then, puffed up like that, you couldn't see it in nobody. Yan and his friends dared each other to shout out his falsename at him—"Night Helicopter!"—to see him let out his breath, let go of his man-self and run mad. Beef was like that too, charging his way through to the Co-op to unload sacks of flour. Hell to trouble. He was short, and square solid muscle. Always barged his way down the street, a belt round his waist too, even if he didn't have a shirt on. Belt on his bare belly and pants tied up below. Might knock you down if you didn't make way for him.

Look-Back had his man-self so covered up it was confusing.

He'd walk and look back. Small mincing steps and look again. Bird movements, his long neck swivelling, his hands jerking everywhere when he talked, eyes darting. Pants belted right up on his chest. The Rastas had a different name for him. They called him "Anti-man" and he'd scuttle past them fast and into his street.

I looked at my brother's man-self. It was like he was just beginning to know he had it. Maybe I could see it better than he could. It was wobbling around in his voice sometimes and making his apple begin to bump out. His hands gripped too hard and surprised him, growing feet kept stumping out toenails. His belly called for more and more food and his man-self came horsing out of his big teeth as he wolfed a whole loaf of bread down, laughing at how much he could eat. Dads must'a noticed it too. Gave him the keys to bring the van into the yard. Let him go to the cinema anytime he wanted, by himself. We had to go with one'a *them*. I was jealous that Yan didn't have to wear a shirt—my chest was flat as his—so I started walking around without one. Just wore a pair of Dads's old pants held up with string for braces. I began to hate Yan's man-self but wanted to stick around him all the time to do the man-things with him.

This was serious business. Our van had to have an engine job and then a body job. Yan and the boys were taking it on. Mikey, Neighbour Mildred's son, was in charge. He was a mechanic. I sat among the black hands and gasoline smell passing spanners. Had the whole range of them laid out in front of me. Half the time I'd be peeping into the dark under the van to where Mikey lay with a torch, trying to see if I could guess which spanner would be needed next. Carburettor was out, loosed apart. Yan explained how it worked. Took his time to teach me how it all went together while Son and Manny greased down parts of the engine. Later, when I explained this important carburettor set-up to Dads, he smiled like he saw a little of my man-self.

Squatting, grinning and greasing with the boys was the best times of simple man pleasures. When they put the engine back in and the sanding began, was even better. They gave me a small dent to sand and fill. I knew I could do it just as good as anyone, feeling it all the time with my fingertips. Was heaven busying up myself with them. The filler smell and hosing and water-sanding. Rubbing my hand on the smooth-smooth surface, sanding again. Laughing when they laughed. Not talking too much, just glad to listen to their shit talk.

I enjoyed my man-self with the boys. Bits of their man-selves soaked into me and I learnt then how to understand the man-self language. Like with Ramesh, flitting from the Great Van Job to his yard-work. His man-self was so soft and gentle and warm, it hurt me to see Dads shouting at him. Or to see him looking at Yan, shame showing on his face for not knowing so much. I knew I could try out how my she-self worked with him and he'd never embarrass me. I could trust him. My eye-contact could bring a faint smile to his mouth.

Or Son who was still a sparkly red boy. The only son of Mr. Baker, the quiet hard-working house painter, and his warish wife from Buxton. Son had broad flat features and glowing skin, and lips that spread into a smile just as easy at me as at Yan or Manny. His man-self was something in his skin and shone out in a friendly comfortable way.

Iggy's brother Manny ignored me. He stored his man-self in his head. It grew as he got older, right there in his head. Made his head big and his hair long. Fancied himself and thought he was well spoken. It made him study and read till he was almost blind.

Mikey was tall, dark and lanky. Black slinky cat but white teeth smiling. He never knew how much I watched his man-self, his tall loose laughy way, made me want more of it. Be near him all the time. Walk and lope around with him. I watched the way he towered over his mother, looked after her since his father's death, protected her from the jumbies in the cemetery on the other side of their fence. And laughed with her about it. Wished I could come out of "Yan's little sister" skin and be out on the street late when he came out bathed and dressed for the night. I'd whistle at him from the upstairs window and he'd whistle back before looking up. It always made him laugh and wave. Damn Buxton Spice* laughed and waved too— mocking me. Had seen me practise stancing in front the mirror in the bedroom. Held in its breath, bent back laughing quietly then craning forward to see my eyes as I followed Mikey's silhouette up the road.

As I was learning the man-self language, I understood Judy's hardness better. But in Sammy I could see no man-self at all. Out'a the four a'we, she was the delicate one: legs skinnier than mine, turned-up mouth and eyes that could blink good. She had a way that could make you give her anything she wanted. She knew I recognized it and, later, when she got to growing her she-self, she'd flash her long straight she-fingers in my face—nails already growing—just to irritate me. She didn't want to miss out on anything even when me and Judy played as rough as we could to try to stop her joining in. Saskia was only two years younger than her but the two a'them couldn't be left in the same room for long. In no time Saskia'd beat her up or t'ief her books or something. Saskia must'a seen that "get what I want" shape of her mouth or look in her eye. Sometimes I felt sorry for Sammy. Guilty bout how we'd use her to get to go to the cinema and then treat her like she really too small to come. Never felt sorry for too long though. At the dinner table, she'd be giving everybody news. Miss Guyana Broadcasting Corporation: who buried today, who went to the funeral, where the grave is in the cemetery, what the dead face look like. Things we all saw together, she'd be letting out without knowing it. Got us in trouble too. If that was what she-self was all about, I go keep my man-self till I old.

* Damn Buxton Spice: the name given to the large mango tree outside Lula's window

THE LOST CHILD: AN ALGERIAN CHILDHOOD

Albert Bensoussan

TRANSLATED BY MARJOLIJIN DE JAGER

In this deceptively simple tale based on Albert Bensoussan's life, a six-year-old Jewish boy is traumatized upon losing his mother in the Casbah (old market district) on the eve of Rosh Hashanah. While waiting to be found, the boy is befriended by an Arab girl a few years his senior, and for the next three years, he visits every market day, the girl opening for him an entire world of honeyed sweets and culture ("it was Fatiha, the daughter of my Arabic family, who taught me the folklore of the country in which I live and survive today"). Upon the abrupt termination of their friendship, the child's confusion merges with the adult narrator's lament.

With family roots in Algeria, Morocco, Spain, and Majorca, Albert Bensoussan was born to a lower-middle-class family in Algiers in 1935. His upbringing in Algeria was "divided harmoniously" between the Judaism of home and synagogue and the Francophone culture of school. He earned a doctorate in Iberian studies, becoming a translator of Spanish literature and teaching in Algeria and France. He published his first novel at age thirty, has authored twenty works, and is currently a professor at the Université de Haute-Bretagne.

"The Lost Child" reveals Bensoussan's preoccupation with exile, which he views as "not only the passage to another bank—adulthood and maturity—but physical passage" to another country. This boundary crossing introduces another motif in his writing—the cultural exchange (and clash) resulting from centuries of Berber, Muslim, Arab, Ottoman, and French influence in Algeria. The imagistic text is layered with references to Jewish and Arabic foodways and traditions. In addition to this code-switching, the narrative switches voice, from first to third person when losing the mother, and into second when mourning the loss of Fatiha. The fact that the narrator is male makes his regret about the restrictions placed on girls, including wearing the burqa, *a garment leaving only the eyes uncovered, all the more poignant. You may wish to compare it to "The Women's Swimming Pool," Hanan al-Shaykh's story about an Arab Muslim girl negotiating public space, or the excerpt from* Shadows of a Childhood, *in which Elisabeth Gille writes about a Jewish girl searching for her parents in Paris after the war, or "Kindergarten," Victor Perera's tale of a Jewish boy's trials at an international school in Guatemala.*

For Rosh Hashanah*—which is the beginning of the year—you must eat jujubes. That is the tradition. "The Ada,"† Mama says, as she pulls me along in the rue de la Lyre, very lively on this October afternoon. Stalls against the walls everywhere: a stool with a basket on it in which the newspaper cones are lined up that every Jew in the city

---

* Rosh Hashanah: Jewish New Year; literally the "head of the year"
† 'ada: a Judeo-Arabic word meaning "tradition"

will buy because custom requires that on the first evening of Tishri*
the jujube fruit melt in the mouth of Israel (and besides, in my dic-
tionary *jujube* comes right after *juiverie*—Jewry—so there!). My
mother argues on principle and does so in the language of the country
of which I only grasp the "*shral*"† and the "*achrène douro*,"‡ but I don't
understand Arabic very well and then, too, I am so little and already
overloaded with words. She entrusts to me the cone containing the
dozen pieces of red fruit that taste like dates, and I clutch it against
my chest with one hand, while the other connects me to Mama's left
hand holding the shopping bag. Then we turn into the rue Ben-
Acher—or is the rue Porte-Neuve?—and there we are right in the
heart of the Casbah with the rivulet in the center, always full of all the
waste water that comes rushing down from the citadel. The butchers
are displaying their *bouzelouf*,§ barely cut off from the sheep's body
and still bleeding. If you only want the brain, the sheep's head is
thrown on a block and the skull smashed with an ax, then hooked fingers delicately loosen the two lobes quivering with small veins and
wrap them up in newspaper. We only buy meat at Sylvain's of Bab-el-
Oued, in the rue Suffren, where the blood never flows because the
rabbi has forbidden that. Besides, as soon as she comes home, Mama
puts the meat under the faucet in a bowl with a large pinch of salt so
that it can finish soaking. For us blood is *trefe*,‖ since the soul, you
might as well say Elohim's** breath, circulates through the blood. So
how could we eat the good Lord as the *Roumis*†† do?

---

* Tishri: the first month of the Jewish calendar
† *shral*: colloquial Arabic: "how much?"
‡ *achrène douro*: colloquial Arabic: "a hundred francs"
§ *bouzelouf*: colloquial Arabic: "sheep's head"
‖ *trefe*: Hebrew for forbidden on religious grounds
** *Elohim*: Hebrew word for God
†† *Roumis*: Muslim term for Christians (from "Rome," originally referring to Roman Catholics specifically)

The jujubes are red and moist with the syrupy taste of dates. "Just one," says Mama, who knows I'm greedy, gluttonous even, "because it's for the celebration." The beginning of the year is signaled by the sweetness of good omens: apples cut in quarters will also be soaked in honey. And then we will eat the head of a ram in memory of Isaac's sacrifice and also so we can wish for being at the head and not at the tail end of things throughout the year. And then we'll eat fish, in the desire to be prolific and fertile—without understanding it too well, I will repeat all the words Papa speaks. And we never consume bitter herbs or sour dishes as we do at Pesach,* which commemorates our slavery in Egypt. We don't even eat hazelnuts and other nuts that evening, because they irritate the mouth. No, what is needed is sweetness, calm, and trust. And I was trusting when I was six, my nose in Mama's skirt and holding her hand . . . until we stopped to buy poultry. For Tishri also is the month of atonement, prelude to the dreadful days that culminate in the fast (which I might do next year if I can), the Kippur.† The rooster will spin around on the head of the little male and will shield him from all harm throughout the year: the rooster's blood will be spilled at his feet and the sacrifice consumed. He explained this to me so carefully, Papa did, and I understood it all, so I move on fearlessly in the street, counting the flowers on Mama's dress my only concern.

With one hand Mama is holding the shopping bag, with the other the tied feet of a rooster and hen to be sacrificed, one on behalf of the boys, the other for the well-being of the girls. "It is the Ada," she repeats to dodge my questions and bustles about in the dark alleys, while I hold her skirt and try not to trip over the irregular cobblestones as we go down from the Randon market. There we are again underneath the high arcades of the Lyre. Mama quickens

* Pesach: Passover
† Kippur: the Day of Atonement (the tenth of the month of Tishri)

her pace to catch the green double streetcar on the place du Cheval. I trot behind her, holding out my hand in front of me, intent on the blue and white flowers of her skirt, which I squeeze, which escapes my grip, and suddenly in the blinding crowd my hand clutches nothing but emptiness. I stand motionless, looking distraught, in one fell swoop stripped of all my trust in the world. I look, pivot around, turn my small hand in the air again and again. Seeing nothing anymore and almost drowning in the human flow still bustling about in the avenue, what else can I do but shout my hate. So my lungs swell and unendingly I shriek "Ma-a-ma-a . . . !"

That October day, and it was Thursday because I had no school, on the eve of the beginning of atonement, in my sixth year, I had lost Mama. Was it my fault? Was I that little, that featherbrained, too trusting? So with all the breath I could muster, with all my hate: "Ma-a-ma-a! Ma-a-ma-a!" A hand grabbed mine and pulled me into an adjacent alley. The old man bent down to my thrashing and shrieking height, and with the voice of an oak tree questioned me in Arabic. I didn't know what to say, I hardly understood him, but I already knew the basic words, the Sesame. Forcing back my tears as he stroked me, I could only utter one word: "Imma!"*

The old man took the child by the hand—the child whose mother had betrayed him, whose trust she had destroyed—and murmured a few soothing words. We had to retrace our steps. We went back up the rue de la Lyre, then back down again, and already the jujubes were making me sick, bursting forth from the many cones like the chili pepper on a dog's underbelly. And we went back up the street again. "*Ouallou!*"† he kept saying as he spread his empty hand. Yes, I was very much lost. I followed the man home, very close by, in the alley that was once again becoming the place of

* *Imma*: "Mama" in Arabic
† *Ouallou*: colloquial Arabic: "there is no more"

trust, the rue du Divan. There, indeed, he put me down on the mats on the tiled floor right inside the entrance as he loudly called, "Fatiha! Fatiha!" Then from behind a curtain, which must have divided the room in two—and surely that was the kitchen because of the good smell of the couscous and the steam—a young girl emerged, barely older than I, or perhaps eight or nine, with her hair in a single braid touched up with henna reaching down to the hem of her apron. The father explained the ins and outs to his daughter in his language, which escaped me, but the gestures he made with his hands as he let his fingers take flight made Imma's desertion quite clear. Then the little girl came closer to the still tearful child lying there and in a voice like *galbelouze**—the cake dripping with honey, which she brought me right away in the palm of her hand—said to him, "Don't be afraid [is what she said in her childlike language], your mam-ma is going to come back." Then she added, "Let's play." She unhooked a rope from the wall and started to jump in the middle of the hallway and when she was going so fast that the rope was whipping against the tiled floor, I had to encourage her by yelling, "Vinegar! Vinegar!" Then, as she extended the rope and made it trace a wide circle in the air, she took me by the hand and said: "Come, join in the dance . . . this is how you do it . . . one, two, three and there you are." After that she sped up the rotation of her rope and forced me to lift my heels faster and faster and once again we had to yell it together: "Vinegar! Vinegar!" as we doubled up with laughter. When we were completely out of breath, she left me half limp on the mat and went behind the curtain to get a large round ceramic plate loaded with *mekrouds*,\[†\] *zalabias*,\[‡\] and the famous *galbelouzes*, and invited me to coat my lips with them. While

* *galbelouze*: Arabic pastry of Algeria, with a base of flour and honey
\[†\] *mekroud*: Arabic pastry of Algeria, with a base of semolina and honey (sometimes dates as well)
\[‡\] *zalabia*: typical Arabic cake, entirely drenched in honey

chewing the honeyed semolina, I was telling her that Mama would make *mekrouds* stuffed with dates and that Antoinette, who lived on place de Chartres in the lower Casbah, always brought them to me when she came to visit us. Antoinette was the daughter of a general (of the Conquest?) who had left her with her Moorish mother and so, while growing up as the general's daughter, she cleaned house for the Jewish middle class to ensure her daily living. "So we eat the same cakes, then, Benyamine?"—she had remembered my name. "Not the *galbelouzes*," I told her and felt a little foolish because I didn't understand why I knew all the Arabic cakes except for that one.

When the door opened and my father rushed in to take me into his arms while covering me with wet kisses, I was incapable of telling what time it was or of how much time had passed. While I was playing with Fatiha, her old father—whom I was to call *Sidi Lardjouz** from then on—probably phoned my father. I didn't recall having told him my name or where I lived, but it is true that I had been taught to rattle all that off should the need arise. Fatiha kissed me on the cheek and I gave her my cone with jujubes. That was why we didn't taste any jujube fruit that particular Rosh Hashanah evening, which is the beginning of the year when one must eat dishes of good omen. But I didn't care because my lips had dripped with honey and my mouth was moist, and Fatiha and I had warded off disaster by shouting "Vinegar!" within the sky-high circle of time.

After this, every Thursday when Mama put on her flowered dress and took her shopping bag, I held her hand but remained uncommunicative during the errands—even now, I have to be dragged into town and I balk when running from store to store, and I grumble and stamp my feet, no, I don't much care for that great rush of markets and for crowds—and then we'd get off at the stop by the theater, we'd

* *Sidi Lardjouz*: colloquial Arabic: literally "the Old Gentleman"

go up the stairs behind it to the place de la Lyre and then go down underneath the arcades to the rue du Divan. There, where the door was tattooed with a hand of five fingers close together with a starry eye in the palm, she would let me tap on the door and I would make a fist and knock hard three times, shouting "Vinegar! Vinegar!" at the top of my lungs. More often than not it was Fatiha who opened the door or it was her mother, who wore baggy pants and walked on the tiled floor in bare feet, a simple scarf covering her hair. And sometimes Sidi Lardjouz passed by, laughing in his mustache and he would let his fingers flutter in front of his hands as if to remind me of the day we met. I would snuggle up against him and he'd stroke my forehead, mumbling a whole pious litany in Arabic. My mother would leave me there in good company and, after she had done her shopping at the Randon market, she would come to pick me up. She would bring a necklace of jasmine for Fatiha or else she'd give us each a large fritter dripping with oil in newspaper. First we'd jump rope, then we'd play pastry shop: Fatiha behind her stall with *galbelouzes* and I'd be the customer, then the greedy one, and finally the glutton. We'd always end with playing school, but Fatiha would be the mistress because she was something like two years older than I and then, too, she was tall, thin as a reed, standing straight in her apron and, in contrast to her mother, she always wore sandals on her bare feet with just a little henna on her nails. Of course, sometimes she'd also pretend to be a hairdresser, a masseuse in the *hammam*,* and there, if it was henna day, the whole family would drop by, myself included, and when Mama came back to get me I would boldly show her the gold louis that Fatiha had drawn in the palm of my hand. To her, being a schoolmistress always meant singing a song, and I went down with her into my garden to pick rosemary, I was with her when Joan of Arc brought her cows to pasture, I held her lovely three-colored ribbon,

---

* *hammam*: the public bath

with her the Eiffel Tower was always four hundred meters high, and we'd crisscross France's beautiful roads, flowers in our hats, a song on our lips, our hearts joyful and sincere. When I think about it, it was Fatiha, the daughter of my Arabic family, who taught me the folklore of the country in which I live and survive today. She was very gifted, even in arithmetic, and with one glance you had to guess how many *galbelouzes, zalabias*, and *mekrouds* there were on the ceramic plate and if I was wrong, well, it was very simple, she would get to eat one more. As I was greedy and a glutton even, in the long run being wrong was no longer a question. Fatiha taught me to read, count, sing, and laugh. Because I was Mama's very last child and she was growing a bit older and losing me in the streets, and then my sisters were too big already to deign to play with the six-year-old little brat that I was. Seven, eight, and nine years old.

Yes, until I was nine and the day arrived when Lalla Zohra came to see my mother and they spoke Arabic in the kitchen and I didn't understand a thing. But after her visit Mama no longer took me to the rue du Divan on Thursdays and that was when—because I was quite sad—I started to hang out with all the urchins of the Jewish Alliance in the rue Bab-el-Ouad to learn Hebrew, religion, and to prepare my communion—as they said to put it nicely. But what became of you, Fatiha, my friend? Nobody told me, or rather, I was made to understand that she had left, that she was sick, that I could no longer see her. But it was not until later, much later, that I understood. Once she had passed the age of eleven, Fatiha had become a woman and she would never again show herself with uncovered face to a boy. The veil, discretion, the cloistered life were hers. Later on, how many of these little girls did I not see in my neighborhood in the rue Danton and the rue de Mulhouse where a few Muslim families lived, little girls who used to play in the street with braids down their backs and jump rope as they yelled—and I'd sing along with them, using my Latin version: "Vinegar! Vinegar!" and I'd pick

it up in their voices—even as I was sweating over that Kantian*
thesis: *joli coquelicot,*[†] *Madame* . . . Sweet little girls playing, squealing, and one fine day they would disappear, and way down there at
the end of the street one would see frail and awkward silhouettes,
wrapped in a white sheet and with the small veil that hides nose and
mouth, leaving nothing visible but two dark eyes that had forever
lost their guile.

* Kantian (from the German eighteenth-century philosopher Immanuel Kant):
placing the human subject at the center of what we can understand about the
world, and suggesting that the rational order of the world is determined by the individual mind's experience of it

[†] *joli coquelicot*: pretty poppy

CLOSER

David Malouf

David Malouf's "Closer," told in the voice of a nine-year-old girl, Amy, who belongs to a family of Pentecostals—Christians who emphasize the reliability of the Bible and the need for the transformation of an individual's life with faith in Jesus— exposes a message of faith and hope in a world that ironically focuses on unchristian exclusion. Malouf makes home-schooled Amy use literal biblical language to emphasize the deeper truths of the story: that a beloved uncle, lost to "Sodom," or city life in Sydney, becomes an exile from his extended rural family, unloved in principle but not in memory, especially in the memory of his mother and in Amy's dreams. Forbidden by the grandfather to venture beyond the "home-paddock" fence, the glorious, golden Uncle Charles nevertheless makes the pilgrimage twice a year, at Christmas and at Easter, to visit—that is, to stand on the other side of the fence—charting his progress toward this goal with telephone announcements of his driving progress that offer the only concrete hint of the reason for his banishment in the form of a license plate identification: "This is GAY 437 . . . I am approaching . . ."

Amy's dream, the singular event of the story, occurs only af-ter Uncle Charles no longer comes one Easter. In it, Malouf con-veys a deeper truth lost on the rest of the Morpeth family: that love thwarted and withheld can be transcended by opening the heart, that the grass growing on both sides of the fence is the same, and that the will to remember trumps the injunction to forget. Ultimately, he reveals, we can move closer to one another.

Born in Brisbane, Queensland, in 1934, David Malouf divided his time between Britain and Australia until his repu-tation as a writer was established by numerous books of poetry, short fiction, opera librettos, drama, and fiction. Currently liv-ing in Australia and Tuscany, Malouf has spent much of his writing career focusing on the immigrant history of Australia, perhaps because his father's family immigrated there in the 1880s from Lebanon, while his mother's family immigrated from London just before World War I. He also writes about the relationship between city dwellers and rural dwellers, what he has called the dialogue between the notion of ourselves as citi-zens and the notion of ourselves as free wild creatures, evident in this story in the connection between Amy and her uncle.

This story, with its attempt to define a more humane no-tion of truth through the dream and with its distinct language, can be compared to those same elements in Yu Hua's "On the Road at Eighteen," where the language of truth ironically un-derscores the narrator's dreamlike learning experience, or to Faith Adiele's "Black Men," in which identity expectations and emotional realities cannot be confined by the language of race.

There was a time, not so long ago, when we saw my Uncle Charles twice each year, at Easter and Christmas. He lives in

Sydney but would come like the rest of us to eat at the big table at
my grandmother's, after church. We're Pentecostals. We believe that
all that is written in the Book is clear truth without error. Just as it is
written, so it is. Some of us speak in tongues and others have the gift
of laying on hands. This is a grace we are granted because we live as
the Lord wishes, in truth and charity.

My name is Amy, but in the family I am called Ay, and my
brothers, Mark and Ben, call me Rabbit. Next year, when I am ten,
and can think for myself and resist the influences, I will go to school
like the boys. In the meantime my grandmother teaches me. I am
past long division.

Uncle Charles is the eldest son, the firstborn. When you see him in
family photographs with my mother and Uncle James and Uncle
Matt, he is the blondest; his eyes have the most sparkle to them.
My mother says he was always the rebel. She says his trouble is he
never grew up. He lives in Sydney, which Grandpa Morpeth says is
Sodom. This is the literal truth, as Aaron's rod, which he threw at
Pharaoh's feet, did literally become a serpent and Jesus turned water
into wine. The Lord destroyed Sodom and he is destroying Sydney,
but with fire this time that is slow and invisible. It is burning people
up but you don't see it because they burn from within. That's at the
beginning. Later, they burn visibly, and the sight of the flames blistering and scorching and blackening and wasting to the bone is horrible.

Because Uncle Charles lives in Sodom we do not let him visit. If
we did, we might be touched. He is one of the fools in Israel—that
is what Grandpa Morpeth calls him. He has practised abominations.
Three years ago he confessed this to my Grandpa and Grandma and
my Uncle James and Matt, expecting them to welcome his frank-
ness. Since then he is banished, he is as water spilled on the ground
that cannot be gathered up again. So that we will not be infected by
the plague he carries, Grandpa has forbidden him to come on to the
land. In fact, he is forbidden to come at all, though he does come, at

Easter and Christmas, when we see him across the home-paddock fence. He stands far back on the other side and my grandfather and grandmother and the rest of us stand on ours, on the grass slope below the house.

We live in separate houses but on the same farm, which is where my mother and Uncle James and Uncle Matt, and Uncle Charles when he was young, grew up, and where my Uncles James and Matt still work.

They are big men with hands swollen and scabbed from the farm work they do, and burnt necks and faces, and feet with toenails grey from sloshing about in rubber boots in the bails. They barge about the kitchen at five o'clock in their undershorts, still half asleep, then sit waiting for Grandma to butter their toast and pour their tea. Then they go out and milk the herd, hose out the bails, drive the cows to pasture and cur and stack lucerne* for winter feed— sometimes my brothers and I go with them. They are blond like Uncle Charles, but not so blond, and the hair that climbs out above their singlets, under the adam's apple, is dark. They are jokers, they like to fool about. They are always teasing. They have a wild streak but have learned to keep it in. My mother says they should marry and have wives.

Working a dairy farm is a healthy life. The work is hard but good. But when I grow up I mean to be an astronaut.

Ours is a very pleasant part of the country. We are blessed. The cattle are fat, the pasture's good. The older farmhouses, like my grandfather's, are large, with many rooms and wide verandahs, surrounded by camphor-laurels, and bunyas and hoop-pines and Scotch firs. Sodom is far off, but one of the stations on the line is at the bottom of our hill and many trains go back and forth. My Uncle Charles, however, comes by car.

His car is silver. It is a BMW and cost an arm and a leg. It has

* *lucerne*: alfalfa

sheepskin seat covers and a hands-free phone. When Uncle Charles is on the way he likes to call and announce his progress.

The telephone rings in the hallway. You answer. There are pips, then Uncle Charles says in a jokey kind of voice: "This is GAY 437 calling. I am approaching Bulahdelah." The air roaring through the car makes his voice sound weird, like a spaceman's. Far off. It is like a spaceship homing in.

Later he calls again. "This is GAY 437," the voice announces. "I am approaching Wauchope."

"Don't any one of you pick up that phone," my grandfather orders.

"But, Grandpa," my brother Ben says, "it might be Mrs. McTaggart." Mrs. McTaggart is a widow and our neighbour.

"It won't be," Grandpa says. "It will be him."

He is a stranger to us, as if he had never been born. This is what Grandpa says. My grandmother says nothing. She was in labour for thirty-two hours with Uncle Charles, he was her first. For her, it can never be as if he had never been born, even if she too has cast him out. I heard my mother say this. My father told her to shush.

You can see his car coming from far off. You can see it *approaching*. It is very like a spaceship, silver and fast; it flashes. You can see its windscreen catching the sun as it rounds the curves between the big Norfolk Island pines of the golf course and the hospital, then its flash flash between the trees along the river. When it pulls up on the road outside our gate there is a humming like something from another world, then all four windows go up of their own accord, all together, with no one winding, and Uncle Charles swings the driver's door open and steps out.

He is taller than Uncle James or Uncle Matt, taller even than Grandpa, and has what the Book calls beautiful locks. They are blond. "Bleached," my grandfather tells us. "Peroxide!" He is tanned and has the whitest teeth I have ever seen.

The corruption is invisible. The fire is under his clothes and inside him, hidden beneath the tan.

The dogs arrive, yelping. All bunched together, they go bounding over the grass to the fence, leaping up on one another's backs with their tails wagging to lick his hands as he reaches in to fondle them.

"Don't come any closer," my grandfather shouts. "We can see you from there."

His voice is gruff, as if he had suddenly caught cold, which in fact he never does, or as if a stranger was speaking for him. Uncle Charles has broken his heart. Grandpa has cast him out, as you cut off a limb so that the body can go on living. But he likes to see that he is still okay. That it has not yet begun.

And in fact he looks wonderful—as far as you can see. No marks.

Once when he got out of the car he had his shirt off. His chest had scoops of shadow and his shoulders were golden and so smooth they gave off a glow. His whole body had a sheen to it.

Uncle James and Uncle Matt are hairy men like Esau, they are shaggy. But his chest and throat and arms were like an angel's, smooth and polished as wood.

You see the whiteness of his teeth, and when he takes off his sunglasses the sparkle of his eyes, and his smoothness and the blondness of his hair, but you do not see the marks. This is because he does not come close.

My grandmother stands with her hands clasped, and breathes but does not speak. Neither does my mother, though I have heard her say to my father, in an argument: "Charlie's just a big kid. He never grew up. He was always such fun to be with."

"Helen!" my father said.

I know my grandmother would like Uncle Charles to come closer so that she could really see how he looks. She would like him to come in and eat. There is always enough, we are blessed. There is an ivory ring with his initial on it, C, in the dresser drawer with the napkins, and when we count the places at table she pretends to make a mistake, out of habit, and sets one extra. But not the ring. The place stays empty all through our meal. No one mentions it.

I know it is Grandpa Morpeth's heart that is broken, because he has said so, but it is Grandma Morpeth who feels it most. She likes to touch. She is always lifting you up and hugging. She does not talk much.

When we go in to eat and take up our napkins and say grace and begin passing things, he does not leave; he stays there beside his car in the burning sunlight. Sometimes he walks up and down outside the fence and shouts. It is hot. You can feel the burning sweat on him. Then, after a time, he stops shouting and there is silence. Then the door of his car slams and he roars off.

I would get up if I was allowed and watch the flash flash of metal as he takes the curves round the river, past the hospital, then the golf course. But by the time everyone is finished and we are allowed to get down, he is gone. There is just the wide green pasture, open and empty, with clouds making giant shadows and the trees by the river in a silvery shimmer, all their leaves humming a little and twinkling as they turn over in a breeze that otherwise you might not have felt.

Evil is in the world because of men and their tendency to sin. Men fell into error so there is sin, and because of sin there is death. Once the error has got in, there is no fixing it. Not in this world. But it is sad, that, it is hard. Grandpa says it has to be; that we must do what is hard to show that we love what is good and hate what is sinful, and the harder the thing, the more love we show Him.

But I don't understand about love any more than I do about death. It seems harder than anyone can bear to stand on one side of the fence and have Uncle Charles stand there on the other. As if he was already dead, and death was stronger than love, which surely cannot be.

When we sit down to our meal, with his chair an empty space, the food we eat has no savour. I watch Grandpa Morpeth cut pieces of meat with his big hands and push them between his teeth, and chew and swallow, and what he is eating, I know, is ashes. His heart is closed on its grief. And that is what love is. That is what death is. Us inside at the table, passing things and eating, and him outside, as if he had never been born; dead to us, but shouting. The silver car with its dusky windows that roll up of their own accord and the phone in there in its cradle is the chariot of death, and the voice announcing, "I am on the way, I am approaching Gloucester, I am approaching Taree"—what can that be but the angel of death?

The phone rings in the house. It rings and rings. We pause at the sink, in the middle of washing up, my grandmother and my mother and me, but do not look at one another. My grandfather says: "Don't touch it. Let it ring." So it keeps ringing for a while, then stops. Like the shouting.

This Easter for the first time he did not come. We waited for the telephone to ring and I went out, just before we sat down to our meal, to look for the flash of his car along the river. Nothing. Just the wide green landscape lying still under the heat, with not a sign of movement in it.

That night I had a dream, and in the dream he did come. We stood below the verandah and watched his car pull up outside the fence. The smoky windows went up, as usual. But when the door swung open and he got out, it was not just his shirt he had taken off, but all his clothes, even his shoes and socks. Everything except his sunglasses. You could see his bare feet in the grass, large and bony, and he glowed, he was smooth all over, like an angel.

He began to walk up to the fence. When he came to it he stood still a moment, frowning. Then he put his hand out and walked on, walked right through it to our side, where we were waiting. What I thought, in the dream, was that the lumpy coarse-stemmed grass was the same on both sides, so why not? If one thick blade didn't know any more than another that the fence was there, why should his feet?

When he saw what he had done he stopped, looked back at the fence and laughed. All around his feet, little daisies and gaudy, bright pink clover flowers began to appear, and the petals glowed like metal, molten in the sun but cool, and spread uphill to where we were standing, and were soon all around us and under our shoes. Insects, tiny grasshoppers, sprang up and went leaping, and glassy snails no bigger than your little fingernail hung on the grass stems, quietly feeding. He took off his sunglasses, looked down at them and laughed. Then looked across to where we were, waiting. I had such a feeling of lightness and happiness it was as if my bones had been changed into clouds, just as the tough grass had been changed into flowers.

I knew it was a dream. But dreams can be messages. The feeling that comes with them is real, and if you hold on to it you can make the rest real. So I thought: if he can't come to us, I must go to him.

So this is what I do. I picture him. There on the other side of the fence, naked, his feet pressing the springy grass. *Stretch out your hand*, I tell him. *Like this.* I stretch my hand out. *If you have faith, the fence will open for you, as the sea did before Moses when he reached out his hand.* He looks puzzled. *No*, I tell him, *don't think about it. Just let it happen.*

It has not happened yet. But it will. Then, when he is close at last, when he has passed through the fence and is on our side, I will stretch out my hand and touch him, just under the left breast, and he will be whole. He will feel it happening to him and laugh. His laughter will be the proof. I want this more than anything. It is my heart's desire.

Each night now I lie quiet in the dark and go over it. The winding up of the smoky windows of the chariot of death. The swinging open of the door. Him stepping out and looking towards me behind his sunglasses. Me telling him what I tell myself:

Open your heart now. Let it happen. Come closer, closer. See? Now reach out your hand.

School Days

FROM *BABY NO-EYES*

KURA

Patricia Grace

"Kura" is a chapter from Baby No-Eyes *(1998), a novel by Patricia Grace. Shane, a young Maori man, goes home to the village and demands to know his real Maori name, asking why he was given "a movie name, a cowboy name." His grandmother Gran Kura says it was to protect him, and she tells a story from her childhood to explain. We learn that as a young girl, she attended school with her cousin Riripeti, a six-year-old who was abused by the teacher for not understanding English or the rules. Similar to students in early schools for Native Americans, Aborigines, and Africans, Maori children were given English names and prohibited from speaking their native tongue. This severing of Riripeti/Betty from her true identity, symbolized by the departure of her spirit, results in disaster.*

Novelist, short-story writer, and children's author Patricia Grace was born of Ngati Toa, Ngati Raukawa, and Te Ati Awa heritage in Wellington, New Zealand, in 1937. After graduating from Wellington Teachers' Training College, she started writing while teaching school and raising seven children. Her first book, Waiariki *(1975), was the first short-story collection*

by a Maori woman. One of the leading figures in Maori litera-
ture, Grace has been awarded the PEN Award, New Zealand
Book Award, Literaturpreis (Germany), Queen's Service Order,
Kiriyama Pacific Rim Book Prize, and Deutz Medal. In 2005
she was honored as a living icon of New Zealand art. She cur-
rently lives in Plimmerton, near Wellington.

Though Maori oral literature has a long history, written
novels and short stories first appeared in the 1970s. As the
Maori were undergoing crises stemming from the death of spo-
ken Maori (only recognized as an official language in 1987)
and rapid urbanization, the challenge for Grace and other
Maori Renaissance writers was how to capture their worldview
in English. Grace accomplishes this through code-switching—
switching from deliberately untranslated Maori to proper
school English and to Maori English (similar to Black English
in that it bends idiom, rhythm, and syntax to make the lan-
guage its own)—and innovative structures that re-create the
experience of an elder telling a nonlinear talking-tale. You may
wish to compare "Kura" to the excerpt from Buxton Spice,
Oonya Kempadoo's talk-story written in Guyanese patois;
Charles Mungoshi's "Shadows on the Wall," also about a child
who abandons language; Patrick Chamoiseau's School Days,
also about being forced to learn a colonial tongue at school; and
Tiffany Midge's "Beets," also about the tensions native people
experience between school and home.

There was a school. Our grandfather gave land for it so that we could have our education. It was what we wanted. The school was along by the creek where Staffords live now. It was there for our parents and us, and then for our children. But after our children grew up our school was left empty because many people had left the area by then. Their land was gone, and the children's children, who were only a few, had to travel by bus to the big school in town.

Our grandfather's mother was the eldest daughter of Te Wharekapakapa and Kapiri Morehua, both people of high birth and status—so it was through her parents that our great-grandmother came to have jurisdiction over land from beyond the foothills to the sea, and from Awakehua to Awapango. I mention this not to be boastful but only to tell you that we did not come from slaves.

Our school was painted light brown with dark brown window frames and door. There was one big room with a high roof, and a low porch on one end. Joined to it at the other end was a little low-roofed shelter. The big children were taught by the headmaster in the big room with its blackboards and big windows, its polished wood floors and varnished walls, while the primer children were taught by the headmaster's wife in the little joined-on room.

When I first started school this primer room had a board floor and one little window. Inside was a blackboard on an easel. Beside it was the teacher's desk. There were six desks in a row for the older children, and a table with forms on either side where the littlest ones sat. By the time Riripeti started school I was eight and had a desk of my own. When I took Riripeti to school on her first day I took her to the table where the little ones sat. That's where I put her. I believed it was the right thing to do.

I was up early that day. I hurried all morning because I had this important work to do—to take Riripeti to school. My mother and Riripeti's father were sister and brother, which in those days made Riripeti a sister to me. She was my teina.

That morning before I went to get Riripeti my mother said, "Look after your little sister at school, help her, teach her what to do." All right I was very happy. I was proud of this work I'd been given.

When I arrived at Riripeti's place she was ready, wearing a new dress that Grandmother had made for her. Her hair had been plaited and tied with ribbons made from strips of the dress material. There was a hanky in her sleeve and a bandage on her knee.

Grandmother was there with Aunty Heni and Uncle Taare to see Riripeti off to school. "Look after your teina, take her by the hand," Grandmother said to me. "Do as your tuakana says," she said to Riripeti. "Your tuakana will help you so that you'll know what to do. Listen to what she says."

Then our grandmother said to me, "We know you're a good girl. We know you'll do what you're told, we know you'll help your little sister and look after her. We don't want our children to be hurt at school. That's why you have to be very good. You have to listen, you have to obey. We know that you're clever and we know you'll learn. That's what our school is for, for you to learn, for our children to learn. You're very lucky to have a school and to be allowed to go to school. Look after your little sister."

Perhaps I was told to take Riripeti to the headmaster or the teacher before taking her into the classroom, perhaps I forgot this, being too excited to hear.

Sixty years ago I was a tiny girl, small for my age. See that leaf— like that. Thin like that, without weight. You could see through me those days, just as you can see through that leaf now, but I was not too light and leafy to have this important job. I was this important girl, this happy leaf, and I loved my teina with her new clothes, her hair in pigtails, a rag hanky in her sleeve. She was a black girl, six years old.

The teacher didn't notice Riripeti marching into school with me, and was busy writing on the blackboard when I stood Riripeti by Tihi at the little children's table. I was the one who told her to stand there. I straightened her, put her feet together, put her shoulders back and went to stand by my own desk. We said our good mornings to the teacher before we all sat down.

"Who is this?" the teacher said when she saw Riripeti sitting on the form. I put my hand up because that was the right thing to do, but the teacher didn't look at my hand. "Who are you and where are your manners, coming in and sitting down as though you own the place?" she said to Riripeti, but Riripeti didn't know what the teacher was saying. "Stand up when you're spoken to," the teacher said. I wanted to whisper in our language so this teina of mine would know what to do, but I knew I wasn't allowed to speak our language so I made a little movement with my hands trying to tell her to stand. She didn't understand and sat there smiling, swinging her shoulders, swinging her eyes—to me, then back again to the teacher.

I knew Riripeti shouldn't smile so much. I knew she shouldn't fidget herself or roll her eyes. At that moment I didn't want her to be a girl so black that it would make the teacher angry.

"Get that smile off your face. Do you think this is a laughing matter?" the teacher said, taking Riripeti by the arm and standing her.

Riripeti could speak some English. Of course. We all could. But Riripeti had not heard words like the words she was now hearing. "Go and stand in the corner until you learn better manners," the teacher said, but Riripeti didn't know what she was being told to do. I wanted to call out to her but speaking wasn't allowed.

The teacher turned Riripeti and poked her in the back while she shuffled forward, but not fast enough, not fast enough, still swerving her head and eyes towards me—until she was standing in the corner at the front of the room where bad children always stood.

But how was she to know she was bad? She had said no words that would make her bad, spelled nothing wrong to be bad, given no answers to be wrong. "Face the corner," the teacher said, because Riripeti was still twisting her neck to look at me. She didn't know what she had been told to do. The teacher jolted her head round and gave her a smacking on the legs, then Riripeti stood stiff and still without moving, facing the corner.

At playtime, I ran with our cousins Kuini, Hama and Jimmy to hide in the bushes, where we put our arms round each other. No one from the little classroom played that morning. The ones not crying sat close together eating bread, turning the balls of their feet into the ground, watching their feet make dents in the dust.

After play the teacher turned Riripeti round and asked her for her name but Riripeti wouldn't say it. Instead she smiled and smiled and moved her eyes from side to side. So the teacher asked Dulcie, who was the eldest in our class, what Riripeti's name was. But then the teacher became angry with Dulcie too because she wouldn't speak the name slowly and loudly enough. The teacher gave Dulcie a piece of paper to take to Riripeti's family. Full name, date of birth, English name, it said. She turned Riripeti into the corner again, but allowed her to come out with us at lunchtime.

After school, Dulcie, who didn't live anywhere near Riripeti or me, gave the note to me to take home to my aunty and uncle. Her family was where the Beckets are now—that was their land then. I took the paper home and the next day gave it back to Dulcie to give to the teacher. It gave Riripeti's name, her date of birth and her English name, Betty.

On the way to school we taught Riripeti to say, "Yes Mrs. Wood, No Mrs. Wood, Yes please Mrs. Wood, No thank you Mrs. Wood." We thought it very funny that our teachers were called Mr. and Mrs. Wood, and once we were out of the school grounds Mr. Mrs. Rakau is what we called them. We had this silly song to make ourselves laugh: "Mr. Mrs. Rakau, patu patu *wood*." *Wood* was the loud word. It was the word to scare anyone with. We'd call it out to the kids we didn't like, call it out to the ones chasing us, or we'd jump out from a tree where we'd been hiding and call, "Mr. Mrs. Rakau, patu patu *wood*," and off we'd run.

It was no good. School turned out no good for Riripeti. How did she know her name was Betty? That second day she was in the bad corner for not answering when her name was called, and for not speaking when she was spoken to. On the way to and from school we'd tell her the right things to say, but even though she tried she still couldn't say the words the teacher wanted. She spent most of her time in the corner. Every day she was given smackings by the teacher.

Other children were smacked and caned and punished too, but not as much as Riripeti. We were much naughtier children than what she was, that's how we knew what to do. I knew my name was Kate at school. Minaroa knew her name was Dulcie. And we had ways of sending messages to each other with our faces, ways of guessing the teacher's mind, knew which lies were the right ones to tell. If the teacher gave us a lesson about the right food to have for breakfast, when questioned we would tell her that's what we had— bacon, egg, toast, class of milk. It was the right answer—bacon, egg, toast, class of milk. "*Glass, glass, a glass* of milk," the teacher would say. After a while we could say it, making this choking *g* sound right down in our throats. But we didn't know it meant milk in a glass, didn't know what it meant. Didn't know a glass was right for milk and a cup was right for tea, because at home we had enamel plates and enamel mugs for everything. We didn't speak until we'd learned, didn't speak unless we had to because we were afraid our bad language might come out, but we became good at guessing the answers we had to give.

Riripeti was too good to guess what to say, too good to know what lies to tell, too good to know what to do. It was so difficult for me to be her tuakana. It was so difficult to take her to school every day with her footsteps getting slower and slower the nearer we came. By the gate she'd say, "Kura, Kura, he puku mamae," and she'd hold her stomach and bend over. Her face would be pale.

"Never mind, never mind," I'd say. "You got to go to school every day. We got to learn so we be clever." I'd pull her along so that I wouldn't be in trouble with our mothers. I was trying so hard to do this important work that my grandmother had given me to do.

All the way to school I'd talk to her, tell her what to say and what to do. And she did know, she did learn. She was very brave and tried to do everything I told her. She remembered to speak in English, except that the teacher didn't know it was English she was speaking because Riripeti was too afraid to make the words come out loudly. "Do I have to shake that language out of you, do I do I?" the teacher would say, shaking and shaking her. Then Riripeti would be smacked and sent to stand in the bad place. She did mimi there sometimes. Sometimes she sicked there, then cleaned it all up with a cloth and bucket. I would've helped her if I'd thought I'd be allowed. After a while it was only Riripeti who went to the bad corner. It became her corner. She smelled like an animal and spoke like an animal, had to go to the corner until she stopped being an animal. I could see that she was getting smaller and that it was only her eyes and her teeth that were growing. We didn't tell our mothers, or anyone, what was happening, but sometimes Riripeti was told off at home for her dirty wet clothes.

One morning Riripeti sat down by the track and said she couldn't go to school any more. Usually when she did that we would manage to persuade her, but that day I believed her. It was true that she couldn't go to school. Her spirit was out of her, gone roaming. Her hair was as dry as a horse's tail, rough and hard, her eyes were like flat shadows, not at all like eyes. I had seen a dying dog look like that, which made me think it might be true what the teacher said, that my teina was changing into an animal. "Go home to aunty," I said.

"No, I'll wait for you."

"Go in the trees."

So she agreed and I gave my bread to her. Down the bank she went, across the creek and into the trees where perhaps she would become an animal, a bird.

When Mrs. Wood asked where Betty was I said she was sick, so Mrs. Wood asked the other children too where Betty was, to see if I was telling the truth. "Betty is sick Mrs. Wood," was what each of the children replied, but Mrs. Wood was not happy with this answer. She became angry because how did we all know Betty was sick when we all lived in different directions? Sometimes it was difficult to know the right words to say.

After school I called to Riripeti by the track and I heard her coming. When she came up the bank I could see that her spirit had returned to her. It was looking at me out of her eyes, pleased to see me.

So that's what Riripeti did every day after that, hid in the trees. Mrs. Wood was waiting for her to come back to school with a note and I felt afraid that we'd be found out. But the end of the year came. We had long holidays and Riripeti and I went to stay with our grandmother.

When our grandmother went to town she wore a grey suit and a cream blouse with a high collar and pintucks across the front. She had black Red Cross shoes which she polished the night before, on paper spread on the floor by the hearth. She had a black hat with a small turned-up brim.

In those days no one would take a Maori bag to town or to the shop, not even to a tangihanga, not even to land meetings. It wasn't like these days when you see these baskets everywhere—all colours, all sorts of patterns, not always pretty either. Sometimes they're ragged like the old ones we used for getting pipi, but even a Pakeha will carry a Maori bag now, paying a lot of money for one. In those days all the kete were on top of people's wardrobes with photos in them, or hanging on nails behind the bedroom doors.

Our grandmother had a good leather handbag for her money and combs and handkerchiefs. She had a deep cane basket with black and orange stripes around it for the shopping. Riripeti and I liked to carry the shopping. We were happy to go to town with our grandmother and to carry the basket between us.

We didn't go to town often because in those days we had our own store down the road with everything we needed. We all had our own killers, our own gardens and our own milking cow. So nobody went to town much, but our grandmother sometimes had business there and she'd take us with her for company. When she'd finished her business we'd go and buy whitebait, or whatever she wanted to take home, and then we'd make our way to the railway station where she'd let us buy something to eat. Not for herself. Our grandmother would never eat in town but she would let us buy a sandwich and a melting moment, which we would eat while we waited for the train.

That day Grandmother took us to a shop that sold dress materials and bought remnants to make new dresses for Riripeti and me to wear to school. One of the pieces of material was brown with white spots on it, the other was plain dark blue. What a good day it was.

But on our way to the railway station Riripeti's feet began to slow down. "Come on, catch up to Grandmother," I said. Our grandmother was already going up the steps to the station. Riripeti stopped walking, "I don't want a dress," she said.

"Come on, come on," I said pulling her by the hand and talking about the sandwich and the cake. I knew she was thinking about school.

There was a woman in our village who was good at making dresses. We only had to take material to her and she would make anything we asked, but it was our grandmother who wanted to make these dresses for Riripeti and me. Riripeti didn't want to watch

Grandmother make the dresses or to have her dress tried on. Didn't want to talk about the dresses. She told me she wanted to go back to her mother and father and kept urging me to ask our grandmother if she could go home, but I wouldn't. I wasn't old enough to ask our grandmother a thing like that.

Riripeti's dress was the spotted one, mine was the plain blue. When they were finished we went home to our parents. The day after that was the day school began again.

Riripeti wanted to hide down by the creek on that first day but I wouldn't let her because I didn't want to be in trouble and didn't want to have to tell lies to the teacher. "I'll tell aunty and uncle if you don't come," I said. "I'll tell Grandmother." She was too good not to listen to me. That was how I made her come to school.

But when we arrived at school we found out something that made us both cry. We found that I was to go into the other classroom, the one for the older children, and that Riripeti was to stay in the little room as before.

There were plenty of children crying that day—little children, big children. I don't know what for but some of it was to do with Waana who was Dulcie's little brother, brought up by their grandfather. The grandfather had brought Waana to the steps of the classroom and was talking to him, trying to make his grandson let go of his leg. The headmaster came out and said in a loud voice, "I'd like to remind you Mr. Williams that I don't allow any of that language in my school or in these school grounds." We all got a fright because Waana's grandfather took no notice of the headmaster and kept talking to Waana. The headmaster became angry. "I'm asking you to leave these grounds at once," he said. "Off you go and take your language with you. We're not having any of that in *my* school and in front of these children."

"I go, yes, take my grandson too," the grandfather said to him in English. He lifted Waana and off he went. Waana never came to school again. His grandfather hid him from the authorities, telling them that Waana had gone to live somewhere else.

Riripeti was silly, because when it was time for me to go to the other classroom she cried and put her arms around me. I promised her my bread, I promised her my dress, but she wouldn't let go. In the end I had to wriggle myself away, had to pull her hands off me and run because I could see the teacher coming.

It was when I ran off that Riripeti called out to me but forgot to speak in English. Well, all the holidays we had been speaking in that Maori language of ours, so perhaps that's why she forgot. Mrs. Wood grabbed Riripeti by the shoulders and brought her to Mr. Wood for the cane. We all had to stand in our lines and watch this caning so we would learn how bad our language was.

Riripeti wouldn't hold her hand out, which I knew was from fear and not from being stubborn. She had her eyes shut and stood without moving while Mr. Wood gave her a caning round the legs, then Mrs. Wood got her by the arm so she wouldn't run away. I thought what an evil thing our language was to do that to my teina.

It was a bad time for all of us. Some of us learned to be good and to keep ourselves out of trouble most of the time. Others were bad—swore at the teachers, got canings, or were sent home and not allowed to return.

Riripeti came to school every day. She didn't try to go and hide any more, and even though she began vomiting each day as we came near to school, still she came. She was always good. We were known as a good family. I'm not saying that to be boastful but just to let you understand about Riripeti.

One day during the holidays our grandmother said to Riripeti, "Why are you small? Why are you thin?" And she took Riripeti to live with her, gave her wai kohua, gave her malt and Lane's emulsion and meat. Riripeti was all right too. For a while she was happy and we played together, then when it was near time to go to school again she became sick and couldn't eat. Her throat closed and wouldn't let any food go down. Her skin was moist all the time and she couldn't get out of bed.

Not long after that she died.

Killed by school.

Dead of fear.

My heart broke for my teina. Oh I cried. She was mine, she was me, she was all of us. She was the one who had died but we were the ones affected, our shame taking generations to become our anger and our madness. She was my charge, my little sister, my work that I'd been given to do, mine to look after. What an evil girl I was to let her die.

We never told our mothers and fathers what we knew. They thought Riripeti had a Maori sickness, thought some angry person had put a makutu on her—which was right perhaps, but they didn't know who. Or they thought it could've been part of the cursing of Pirinoa that was still being handed down and affecting us all.

After that I became sick too. I couldn't eat and I couldn't go to school. I went to bed and couldn't get up, just like Riripeti. I think I nearly died too. There were people coming and going, talking to me, talking amongst themselves, putting their hands on me, speaking that language over me—that evil language which killed my teina and which I never spoke again.

One day my grandmother took me out of bed, wrapped a blanket round me and sat in an armchair with me on her knee. She held me against her and rocked me. I think we stayed like that for days and nights. While she held me and rocked me she spoke to me of God's Kingdom. She told me about Riripeti's special place in God's Kingdom with the Lord, who alone was merciful, who alone was good. Riripeti was heaven's bright gold. She talked about the journey that is life, how we must walk its pathways in goodness and righteousness, how we would all be together one day in glory. We all prayed together and the Lord answered our prayers.

Soon I was able to eat. Soon I could sit in the armchair on my own with pillows round me. After a time I was able to get up. Three months after Riripeti died I returned to school with God in my heart. There were new teachers there who were different in their ways, but I only stayed at school for two more years because I was needed at home.

So we children never spoke of what had happened to Riripeti. It became our secret and our shame. It's a story that has never had words, not until today. Today the words were jolted from my stomach by Shane, where they have been sitting for sixty years. They came to my throat, gathering there until the sun went down, when they spilled out on to the verandah in front of the children's children, who may not be strong enough for them.

We keep our stories secret because we love our children, we keep our language hidden because we love our children, we disguise ourselves and hide our hearts because we love our children. We choose names because we love our children.

Shane.

FROM *RITES:*
A GUATEMALAN BOYHOOD

KINDERGARTEN

Victor Perera

"Kindergarten," excerpted from Victor Perera's autobiographical Rites: A Guatemalan Boyhood, *presents the author's earliest encounters with friendship (with Jorge, an "idiot boy" who is soon institutionalized), hero worship (the platoon of uniformed guards marching past young Victor's house every afternoon), sex (his Indian nursemaid's passionate murder by her would-be lover), violence (the school playground bullies), and religious discrimination ("My mother says you are a Jew. . . . My mother says the Jews killed Christ"). Along the way, Victor learns that to enter kindergarten just short of five is to be vulnerable to derision, alienation, and girls for whom difference becomes motive enough for hatred.*

Born in Guatemala in 1934 of Sephardic Jewish heritage, Victor Perera was the author of six books and an active journalist and teacher. When he was twelve, his family moved to Brooklyn, where Perera attended Brooklyn College before going on to the University of Michigan for graduate school and then to a series of writing stints for such publications as the

New Yorker *and the* New Republic. *Next, he moved west,*
making his home in the San Francisco Bay area and teaching on
the faculties of the University of California campuses at Santa
Cruz and Berkeley. In 1998, he suffered a crippling stroke
from which he never fully recovered. He died in 2003, leaving
behind, in addition to his publications, the Los Angeles–based
Ivri-NASAWI, an organization intended to promote Sephardic-
Mizrahi culture. Sephardic Jews originate from the Iberian
peninsula (Spain and Portugal), including those Jews subject
to expulsion from Spain by order of the Catholic monarchs
Ferdinand and Isabella (as codified in the Alhambra decree of
1492) or from Portugal by order of King Manuel I in 1497.
Mizrahi Jews are descended from Jewish communities of the
Middle East. They are non-Sephardic Jews from the Arab
world and from other Muslim countries.

Perera's passionate advocacy of underdog causes can be
traced back to his Sephardic roots and the way that they influ-
enced his Guatemalan childhood as well as his later experiences
as a United States immigrant and as a Latino member of a re-
ligion where non–Eastern Europeans are a minority. Questions
about cultural identity inform much of his writing, evident
here in young Victor's confusion over whether his being a Jew
has been the actual cause of his beloved nurse's death and in his
shocked speculation that his circumcised penis is enough to
make one of the kindergarten girls hate him.

This excerpt, with its emphasis on exclusion and otherness,
has obvious connections to the Elisabeth Gille selection, from
Shadows of a Childhood, *but Perera's struggle to make sense of*
himself in an environment both familiar and alien also can be
compared to Alexandra Fuller's similar confusion in the excerpt
from Don't Let's Go to the Dogs Tonight, *to the narrator's*

confusing sexual discoveries in the excerpt from Buxton Spice *by Oonya Kempadoo, and to Faith Adiele's reassessment of race in "Black Men."*

M y earliest images are geometrical: the narrow bars of the bedstead that I amazed everyone by squeezing through one windy night when I was frightened by a sheet flapping on a clothesline and wanted my mother; the perfect rectangle of Parque Central, with its octagenal tiled benches, encircled fountains, chequered flagstones. And across the way the twin towers of the cathedral, housing a dark mystery of candles and painted idols that would forever be barred to me.

In my pedal-car I explored the limits of my universe, always certain that beyond our doorstep and the park's four borders lay unnamed terrors. I was especially fond of a wooded labyrinth in the park's northern end, a dark, sinuous place where I could act out my heroic reveries unseen by Chata, the Indian girl with long braids and sweet-smelling skirts who looked after me. To my five-year-old's eyes Chata seemed a rare beauty; she dressed in the vivid, handwoven *huipil** blouse and skirt of her region, and had unusually fine olive skin. Chata was a spirited and mischievous young woman who let me eat forbidden sweets from street vendors and who would gently tease me into fondling her firm round breasts under the thin blouse.

I made friends in Parque Central, the year before my second branding. The first I can recall was Jorge, an idiot boy with gray drooping eyes that did not disguise his sunny nature: I liked Jorge

---

* *huipil*: Spanish term for a Mayan woman's traditional blouse, used to identify the specific village of the wearer, her social and marital status, religious background, and beliefs, wealth, authority, and individual personality

because he was affectionate—indeed, he was little else—and disarmed my budding defenses by hugging me uninhibitedly and stroking my face. Jorge taught me to touch another without shame or ulterior motive, and for this I am forever indebted to him. I grew to love Jorge and had begun to interpret his grunts and noises into a modest vocabulary when he stopped coming to the park. Chata found out from his *china** that Jorge had been placed in a home.

That year I acquired my first heroes, the platoon of uniformed guards who marched past every afternoon on their way to the Palacio. I would follow them the length of the park, beating my hands to the beat of the drum, pumping my legs as high as I could to their stride. At the curb I would stop and mark time until they turned the corner and disappeared.

Chata had an admirer, a tall Indian laborer named Ramiro who courted her in the afternoons and on weekends, when Chata would take me to the park. Ramiro wore a straw hat and leather shoes, and used to flash a gold tooth when he smiled or smirked. Chata kept Ramiro on tenterhooks, encouraging his advances and then rebuffing him with a toss of her head, or mocking his confusion with a whinnying giggle that appeared to goad and arouse him. He looked at her at times with a cold, hungering menace that I recognised even then as lust. I disliked and feared Ramiro, but I never dared to intrude on their lovers' play or their frequent spats in the park. Instead, I would retaliate by making Chata admit, when she tucked me into bed at night, that I was her favorite.

I was some weeks short of five, and small for my age, the first time Chata took me to school and abandoned me in the hands of a tall, gaunt woman with hard eyes and a pursed mouth. Her name was Miss Hale, and I detected from her accent that she was foreign.

"Aren't we a little small to be starting school?" she said, in slow,

---

* *china*: nanny

badly slurred Spanish. I understood this to be a taunt, which, on top of my desertion by Chata, brought tears to my eyes. I feared and distrusted Miss Hale all the more when I realized this was the exact reaction she wanted, and my tears had placated her.

The room she led me into was musty and dim. I was presented to my classmates, most of whom seemed strange to me, and very large. Even their names, Octavio, Gunter, Michel, Loretta, had a foreign ring. From my earliest consciousness I had known I was a foreigner in this strange place, Guatemala. Now, in the kindergarten room of the English-American School, I felt an alien among aliens.

"My mother says you are a Jew." It was Arturo, a dark, thickset boy with hooded eyes and hairy legs below his short trousers. Within a week he and Gunter, a tall blond boy with smudged knees who made in his pants, established themselves as the class bullies. We were at recess, which meant I could play with my new friends, plump-cheeked Grace Samayoa and Michel Montcrassi, who was French, and wore sandals on his stockinged feet and a round blue cap. There was a fountain in the patio with goldfish in it, and a rising nymph with mossy green feet who poured water from her pitcher. In each corner of the patio (Mother said it had once been a convent) was a large red flowerpot, with pink and white geraniums. I sensed the question was critical and I must reply with care.

"Yes," I said.

"My mother says the Jews killed Christ."

Now this was a trickier question. Who was Christ? "They did not," I said, but all I could be certain of was that I, at least, had not killed Christ—whoever he was—because I had never killed anyone, at least not knowingly. Then I remembered stepping on a cockroach once, and stomping on ants in the kitchen. Maybe I had killed Christ by accident.

"Prove it," Arturo said.

I told him I would ask Father about it and give him a reply the next day.

That night I asked Father why I was a Jew. He hoisted me up by the armpits, sat me on his knee, and told me a long and complicated story about God, the Bible, and a Jew named Moses. When I asked if it was true that the Jews had killed Christ he frowned and said the Romans had done it. He said I should pay no attention to Arturo.

When Arturo approached me next day Father's story had gone clear out of my head. All I remembered was that the Romans had done it.

"The Romans killed Christ," I said.

"Who are the Romans?" Arturo asked.

I said I wasn't sure, but would ask Father and let him know.

When I asked Father in the evening he was reading a newspaper. He said the Romans did it and that was that, and I was to pay no heed to Arturo. Father was not in a talkative mood, and I did not press the matter. But I was confused, and feared my next encounter with Arturo.

Several days passed, and Arturo did not mention the Jews and Christ. I dared hope the whole subject had been forgotten. In the meantime my friendship with Michel grew. He let me call him "Coco," which was his nickname, because his head was round and hard like a coconut; even his curly blond hair resembled a coconut husk. Coco was as much a foreigner in the school as I was. He was Protestant, and the bigger boys mocked his French accent and played catch with his cap.

Grace Samayoa was a little shy of me, although she liked me to tell her stories I'd made up in the labyrinth. Now and again she gave me an approving smile when I answered Miss Hale's questions correctly—and once she let me stroke her hair. Grace Samayoa was the most attractive female I knew next to Chata and my mother. But

Grace was also my own size, which made her a challenge. I longed to hug her.

One afternoon Chata failed to pick me up at school. That morning Ramiro had followed us to school, as usual, although they had quarreled in the park the day before when he caught her flirting with a young chauffeur.

"He's following us. Don't turn around," I recall Chata saying, glancing behind her without turning her head. They were the last words of Chata's I would ever hear.

It had grown dark outside and my knees were cold when Father finally came for me, after closing the store.

"Chata has gone away," was all he would say. "We will get you another *china*."

After dinner I went into the kitchen and wormed the truth out of Clara, the cook. She said Chata and I had been followed by Ramiro. After she deposited me at the school he waylaid Chata a block away and gave her "*siete puñaladas en el mero corazón*" (seven knife stabs in the very heart). I accepted Clara's story on faith, not at all concerned that her description matched word for word the title of a popular song. I stamped about the house, pumping my legs high like the palace guards and chanting the song title aloud: "*Sié-te Puña-ládas en El Mero Corazón. Sié-te Puña-ládas en El Mero Corazón.*" The resonance of the phrase, its hard metric beat, gave Chata's disappearance a finality I could comprehend.

The fuller import of Chata's death did not dawn on me until the following day, when I was taken to school by her older sister, Elvira, whose braids were neither as long nor as glossy as Chata's, and whose skirts did not smell half as good.

In the days that followed, Chata's violent death and Arturo's hard questions got mixed together in my dreams, and my apprehension grew that Chata had been murdered because of me, and because I was a Jew.

Unlike her younger sister, Elvira was a practicing Catholic, and one Sunday afternoon she sneaked me into the Cathedral across from the park.

"You must pray to our Lord," she whispered, pointing to the pale naked statue, with bloodied ribs and thorns on his head, that hung with arms outstretched from the front wall, in the same place where the Ark would stand in our synagogue; only this place was a lot bigger and scarier.

When I balked at reciting the Pater Noster she had taught me, Elvira rebuked me, "You must pray to our Lord to be forgiven for your ancestors' sins against him. That way you can go to Heaven, even if you're not Catholic."

Choking back tears, I mumbled the Pater Noster, not for myself so much but for Chata, who Elvira said had been punished for her sins.

During recess one noon Arturo again brought up the Jews and Christ. This time Gunter was with him, and there was something in his face I had not seen there before. Gunter's blue eyes never looked right at yours.

"My mother says all Jews have tails and horns," Arturo said, with an accusing look. Now this I knew was absurd, because I had seen myself in the mirror.

"They do not," I said.

"Jews have bald-headed pigeons," Gunter said, with a smirk.

I flushed, because this was true—at least I did, Father did and Uncle Mair, and Mr. Halevi at the Turkish baths, but not Señor Gonzales and the others there that day—their pigeons weren't bald. . . . But then—what business was it of Gunter's anyway?

"It's none of your business," I said. My face was hot.

"My mother says Jews are the devil," Arturo said, and gave me a shove.

Gunter called the other boys over and said, "Look at the Jew who killed Christ." Then they all gathered behind him and Arturo and stared at me.

"Leave him alone," called a thin, furry voice from the back. "He's not the devil." It was Coco.

"You keep still, dirty Frenchy," Gunter said.

"Dirty Frenchy, dirty Frenchy," chorused the other boys. Someone snatched the beret from Coco's head and they all stomped on it, one by one.

"Let's look at his bald-headed pigeon," Gunter said, turning toward me, without looking in my eyes.

I was growing frightened now, but not of Gunter, whom I suspected to be the instigator of all this. I feared the mob.

"He killed Christ," Gunter said, in a rising voice, and the group behind him grew tighter. Arturo shoved me again, harder. Torn between fear and anger, I wanted to punch Gunter in the face. But Gunter was a head taller than I, and out of reach.

I stretched to my full height. "At least I don't make in my pants," I said, and looked Gunter straight in the eye.

He made a grab for my suspenders and I swung at his face. But Arturo held me fast and then all the other boys fell on top of me. I kicked and scratched and defended myself, but they were too many. When they had stripped off all my clothes—except my shoes and socks—they stepped back to look at me.

"He lost his tail," Arturo said, almost in relief.

"But he has a bald-headed pigeon," Gunter said. A giggle came out of his face that was unlike any sound I had ever heard from a boy, or anyone else.

I turned toward the wall. My chest ached from the effort to hold back tears. Several of the boys had drifted away, as if they wished to distance themselves from the two leaders.

Silence, except for the trickle of the fountain and the heaving of my chest. Coco came forward and offered me his crushed beret so I could cover myself.

More boys moved away and I saw that the girls had all gathered at the far end of the patio, behind the fountain—all except Grace Samayoa. She sat on the rim of the fountain, and stared at me.

"Don't look," I said to Grace Samayoa, and turned to one side. But she kept on looking.

Then Grace Samayoa said, "I hate you," and walked toward the girls at the far end of the patio.

I covered myself with Coco's cap, and I cried. I cried at the top of my lungs until Miss Hale came. She cleared everyone from the patio and told me to get dressed.

The following year I was left back in kindergarten. Miss Hale and my parents agreed I was underage for the first grade.

BEETS

Tiffany Midge

Tiffany Midge's short story "Beets" employs wry humor to express the complexities of growing up of mixed Sioux and white race: having parents with very different backgrounds and visions; living among a mainstream culture whose associations with Indians are mostly restricted to the Eastern tribes who helped the Pilgrims with Thanksgiving; confronting racism founded on the assumption that Indians are black.

Midge herself is no stranger to this experience. Born of Hunkpapa Sioux and German ancestry, she grew up in the Pacific Northwest and currently lives in Seattle. She is an enrolled member of the Standing Rock Sioux Tribe and serves on the board of directors for Red Eagle Soaring, a Native American outreach theater company. She is also poetry editor for the multicultural arts magazine the Raven Chronicles.

The story's setting in the early 1980s, during the period when the United States began what Midge calls its "hyperecological awareness," becomes a sore point of reference for the narrator. Her Plains Indian heritage suffers a blow from environmental politics. The historical Plains Indians lived in an area from the

*Mississippi River to the Rocky Mountains and from Canada to
Mexico. The most important tribes, the Sioux, Blackfoot,
Cheyenne, Crow, Kiowa, and Comanche, survived dry summers hotter than 100 degrees when rains often brought floods,
and winters with heavy snows that saw temperatures sometimes
drop to 40 degrees below zero. They hunted buffalo and other
game all year long; they also ate a variety of wild berries, greens,
and roots, as they did not plant crops. In fact, as the narrator
points out, the government's attempts to change these habits did
not ever succeed in converting the Plains tribes into willing, en-
thusiastic, or even able farmers. But the white father in this story
is determined to make a go of farming, even if he knows only as
much about it as his Sioux wife—perhaps less. Within this
family and outside, the narrator and her sister must negotiate a
world where elementary-school citizenship trumps well-meaning,
if obsessive, environmental efforts. Midge, in a brilliant final
scene, shows how a sense of humor can be the most valuable survival tool of all.*

*Midge's use of humor as the narrative fulcrum for her story
can be compared with Chamoiseau's very different use of humor
in the excerpt from* School Days, *where it serves to emphasize the
cultural imposition of colonial language, or even to Chang-rae
Lee's subtly humorous account of a disastrous gustatory culture
clash in "Sea Urchin." Another important element of "Beets" is
the relationship between the narrator and her sister, its hidden
tenderness similar to the more openly tender relationship among
the sisters in Aputis' "The Glade with Life-Giving Water."*

In fourth-grade history class I learned that the Plains Indians
weren't cut out to be farmers; that the government tried to get

them to plant corn and stuff, but it was one of those no-win situations, meaning that no matter how hard the Indians fought against progress and manifest destiny, they'd never win.

This history lesson occurred around the same time the United States began its hyperecological awareness, which soon seeped into the media. Theories and speculations were developed that asserted that the earth was heading for another ice age. Whereas today scientists tell us that the earth is getting hotter. It was during this time that my father's convictions regarding the demise of the twentieth century began tipping toward fanaticism. *The Whole Earth Catalog** took up residence in our home and he began reciting from it as if it were Scripture. He wanted us all to get back to nature. I think he would have sold the house and moved us all into the mountains to raise goats and chickens, but my mother, who didn't have much of a say in most of the family decisions, must have threatened to leave him for good if he took his plan to fruition. So he settled with gardening. Gardening is too light a word for the blueprints he drew up that would transform our backyard into a small farming community.

One day I returned from school and discovered my father shoveling manure from a pile tall as a two-story building. I couldn't help but wonder where he ever purchased such a magnificent pile of shit, and impressive though it was, I doubt the neighbors shared in my father's enthusiasm. I wouldn't have been surprised if they were circulating a petition to have it removed.

"Good, you're home!" my father said. "Grab a rake."

Knowing I didn't stand a chance in arguing, I did just as he ordered. And I spent the rest of the day raking manure, thinking the Plains Indians opted not to farm because they knew enough not to.

---

* *The Whole Earth Catalog*: a catalog published between 1968 and 1998 that provided practical information with an ethical and moral ecological agenda; Steve Jobs at Apple has called it a conceptual forerunner of a Web search engine

I think my father would have kept us out there shoveling and raking till after midnight if my mother hadn't insisted I come in the house and do my homework. The next day I had blisters on my hands and couldn't hold a pencil.

"Hard work builds character," my father preached. "Children have it too easy today. All you want to do is sit around and pick lint out of your belly buttons."

I was saved from hard labor for the next week because the blisters on my hands burst open and spilled oozy blood all over the music sheets in singing class. The teacher sent me home, back to the plow.

"No pain, no gain," Father said. "Next time wear gloves."

The following weekend our suburban nuclear unit had transformed into the spitting image of the Sunshine Family dolls. I began calling my sister Dewdrop. Myself, Starshine. I renamed my mother Corn Woman and my father Reverend Buck. Reverend Buck considered it his mission in life to convert us from our heathen Hungry-Man TV dinner, Bisquick and Pop-Tart existence.

"Do you realize that with all these preservatives, after you're dead and buried, your body will take an extra few years to completely decompose?" Father preached.

"I don't care," my sister said, "I plan on being cremated."

As the good reverend's wife and children, we must have represented some deprived tribe of soulless, bereft Indians and he designated himself to take us, the godless parish, under his wing.

Mother resigned herself to his plans. And we trudged along behind her. When she was growing up on the reservation, her family had cultivated and planted every season, so gardening wasn't a completely foreign activity. The difference was, her family planted only what could be used. Their gardens were conservative. But my father's plans resembled a large Midwestern crop, minus the tractors. He even drew up sketches of an irrigation system that he borrowed from *The Whole Earth Catalog*. It was a nice dream. His heart was in the right place. I'm sure the government back in the days of treaties, relocation and designation of reservation land thought their intentions were noble too. I kind of admired my father for his big ideas, but sided with my mother on this one. Father was always more interested in the idea of something rather than the actuality; to him, bigger meant better. My father liked large things, generous mass, quantity, weight. To him, they represented progress, ambition, trust. Try as he might to be a true renegade, adopt Indian beliefs and philosophies, even go so far as to marry an Indian woman, he still could never avoid the obvious truth. He was a white man. He liked to build large things.

"What do you plan to do with all these vegetables?" my mother asked him.

"Freeze and can 'em," he replied. Mother was about to say something, but then looked as if she'd better not. I knew what she was thinking. She was thinking that our father expected *her* to freeze and can them. She didn't look thrilled at the prospect. Father may have accused her of being an apple from time to time, even went so far as to refer to her as apple pie, what he thought to be a term of endearment, but Mother must have retained much of that Plains Indian stoic refusal to derive pleasure from farming large acreage.

Father assigned each of us a row. Mother was busily stooped over, issuing corn into the soil, as if offering gems of sacrifice to the earth goddess. I was in charge of the radishes and turnips, which up until that day I'd had no previous experience with, other than what I could recall from tales of Peter Rabbit stealing from Mr. McGregor's garden. I bent down over my chore, all the while on keen lookout for small white rabbits accessorized in gabardine trousers.

My sister was diligently poking holes in the soil for her onions when our adopted collie began nosing around the corn rows looking for a place to pee. "Get out of the corn, Charlie!" I ordered him.

Father chuckled and said, "Hey, look, a scorned corndog!"

Mother rolled her eyes and quipped, "What a corny joke!"

My sister feigned fainting and said, "You punish me!"

Yeah, we were an image right out of a Rockwell classic* with the caption reading, *Squawman and family, an American portrait of hope.*

In school we learned that the Indians were the impetus behind the Thanksgiving holiday that we practice today. This legend depicts that the Eastern tribes were more reverent and accepting of the white colonists than any fierce and proud Plains Indian ever was. My father challenged this theory by suggesting I take armfuls of our sown vegetables to school. "It'll be like helping out the Pilgrims," he told me. I brought grocery sacks of turnips to class one day and offered them as novelties for our class show-and-tell activity. Everyone was left with the assumption that it was the Sioux Indians who were farmers and who had guided and helped the Pilgrims in their time of need. Mrs. Morton didn't discourage this faux pas† but, rather, rattled on about how noble, how Christian, of the Indians to assist the poor colonists in the unsettling and overwhelming wilderness they'd arrived at. My classmates collected my offering of turnips and at recess we rounded up a game of turnip baseball. Lisa Parker got hit in the face with a turnip and went bawling to the school nurse. Mrs. Morton ignored me the rest of the day and sent me home with a note to my parents, which said, *Please do not allow this to happen again.*

At Father's suggestion, my sister engineered a baking factory.

---

* Rockwell classic: refers to Norman Rockwell, an early-twentieth-century American painter famous for his ability to capture traditional American values in his paintings of everyday Americans and everyday American life

† *faux pas*: French for "false step"

Every evening after dinner she would bake loaves of zucchini bread. These baked goods went to the neighbors, coworkers and the public just happening by. My father had suggested she sell them at school, but Mother firmly reminded him that the teachers weren't supportive of free enterprise in the elementary schools. "Well, she could organize a bake sale and the proceeds could go to charity," my father offered. So the following week Helen Keller Elementary School had a bake sale in the school gymnasium. Tables were loaded up with flour-and-sugar concoctions of every creed and color. Cookies, cupcakes, strudel, fudge, brownies and whole cakes. My sister's table was the most impressive and I felt swelled up with pride at her arrangement. She had a banner struck across the wall behind the table that read *zucchini's R R friends*. And then along with her stacks of loaves she also had our season's bounty of zucchini. I even snuck in a few turnips for color. The teachers milled around her table praising her for her fine ingenuity.

Mrs. Morton asked me, "How did your family ever come into so many zucchinis?" As if zucchini was old money we had inherited.

"Oh, zucchini is a fast-growing vegetable," I told her. "My father says that it breeds in the garden like rabbits, really, really horny rabbits that multiply exponentially."

Mrs. Morton ignored me for the rest of the day and sent a note home to my parents that read, *Please do not allow this to happen again.*

In school we learned about the fur trappers and traders who migrated all over the frontier trading with the Indians. We learned about the Hudson's Bay Company and how the Plains Indians bartered with them for the glass beads and shells that modernized and increased the value of their traditional regalia. We learned that before money, folks just traded stuff. Bartered their wares. But then gold was discovered throughout the West and bartering furs and beads took a backseat. The Indians weren't gold diggers.

Aside from the Trouble with Tribbles, zucchini problem in our garden, we had another problem to contend with. The beets. Some evenings I would discover my father stooped down over the beet rows, shaking his head and muttering, "Borscht . . . borscht."

My sister was encouraged to invent a recipe for beet bread, as she had done with the zucchini, but it kept coming out of the oven soggy and oozing red juice, as if it were hunks of animal flesh trickling trails of blood all over the kitchen counters. Not a very appetizing sight. Father had a bit more success with his beet experimentation. Inventing such delicacies as beetloaf and Sunday morning succotash surprise and beet omelets. He'd counteracted the red by adding blue food coloring, so we ended up with purple tongues after eating. My all-time favorite was beet Jell-O. And Mother packed our lunches to include bologna-and-beet sandwiches. We took sacks of beets to our grandparents' house and my German grandmother was delighted with our offering. "Oh, I just love beets!" she exclaimed. "I shall make borscht and pickles."

The beets were beginning to get on everyone's nerves. But there were other cauldrons bubbling in our household, my father's over-stimulated dread of waste. He'd been raised by a tough and hearty Montana farm girl, who in turn had been bred from a stock of immigrant Germans from Russia who had escaped the banks of the Valga River after the reign of Catherine the Great.* As if injected straight through the bloodline, my grandmother Gertrude instilled a heavy dose of "Waste not, want not," medication to my father. My grandfather also ladled out his own brand of practical conservation.

---

* Catherine the Great: Empress of Russia, sometimes referred to as an "enlightened despot," who ruled from 1762 until 1796; she was known for her political savvy, her devotion to the arts, and her colorful personal life

But more out of his penny-pinching and obsessive attention to dollars and cents, not out of some necessity imprinted from childhood to "Save today, you'll not starve tomorrow." The examination of water and electric bills was one of my grandfather's favorite hobbies. Either wattage fascinated him or he was always expecting to get stiffed. The latter being more true, because he was one of *the* great complainers.

It didn't come as much of a surprise when my father promoted his newest scheme: of bartering our surplus beets door to door. The catch was, we were the ones doing the soliciting, he was going to stay home and watch the World Series. He furthered his cause by explaining to us that the Indians traded long ago and this would be our own personal tribute to an old way of life.

"Yeah, but they didn't sell beets door to door like encyclopedia salesmen," my sister retorted. "I'll feel so stupid!"

"Nonsense!" my father said. "It's a fine idea. Whatever money you make, I'll just deduct from your allowance. And if you make more than your allowance, you can keep the difference. Save up for a bike or mitt or something."

I couldn't help thinking that if only my mother had stopped my father when he'd decided to become Reverend Buck and toil and sweat in the garden, none of this would be happening. This was a bad episode from *Attack of the Killer Tomatoes*, and my father's ambition and insistence on doing things only on a large scale didn't seem to justify the humiliation and embarrassment that resulted when we were coaxed to distribute the fruits of our labor. However, his latest plan I was for the most part agreeable to, but only because I was so completely eager to do anything that would levitate me in his eyes as angelic and perfect and because, secretly, I enjoyed witnessing my sister's discomfort.

We filled up grocery sacks with surplus. Father had suggested we fill up the wheelbarrow, but Julie wouldn't hear of it. "For cripe's sake, with that wheelbarrow filled with beets we'd look pathetic!" she argued. "We'd look like Okies* from *The Grapes of Wrath*!" My father was a fanatic about Steinbeck. He taught my sister to read "The Red Pony" before she entered the second grade. I, on the other hand, was considered the *slow* one.

We set out. Our own personal tribute to Indians of long ago. We weren't very conspicuous. Nothing out of the ordinary, just a couple of brown-skinned kids in braids walking grocery sacks down the suburban street. Indians weren't a common sight in residential neighborhoods, and my sister and I had experienced our share of racial prejudice. When my mother wrote out checks at the grocery store, the store manager was always called by the clerk to verify her driver's license. This occurring immediately after a white woman wrote a check to the same clerk but no verification was asked for. Once riding my bike, I heard some kids call me *nigger*. I don't know what hurt me more, the fact that they had called me an ugly name or that they had misrepresented my race. My sister during a Husky game at Hecht Ed Stadium was insulted by a black man when she was buying hot dogs. "Must eat a lot of hot dogs on the reservation, huh?" he told her. Later when we told Father, he responded with "Did you ask him if he ate a lot of watermelon?"

We had walked most of a mile to a neighborhood outside the confines of our own, so as not to be further embarrassed by people we actually knew. When we had come to a point where we felt we were at a safe enough distance, my sister told me to go up to the house with the pink flamingos balanced in the flower bed. "Only if you come too," I told her. So together we marched up to the door and rang the doorbell.

---

*Okies: the name for a resident or native of Oklahoma, often used pejoratively mainly by Californians (like writer John Steinbeck) to describe migrant farmers of white and mixed Indian blood who were forced to flee their farms during the Great Depression of the 1930s

A woman with frizzy red hair answered the door. "Hello?" she asked. "What can I do for you girls?"

My sister nudged me with her elbow. "Would you like to buy some beets?" I asked.

The woman's brows knitted together. "What's that? What's that you asked?"

"BEETS!" I shouted. "WOULD YOU LIKE TO BUY SOME BEETS?!"

I yelled so loudly that some kids stopped what they were doing and looked toward the house.

The woman was having a great deal of difficulty disguising her perplexity. Her brow was so busy knitting together she could have made up an afghan. Finally, some expression resembling resolution passed over her face. "No, not today," and she very curtly closed the door in our faces.

I wasn't going to let her go that easily. "BORSCHT, LADY!" I yelled. "YOU KNOW HOW TO MAKE BORSCHT?!"

My sister threw me a horrified look, shoved me and ran down the street. "HEY JULIE!" I called after her. "YOU SHOULD SEE YOUR FACE, IT'S BEET RED!"

We didn't sell any beets that day. Our personal tribute had failed. After I caught up with my sister, I found her sitting on the pavement at the top of a steep hill, with her face in her hands. I didn't say anything because there wasn't anything to say. I knew that she was crying and it was partly my fault. I wanted to make it up to her. Though I wasn't bothered by her pained frustrations, tears were another matter entirely. When she cried, I always felt compelled to cry right along with her. But on this day I didn't. Instead, I took the grocery sacks filled with beets and turned them upside down. The beets escaped from the bags, and as we watched them begin their descent to the bottom of the hill, I noticed the beginning of a smile on my sister's face. When the plump red vegetables had arrived at the bottom of the hill, leaving a bloody pink trail behind, we were both chuckling. And when a Volkswagen bus slammed on its brakes to avoid colliding with our surplus beets, we were laughing. And by the time the beets reached the next block and didn't stop rolling but continued down the asphalt street heading into the day after tomorrow, my sister and I were displaying pure and uncensored hysterics— laughing uncontrollably, holding our bellies as tears ran down our cheeks, pressing our faces against the pavement and rejoicing in the spectacle that we viewed from the top of that concrete hill.

FROM *SCHOOL DAYS*

Patrick Chamoiseau

TRANSLATED BY LINDA COVERDALE

Patrick Chamoiseau recalls the exigencies of starting school in Fort-de-France, Martinique, in this excerpt from his largely autobiographical narrative School Days. *The little boy recounts his first day with humor and amazement, but also with the painful awareness of his first loss. Lurking behind the usual schoolyard bullies and pompous teachers and headmaster is the revelation of what it means to live in a colonial world, where one's own rhythm and sense of importance are suddenly devalued and replaced by something quite strange and foreign, and where there is no one available to answer questions that themselves are difficult (and sometimes impossible) to articulate.*

Martinique, an island in the eastern Caribbean Sea, colonized by the French in 1635, shares a unique relationship with France. It is an overseas département *as well as one of the twenty-six* régions *of France. As a* département, *it remains an administrative unit of France, roughly analogous to a county.* Départements *were created in 1790 to replace France's former colonies; their purpose was to deliberately break up indigenous historical regions in order to erase cultural differences and build a more homogeneous nation. As a* région, *it does not have legislative autonomy, nor can it issue its own regulations. It can levy taxes, and these tax revenues are used mainly to build schools and pay for equipment.*

Chamoiseau, who studied law in Paris but returned to live in Martinique, has been an extremely influential promoter of Creole identity, especially through his writing style, a freeform, highly complex mixture of French, his own invention, and "creolism." Much of School Days *is also informed by language connected to the spoken word, which, together with Chamoiseau's unique language blend, serves as a way of demystifying how children learn culture through language. In addition, it reveals the disparate yet rich linguistic cultural heritage of Chamoiseau's own traditions.*

This story compares poignantly with Patricia Grace's "Kura," in which school anxiety occurs as part of the Maori girl's first experience, or with Victor Perera's "Kindergarten," in which the narrator's innocence and positive sense of himself are also brought down a notch. The issue of language and how it can redefine one's sense of self also arises in Faith Adiele's "Black Men."

The little boy spent the morning like a potato bug under a bitter leaf. He never dared to look directly at the Teacher. This was a stratagem much favored by the small fry. If ever your eyes met, he might suddenly feel like asking you one of his impossible questions. While in his getting-acquainted phase, he paced back and forth, talking, talking, providing information of which his little troop (except, perhaps, for a few of us who were naturally gifted at this sort of thing) could make neither head nor tail. Sometimes he stopped in front of the first rows, trying to catch some furtive eye. At the door, he would gaze out at the silent playground now abruptly filled with his voice, then whirl around to stride back across the room. Suddenly, he advanced down the center aisle. Half huddled beneath his bench, gaze glued to the floor, the little boy listened in dismay as the voice drew closer. After a moment's hush, an iron hand jiggled his shoulder: *Sit up strraight, my frriend, mind your posture, for goodness' sake* . . . Back at the blackboard, the Teacher snatched up the chalk and began the ritual that would from now on set the tempo of endless hours of school: *Who can tell me what day, of what month, of what year it is?*

A thoughtful silence fell.

The little boy had never considered the world from that angle. He knew about church days, Mam Ninotte's washdays, All Saints' Day,* Christmas Day, New Year's Day . . . Life was given its rhythm by sunshine or rainy weather, by redfish season and whitefish time . . . and Mam Salinière had never asked that kind of question. One little squirt in the front row stood up, however, and reeled off the day-month-year, earning incomprehensible congratulations from the Teacher (*O gleam of humanity in an ocean of barrbarrism!*), who wrote the answer in a fine hand on the blackboard. It was a Monday. In the month of September. In the devil only knows what year.

"I drraw your attention, gentlemen, to what I have just wrritten. Do you not observe, a certain elegance in the way these lines grrow sometimes fat and sometimes slender? Is this not so? . . . For your inforrmation, these are called upstrrokes and downstrrokes. No wrriting without upstrrokes and downstrrokes . . ."

*All Saints' Day: sometimes known as "All Hallows" ("hallow" meaning "holy"), and so related to our Halloween, this is a Roman Catholic holiday that falls on November 1 and commemorates the close of the Easter season; it honors all saints, known and unknown

---

The little boy's life was saved by the bell. From that day forward he would learn to welcome it with a deep, invigorating breath. This ringing set off a terrific din upstairs—you could just feel the classrooms explode. The stairwells filled with liberated hordes, and after a slight, pregnant pause, pandemonium would erupt into the courtyard.

Time for recess . . .

Some dummy had the misfortune to pop right up out of his seat. The Teacher pounced on him like a red wasp: *Who told you to rrise? Are you in charge here? Sit, scoundrrel, good-for-nothing, budding wrretch, diminutive scalawag of a rrapscallion!* They were stunned to learn that, captain of his ship by divine right, the Teacher ran absolutely everything. He and he alone gave permission to stand up. To sit down. To open one's mouth. When he spoke, all eyes and ears were to be trained on him. Pay attention, look alive, and sit up straight. The Teacher was to be spared any bunny-mumbles, any bovine, sun-drowsy yawns, any stupid-ass-molasses-lapping grins, any barnyard cackles from beneath the desks. All bladders—and the neighboring tubes—were to be emptied before entering this sanctuary, thus obviating the need to ask anything that did not pertain to pure knowledge. A raised finger was to be the outward and visible sign of a flash of intelligence rather than the always irritating announcement of a scatological emergency. Not even a fly should buzz without permission. After class had begun, no one should have anything more to say—not to himself, not to the devil or the Goodlord, and absolutely not to his neighbor.

"A classroom is not a bedlam, gentlemen! Order! Discipline! Rrespect! Now, the first rrow will rrise and file out silently, in an orderly and disciplined fashion. Good. Now the second rrow . . ."

Thenceforward the sound of the bell produced nothing more in them than an irrepressible shudder of pleasure, which they had to learn to conceal from the Teacher's newly watchful eye. Out on the playground, the little boy found himself instantly surrounded by several bullies (probably embittered pupils repeating first grade because of their awkwardness at reading *B-a-Ba*) who ran through the list of animals in his name, while other rough boys made fun of his lisp. He could see that his usual defenses would not work here: going stiff-as-a-stone, flopping to the ground in tears, twitching with the ague, looking woebegone—nothing doing. So he spat at them. Ptooey! The frisky monsters dodged his spit gobs. They barred his way in front, they blocked him off behind, they capered in a circle around him when he stood stock still. Hard pressed, the little boy was at a total loss. His breath came in shuddering gasps, his shoulders shook, his heavy heart beat painfully within his heaving breast. He was overwhelmed with shame. Then bang—the pack swooped down on Big Bellybutton, the child who hadn't known his own name. The little boy watched the poor devil take off at bird speed, pursued by a string of bullies in seventh heaven.

Taking advantage of this diversion, the little boy went looking for Paul. He knew his brother was in one of the upstairs classes, and he planned to seek refuge with him against the eventual return of his tormentors. Spotting Paul through the whirl of older students (the new kids were still clumped before their classrooms or standing with their backs to the wall, trying to assess the dangers of this world), he darted toward him. Paul, completely absorbed in his game, turned— unfortunately—just as his brother ran up to him. Bonk! The collision was inevitable. The smaller boy saw swarms of fireflies. Paul wound up flat on his back with a lump on his forehead, limbs every which way, cursing that mole cricket who dogged his steps even on the playground. As for the little boy, he was brave enough not to cry, and pressing a hand over his bruise, he slipped away into the sportive throng before a scornful crowd could gather. A few observant fiends were already pointing at them and shouting nasty things. He spent the rest of his first recess near a row of faucets at which the children sucked relentlessly, as though they'd never seen such a thing before.

Big Bellybutton was still on the run. Every so often the little guy would stop, raise a fist the size of an egg, bare his milk teeth, spit, and try to hide in a corner of the yard . . . *Awa!* The pack stayed right on his heels. *I pa konnèt non'y! . . . I pa konnèt non'y! . . . Doesn't know his own name!* They pushed him. They snatched at him. They shredded him. They plucked him. They minced him. They tripped him. They pinched and tweaked him. They pulled him around by his shirttail. While he was picking up a torn-off button, they knocked him over and sent him tumbling like a soccer ball. All this was drowned out by the general hullabaloo. And so the little boy realized that the playground was a pitiless place of all-out warfare, something like a jungle or a desert, where mass murder could be committed without anyone even noticing. With sudden inspiration, Big Bellybutton took shelter beneath the low roof that covered part of the courtyard, where the Teachers were gathered. The mob evaporated like misty rain on a parched field.

Where are my *Répondeurs?**

---

* *répondeurs*: French for those who are capable of answering or giving answers

Under the roof, the Teachers were talking among themselves. Now and then they would take a step outside their personal domain to break up a fight, slow down a child barreling along too fast, pick up a tot sent flying by a Big Kid. The Teachers wore trousers, vests, jackets, and ties. They walked like senators. They never turned just their heads, always their entire bodies. Their gestures were restrained and seemed intended to give silken wings to their words. When approached by Monsieur le Directeur (a man of their ilk but with a sterner look, gray hair, hands clasped behind his back, shoulders bowed beneath the combined burdens of wisdom and worry), they bowed before him as if in church and, unctuously respectful, hung on his every word. His presence galvanized the Teachers, who then began to keep a closer eye on the children, to venture out into the yard, to dispense advice, to raise an admonitory finger at anyone who forgot to turn off a faucet. Not one of them noticed Big Bellybutton trembling in their protective shadow.

Monsieur le Directeur did not often appear during recess; his arrival usually meant that the bell was about to ring. His eye was all-seeing. He noticed dripping faucets, half-open doors on the toilet stalls, children running around with forbidden treasures—a comic book, a marble, a slingshot . . . He scurried about like a fire ant, busy with emergencies that only he could discern and that vanished as soon as he'd hustled off.

Monsieur le Directeur never spoke to the children except in reprimand. He was not one for *hellos* and *how-are-yous*. He did not look at anyone but would glare witheringly at any insolent boy who forgot to

greet him or at a wild-child too lost in frenzy to notice his approach.
With Monsieur le Directeur, the little boy took some measure of the
trap into which he had crammed himself. The children spoke among
themselves in shrill voices, with their own words, using their native
ways and expressions. The advance of Monsieur le Directeur across
the playground caused abrupt freeze frames all around him. Runners
stopped running. Jumpers stopped jumping. Chatterboxes stopped
chattering. Speechifiers practically swallowed their tongues. He more
or less anesthetized all life. Those who thus modified their behavior
were old hands at this, from the classrooms upstairs.

But not everybody quieted down.

One little live wire, a greenhorn, did not see Monsieur le Directeur coming. He was yammering away about some old neighbor-
lady who could change into a flying sorceress. Hunched over all
twisty-faced and waving his arms around, the Storyteller was still
pouring out his tale when Monsieur le Directeur arrived. Other
oblivious children were listening open-mouthed in a compact circle, fired up by the story. Grasping the Creature by the ear, Monsieur le Directeur dragged him hither and thither: *What do I
hear—you're speaking Creole?* And what do I see—shameless mon-
keyshines? Just where do you think you are?! Speak properly and behave
in a civilized manner* . . . All the young newcomers took serious
note. The passage of Monsieur le Directeur was strewn with cemetery statues.

The little boy never became one of those playground lightning bolts
that streaked pell-mell through the yard, hide-and-seeking, fisticuff-

---

* Creole: from the Portuguese *cioulo*, via Spanish *criollo* and French *créole*; a language that originates from a combination of two or more other languages with its
own distinctive features, not inherited from either "parent" language, and becomes
the native language of a specific community

ing, whirly-dervishing* like rats in a demijohn.† He would sit off in a corner talking with some other kid like himself. Once in a long while he could be seen racing around like a headless chicken, helter-skeltering. But such episodes were rare. And out of character. His nature was contemplative. He watched the others, observed their frights, their joys, their angers, identified the good guys and the bad guys, the savages and gentle souls. Sometimes he wandered over to the front gate, where a candy lady (*O majesty! . . . Answer me . . .*) sold coconut sweeties, sugar twists, peanut caramels, tamarind comfits,‡ lots of confections he could hardly ever buy because Mam Ninotte didn't give him any money. During that first recess, Mam Ninotte appeared at the gate. The little boy ran to her like a madman, ready to wriggle through the bars. He could already see himself, homeward bound. But she explained to him that school wasn't over yet and handed him a *pain au chocolat*.§ A pure marvel that he chewed on sadly, watching her disappear along the enticing streets of Downtown.

> *Répondeurs:*
> Candy Lady
> treasure trove
> store of happiness
> no wrinkle or skinflintiness
> no bitter pennypinching
> could tell against
> the splendors of your tray

* whirly dervishing: from Whirling Dervish—mystical dancers who trace their origins to the thirteenth-century Ottoman Empire and who rotate at a precise rhythm meant to represent the earth revolving on its axis while orbiting the sun
† demijohn: a large glass bottle used for the transport or storage of wine or spirits
‡ comfits: candy containing fruit or nut
§ *pain au chocolat*: French pastry consisting of puff pastry and several strips of chocolate

O majesty!
O sugarplum!

The bell.

The uproar ceased—flap!—and the children lined up double file by classes in front of the row of Teachers. Monsieur le Directeur observed these maneuvers from a distance, waiting for the correct degree of quiet. Waiting. Waiting. Seeing that the requisite hush was long in coming, Monsieur le Directeur frowned his way between the rows of pupils, casting a cold eye on those still horsing around, while the Teachers verified the straightness of each line and checked to see that all partners were holding hands. Waiting. Waiting. Then the waves of happiness receded, stranding the small fry. All energy ebbed from their muscles. All expression drained from their faces. In a spectral silence, Monsieur le Directeur pushed the button of the electric bell. The upstairs classes rippled into motion like tame caterpillars, followed by the ground-floor pupils. Back in his classroom, the little boy found his asphyxia waiting for him right where he had left it.

But everything went well: no one had to speak, to write, to explain this-or-that. It was the Teacher who talked. And now the little boy realized something obvious: *the Teacher spoke French.* Mam Ninotte used snippets of French on occasion (a half-word here, a quarter-word there), bits of French that were automatic and unchanging. And the Papa, when he made a rum punch, ceremoniously unfurled a French that was less a language than an esoteric tool used for effect. As for the Big Kids, their natural mode of expression was Creole, except with Mam Ninotte, other grownups, and most particularly the Papa. A certain respectful distance was maintained through rituals of formality when speaking to them. And everything else for everyone else (pleasures, shouts, dreams, hatreds, the life in life . . .) was Creole. This division of speech had never struck the little boy before. French (to which he didn't even attach a name) was some object fetched when needed from a kind of shelf, outside oneself, but which sounded natural in the mouth, close to Creole. Close through the articulation. The words. The sentence structure. But now, with the Teacher, speaking traveled far and wide along a single road. And this French road became strangely foreign. The articulation changed. The rhythm changed. The intonation changed. Words that were more or less familiar began to sound different. They seemed to come from a distant horizon and no longer had any affinity with Creole. The Teacher's images, examples, references did not spring from their native country anymore. The Teacher spoke French like the people on the radio or the sailors of the French line. And he deliberately spoke nothing else. French seemed to be the very element of his knowledge. He savored this smooth syrup he secreted so ostentatiously. And his language did not reach out to the children, the way Mam Salinière's had, to envelop, caress, and persuade them. His words floated above them with the magnificence of a ruby-throated hummingbird hovering in the breeze. *Oh, the Teacher was French!*

> *Répondeurs:*
> All along the horizon
> on a calm sea
> use your Creole.
> If the weather changes
> surging billows
> wallowing troughs
> gird your loins
> get a grip on your French.

Mama, it's hard . . . Baffled, the little black boy realized that he did not know this language. The chatty lil' voice in his head used a different language, his home-language, his Mama-language, the language he had not learned but rather absorbed with ease as he eagerly explored his world. An alien French streaked through this language in flashes that were fleeting and rare; he had heard these words somewhere and he repeated them on occasions he couldn't quite pin down. Another French that was closer to him, acclimated but just as constricted, was lurking on the edge of the living intensity of his mind. But really speaking—to say something, give vent to an emotion, express yourself, think things over, talk for any length of time—required the Mama-tongue that (ayayaye!) was proving useless in school.

And dangerous.

Oh-so-hard! . . .

The Teacher spoke until the noon bell rang. What did he talk about? Undoubtedly the light shed by Wisdom on benighted minds. Doubtless he praised the public school those of his generation had fought so hard to establish. He urged those with the good fortune to be sitting there to appreciate this extraordinary advantage: a golden opportunity, hard-won, not to be wasted. Or else—the cane fields. Sweeping gutters and thumping drums. Lugging sacks of béke* goods around the waterfront, raking shellfish from the mudflats of Terres-Sainville, dredging the canals of La Levée. Or worse: wind-ing up in the streets, fettered by ignorance and stupidity. The bestial darkness in which one lost forever the idea of Man.

Time-to-time, he'd stop to see what effect this oration was having on his rapt flock. He searched eyes and faces, hoping to read there glim-mers of their inmost feelings. The little boy kept his head down or hurriedly looked away at the Teacher's slightest movement. Several times he felt the latter's gaze directed full upon him and was relieved

---

* *béké*: Creole word for white person

when the intimidating voice, moving from one end of the black-board to the other, would continue as though to itself: *State education, gentlemen, public education—it was a harrd battle, and one that is still being fought every day; we were Caesar, Alexander, and Napoleon, war-rriors and conquerors shaking all the earrth, and no mountain was high enough to stay the course of our thirrst for knowledge* . . .

O comfort beyond measure: holding your mama's hand after a morning at school! You are all made of joy. Quivering with content-ment. Waving bye-bye to the other youngsters, who are escaping just like you. You trot on home as though it were the only place un-scathed in a world turned upside-down. And each step away from school is meant to be forever. And no one looks back. Swarming with schoolchildren, Downtown is recalled to life, and you're happy after all to be a part of it: you've grown up just a bit. Less fearful now, you find you're proud of your experience, and you swing your satchel once again like a jaunty altar boy. I speak of the quiet tri-umph of that homeward journey. *Sweets! Candies, oh!* . . .

The house recovers its former magic. The staircase shadows are once more thronged with seductive spirits. The spider webs shimmer anew with the evanescence of watered silk. The tranquility of the kitchen roof becomes a hideaway where one may contemplate the meaning of life. Everything is dulce. Everything is pleasurable. His spirits soar in a whirl of acclamation.

He takes stock of his familiar world in other ways. He discovers a thousand details. Now he's looking at things he never noticed before. High up on a wall, a picture of Christ suddenly appears: chestnut-brown hair, and blue eyes that move to the left, to the right, watching the little boy. He finally appreciates the fairy-tale scene hanging over Mara Ninotte's bed: near a Chinese junk,* undines† are bathing in water that's unbelievably green; translucent veils add luster to their pale skin; blond cherubs flutter around them, singing and playing the harp with sublime innocence; on the horizon looms a turreted castle that stabs the mauvish sky with a threat of imprisonment; soft outlines of a forest encircle the misty water invitingly . . . You gaze at this Saturnian‡ idyll, you gaze . . . and gaze . . .

And what about this other one, over the buffet?

Country folk, standing in the twilight, heads bowed, hands clasped, farm tools lying scattered on the ground around an old basket. In the distance, haystacks like rolling hills blend into a solemn sunset pricked by the spire of a church tower . . . a magical hour . . . a reverent depiction of working the land, a scene expressing the abiding power of fate, sorrow, courage, tenderness, hope . . . Mesmerized, the little boy can't stop looking at these pictures. Mam Ninotte had bought them from a Syrian shopkeeper. These images adorned every home in the country at that time—and still do today.

After the midday meal, the little boy saw that the hour approached when Mam Ninotte would sit down at her sewing machine. O moment of happiness! He realized with a pang that he had not fully appreciated this moment until now! He began to wait in blissful anticipation—but his vigil was cut short: *Go put your school clothes back on, it's time to leave!*

And everything is distressing.

---

* Chinese junk: Chinese sailing vessal
† undines: in German folklore, water-spirits who like to associate with humans
‡ Saturnian: from Saturn, the Roman god of the harvest

The shirt is a corset.

The shoes and socks become agonizing pincers. Inside the once fantastic satchel lurk secret fears. The little boy (who doesn't dare tell Mam Ninotte how unwilling he is to go back there) looks like a wilted flower. His feet drag. The stairs have grown gigantic. His moist hand does not grip Mam Ninotte's; she is the one holding on to him. His tummy's in trouble. His shoes hurt. Is that a feeble cough? But it doesn't move Mam Ninotte to pity—never mind, she says, it's nothing . . .

Répondeurs:
Gird your loins!
Gird your loins!

Self-Discovery

ON THE ROAD AT EIGHTEEN

Yu Hua

TRANSLATED BY ANDREW F. JONES

*Yu Hua has long been considered one of China's most impor-
tant novelists. One of his novels,* To Live, *was made into a
popular film by Zhang Yimou that won the Grand Prix at the
1994 Cannes Film Festival. "On the Road at Eighteen" represents an earlier phase of his writing career, when he produced
innovative and highly controversial stories and novels that
placed him among a generation of young writers of experimental fiction at the forefront of China's 1980s avant-garde literary scene.*

    *This story reflects Yu's revolutionary disillusionment and
preoccupation with the human capacity for random cruelty
and violence. Its young narrator starts his road trip with his innocence intact, though he's worried about reaching his destina-
tion and becomes increasingly concerned that the road he
travels is going nowhere. Like many of Franz Kafka's stories,
"On the Road at Eighteen" does not seem to take place in any
specific time or place; the narrator never appears to be making
progress, only experiencing constant change. Ordinary objects—
a stalled truck, apples, bicycles, even wheelbarrows—take on*

*mysterious and sinister meaning. The story asks us to move be-
yond our usual ethical, political, and stylistic markers in order
to make sense of a new kind of disorienting realism where the
young may gallop out of the house, ready for adventure, only to
encounter diminished expectations.*

*Born in 1960, Yu grew up in a small town near Shanghai.
After working for five years as a dentist, he turned to short-
fiction writing, publishing his first story in 1984. His most current work is much less experimental than the story represented
here; however, his desire to avoid the ideological manipulation
of the realism that he found in the propagandist literature of his
childhood still makes his characters seem curiously flat, even
while his writing style continues to challenge us to think beyond
the literary structures with which we are familiar.*

*The young narrator in "On the Road at Eighteen" can be
compared with Chang-rae Lee's "Sea Urchin," about a
teenager charged with acquiring his parents' tastes in their
mother country; though Lee's teenager has a purpose, and his
story involves a specific time and place, he too discovers that his
journey takes him to the unfamiliar and that to adjust is not as
easy as he thought.*

The asphalt road rolls up and down like it's pasted on top of
ocean waves. Walking down this little highway in the mountains, I'm like a boat. This year, I turned eighteen. The few brown-
ish whiskers that have sprouted on my chin flutter in the breeze.
They've only just taken up residence on my chin, so I really treasure
them. I've spent the whole day walking down the road, and I've already seen lots of mountains and lots of clouds. Every one of the
mountains and every one of the clouds made me think of people

I know. I shouted out each of their nicknames as I walked by. So even though I've walked all day, I'm not tired, not at all. I walked through the morning, now it's the tail end of the afternoon, and it won't be long until I see the tip of dusk. But I haven't found an inn.

I've encountered quite a few people along the road, but none of them has known where the road goes or whether there's an inn there. They all tell me: "Keep walking. You'll see when you get there." I think what everyone said was just terrific. I really am just seeing when I get there. But I haven't found an inn. I feel like I should be worried about that.

I think it's weird that I've walked all day and only seen one car. That was around noon, when I'd just begun to think about hitch-hiking. But all I was doing was thinking about hitchhiking. I hadn't started to worry about finding an inn—I was only thinking about how amazing it would be to get a lift from someone. I stood by the side of the road waving at the car, trying my best to look casual. But the driver hardly even looked at me. The car or the driver. They hardly even looked at me. All they fucking did was drive right by. So I ran, chasing the car as fast as I could, just for fun, because I still hadn't started to worry about finding an inn. I ran until the car had disappeared, and then I laughed at myself, but I discovered that laughing too hard made it difficult to breathe, so I stopped. After that I kept walking, happy and excited, except that I started to regret that I hadn't picked up a rock before I started waving at the car.

Now I really want a lift, because dusk is about to fall and I can't get that inn out of my goddamned head. But there haven't been any cars all afternoon. If a car came now, I think I could make it stop. I'd lie down in the middle of the road, and I'm willing to bet that any car would come to a screeching halt before it got to my head. But I don't even hear the rumble of an engine, let alone see a car. Now I'm just going to have to keep walking and see when I get there. Not bad at all: keep walking and see when you get there.

The road rolls up and down from hill to valley, and the hills tempt me every time, because before I charge up to the top, I think I'll see an inn on the other side. But each time I charge up the slope, all I see is another hill in the distance, with a depressing trough in between. And still I charge up each hill as if my life depended on it. And now I'm charging up another one, but this time I see it. Not an inn, but a truck. The truck is pointed toward me, stalled in the middle of the highway in a gully between two hills. I can see the driver's ass pointing skyward and, behind it, all the colors of the approaching sunset. I can't see the driver's head because it's stuffed under the hood. The truck's hood slants up into the air like an upside-down lip. The back of the truck is piled full of big wicker baskets. I'm thinking that they definitely must be packed with some kind of fruit. Of course, bananas would be best of all. There are probably some in the cab, too, so when I hop in, I can eat a few. And I don't really care if the truck's going in the opposite direction as me. I need to find an inn, and if there's no inn, I need a truck. And the truck's right here in front of me.

Elated, I run down to the truck and say, "Hi!"

The driver doesn't seem to have heard me. He's still fiddling with something under the hood.

"Want a smoke?"

Only now does he pull his head out from under the hood, stretch out a black, grimy hand, and take the cigarette between his fingers. I rush to give him a light, and he sucks several mouthfuls of smoke into his mouth before stuffing his head back under the hood.

I'm satisfied. Since he accepted the smoke, that means he has to give me a lift. So I wander around to the back of the truck to investigate what's in the wicker baskets. But they're covered, and I can't see, so I sniff. I smell the fragrance of apples. And I think: Apples aren't too bad either.

In just a little bit, he's done repairing the truck, and he jumps

down from the hood. I rush over and say, "Hey, I need a ride."
What I don't expect is that he gives me a hard shove with those
grimy hands and barks, "Go away!"

I'm so angry I'm speechless, but he just swings on over to the
driver's side, opens the door, slides into the cab, and starts the engine. I know that if I blow this opportunity, I'll never get another
one. I know I should just give up. So I run over to the other side,
open the door, and hop in. I'm ready to fight if necessary. I turn to
him and yell: "Then give me back my cigarette!" The truck's already
started to move by now.

He turns to look at me with a big, friendly smile and asks,
"Where you headed?"

I'm bewildered by this turnaround. I say, "Doesn't matter.
Wherever."

He asks me very nicely, "Want an apple?" He's still glancing over
at me.

"That goes without saying."

"Go get one from the back."

How am I supposed to climb out of the cab to the back of the
truck when he's driving so fast? So I say, "Forget it."

He says, "Go get one." He's still looking at me.

I say, "Stop staring at me. There's no road on my face."

With this, he twists his eyes back onto the highway.

The truck's driving back in the direction I just came from; I'm
sitting comfortably in the cab, looking out the window and chatting
with the driver. By now, we're already the best of friends. I've found
out that he's a private entrepreneur.* It's his own truck. The apples
are his, too. I hear change jingling in his pockets. I ask him, "Where
are you going?"

---

* entrepreneur: from the French, meaning a person who takes the risk of organiz-
ing and operating a new business venture

He says, "I just keep driving and see when I get there."

It sounds just like what everyone else said. That's so nice. I feel closer to him. I want everything I see outside the window to be just as close, just as familiar, and soon all those hills and clouds start to bring more friends to mind, so I shout out their nicknames as we drive by.

Now I'm not crying out for an inn anymore. What with the truck, the driver, the seat in the cab, I'm completely at peace. I don't know where the truck's going, and neither does he. Anyway, it doesn't matter, because all we have to do is keep driving, and we'll see when we get there.

But the truck broke down. By that time, we were as close as friends can be. My arm was draped over his shoulder and his over mine. He was telling me about his love life, and right when he'd got to the part about how it felt the first time he held a woman's body in his arms, the truck broke down. The truck was climbing up a hill when it broke down. All of a sudden the squeal of the engine went quiet like a pig right after it's been slaughtered. So he jumped out of the truck, climbed onto the hood, opened up that upside-down lip, and stuffed his head back under it. I couldn't see his ass. But I could hear the sound of him fiddling with the engine.

After a while, he pulled his head out from under the hood and slammed it shut. His hands were even blacker than before. He wiped them on his pants, wiped again, jumped down, and walked back to the cab.

"Is it fixed?" I asked.

"It's shot. There's no way to fix it."

I thought that over and finally asked, "Now what do we do?"

"Wait and see," he said, nonchalantly.

I was sitting in the cab wondering what to do. Then I started to think about finding an inn again. The sun was just falling behind the mountains, and the hazy dusk clouds looked like billows of steam. The notion of an inn stole back into my head and began to swell until my mind was stuffed full of it. By then, I didn't even have a mind. An inn was growing where my mind used to be.

At that point, the driver started doing the official morning calisthenics that they always play on the radio right there in the middle of the highway. He went from the first exercise to the last without missing a beat. When he was finished, he started to jog circles around the truck. Maybe he had been sitting too long in the driver's seat and needed some exercise. Watching him moving from my vantage point inside the truck, I couldn't sit still either, so I opened the door and jumped out. But I didn't do calisthenics or jog in place. I was thinking about an inn and an inn and an inn.

Just then, I noticed five people rolling down the hill on bicycles. Each bike had a carrying pole fastened to the back with two big baskets on either end. I thought they were probably local peasants on their way back from selling vegetables at market. I was delighted to see people riding by, so I welcomed them with a big "Hi!" They rode up beside me and dismounted. Excited, I greeted them and asked, "Is there an inn around here?"

Instead of responding they asked me, "What's in the truck?"

I said, "Apples."

All five of them pushed their bikes over to the side of the truck. Two of them climbed onto the back, picked up about ten baskets full of apples, and passed them upside down to the ones below, who proceeded to tear open the plastic covering the top of the wicker and pour the apples into their own baskets. I was dumbstruck. When I finally realized exactly what was going on, I made for them and asked, "Just what do you think you're doing?"

None of them paid the slightest bit of attention to me. They continued to pour the apples. I tried to grab hold of someone's arm and screamed, "They're stealing all the apples!" A fist came crashing into my nose, and I landed several feet away. I staggered up, rubbed my nose. It felt soft and sticky, like it wasn't stuck to my face any-more but only dangling from it. Blood was flowing like tears from a broken heart. When I looked up to see which of them had hit me, they were already astride their bikes, riding away.

The driver was taking a walk, lips curling out as he sucked in deep draughts of air. He had probably lost his breath running. He didn't seem to be at all aware of what had just happened. I yelled to-ward him, "They stole your apples!" But he kept on walking without paying any attention to what I had yelled. I really wanted to run over and punch him so hard that his nose would be left dangling, too. I ran over and screamed into his ear, "They stole your apples." Only then did he turn to look at me, and I realized that his face was getting happier and happier the longer he looked at my nose.

At that point, yet another group of bicycles descended down the slope. Each bike had two big baskets fastened to the back. There were even a few children among the riders. They swarmed by me and surrounded the truck. A lot of people climbed onto the back, and the wicker baskets flew faster than I could count them. Apples poured out of broken baskets like blood out of my nose. They stuffed apples into their own baskets as if they were possessed. In just a few seconds, all the apples in the truck had been lowered to the ground. Then a few motorized tractor carts chugged down the hill and stopped next to the truck. A few big men dismounted and started to stuff apples into the carts. One by one, the empty wicker baskets were tossed to the side. The ground was covered with rolling apples, and the peasants scrabbled on their hands and knees like ants to pick them all up.

It was at that point that I rushed into their midst, risking life and limb, and cursed them, "Thieves!" I started swinging. My at-tack was met with countless fists and feet. It seemed like every part of my body got hit at the same time. I climbed back up off the ground. A few children began to hurl apples at me. The apples broke apart on my head, but my head didn't break. Just as I was about to rush the kids, a foot came crashing into my waist. I wanted to cry, but when I opened my mouth, nothing came out. There was nothing to do but fall to the ground and watch them steal the apples. I started to look around for the driver. He was standing a good distance away, looking right at me, and laughing as hard as he could. Just so I knew that I looked even better now than I had with a bloody nose.

I didn't even have the strength for anger. All I could do was gaze out at everything that was making me so angry. And what made me the angriest of all was the driver.

Another wave of bicycles and tractors rolled down the hill and threw themselves into the disaster area. There were fewer and fewer apples rolling on the ground. A few people left. A few more arrived. The ones who had arrived too late for apples began to busy themselves with the truck. I saw them remove the window glass, strip the tires, pry away the planks that covered the truck bed. Without its tires, the truck obviously felt really low, because it sank to the ground. A few children began to gather the wicker baskets that had been tossed to the side a moment before. As the road got cleaner and cleaner, there were fewer and fewer people. But all I could do was watch, because I didn't even have the strength for anger. I sat on the ground without moving, letting my eyes wander back and forth between the driver and the thieves.

Now, there's nothing left but a single tractor parked beside the sunken truck. Someone's looking around to see if there's anything left to take. He looks for a while and then hops on his tractor and starts the engine.

The truck driver hops onto the back of the tractor and looks back toward me, laughing. He's holding my red backpack in his hand. He's stealing my backpack. My clothes and my money are in the backpack. And food and books. But he's stealing my backpack.

I'm watching the tractor climb back up the slope. It disappears over the crest. I can still hear the rumble of its engine, but soon I can't even hear that. All of a sudden, everything's quiet, and the sky starts to get really dark. I'm still sitting on the ground. I'm hungry, and I'm cold, but there's nothing left.

I sit there for a long time before I slowly stand up. It isn't easy because my whole body aches like crazy every time I move, but still I stand up and limp over to the truck. The truck looks miserable, battered. I know I've been battered too.

The sky's black now. There's nothing here. Just a battered truck and battered me. I'm looking at the truck, immeasurably sad, and the truck's looking at me, immeasurably sad. I reach out to stroke it. It's cold all over. The wind starts to blow, a strong wind, and the sound of the wind rustling the trees in the mountains is like ocean waves. The sound terrifies me so much that my body gets as cold as the truck's.

I open the door and hop in. I'm comforted by the fact that they didn't pry away the seat. I lie down in the cab. I smell leaking gas and think of the smell of the blood that leaked out of me. The wind's getting stronger and stronger, but I feel a little warmer lying on the seat. I think that even though the truck's been battered, its heart is still intact, still warm. I know that my heart's warm, too. I was looking for an inn, and I never thought I'd find you here.

I lie inside the heart of the truck, remembering that clear warm afternoon. The sunlight was so pretty. I remember that I was outside enjoying myself in the sunshine for a long time, and when I got home I saw my dad through the window packing things into a red backpack. I leaned against the window frame and asked, "Dad, are you going on a trip?"

He turned and very gently said, "No, I'm letting you go on a trip."

"Letting me go on a trip?"

"That's right. You're eighteen now, and it's time you saw a little of the outside world."

Later I slipped that pretty red backpack onto my back. Dad patted my head from behind, just like you would pat a horse's rump. Then I gladly made for the door and excitedly galloped out of the house, as happy as a horse.

SEA URCHIN

Chang-rae Lee

In "Sea Urchin," Chang-rae Lee folds the teenage desire to be-
long at any cost into the strangeness of his return to Seoul, Ko-
rea, for the first time in twelve years. This memory piece,
published in the New Yorker's *August 2003 "firsts" issue, tells*
of Lee's determination to assimilate back into his homeland.
Having lived in the United States for many more years than he
lived in Korea, fifteen-year-old Lee is astonished to find every-
thing about his homeland to be a first-time experience—the
smells, the heat, even the food. His mother's health concerns con-
trast deeply with his father's desire to recapture "something live,
fresh"—in this case, live seafood. Lee's own desire to belong is
stronger than his mother's caution or even his father's nostalgia.

   Lee's visit dovetails with the political unrest in South Korea
in the 1980s. Martial law had been declared after a coup d'état
in 1979 in order to suppress student protest demonstrations
around the country. Students and soldiers confronted each other
in Kwangju, then a city of 600,000 people located 170 miles
south of Seoul, between May 18 and May 27. Angry citizens
joined in, and soon a massacre was under way. Though the death

and arrest numbers became a matter of conjecture, the after-effects of this unrest deepened the chasm among different South Korean provinces and heightened the general distrust of American troop intervention. Though Lee only alludes to this disturbance, his own lack of ease, while emanating from an apparently different cause, seems to mirror the atmosphere of hostile unrest.

Chang-rae Lee was raised in Westchester, New York, attended Phillips Exeter Academy, and graduated from Yale University with a degree in English and from the University of Oregon with an MFA in writing. He worked briefly as a Wall Street analyst before turning to writing full-time. In grade school, Lee toyed briefly with the idea of changing his name to something more Western (such as Tom); he stuck with Chang-rae, but his interest in the challenges of assimilation—the experience of feeling like a perpetual outsider in your adopted country—dominates much of his work. His first novel, Native Speaker, *published when he was twenty-nine, and his second novel,* A Gesture Life, *reflect this concern (though from very different perspectives).*

Lee's experience of displacement in "Sea Urchin" can be compared to that same quality in Elisabeth's Gille's Shadows of a Childhood *as well as Aminatta Forna's* The Devil That Danced on the Water. *His desire to assimilate, yet distinct sense of otherness, is also reflected in David Bezmozgis' "Tapka." The jewel-like crafting of this memory fragment with its evocative reliance on the senses can also be observed in Guadalupe Dueñas' brief pieces "In Heaven" and "Shoes for the Rest of My Life."*

July, 1980. I'm about to turn fifteen and our family is in Seoul, the first time since we left, twelve years earlier. I don't know if it's different. My parents can't really say. They just repeat the equivalent of "How in the world?" whenever we venture into another part of the city, or meet one of their old friends. "Look at that—how in the world?" "This hot spell, yes, yes—how in the world?" My younger sister is very quiet in the astounding heat. We all are. It's the first time I notice how I stink. You can't help smelling like everything else. And in the heat everything smells of ferment and rot and rankness. In my grandfather's old neighborhood, where the two- and three-room houses stand barely head-high, the smell is staggering. "What's that?" I ask. My cousin says, "Shit."

"Shit? What shit?"

"Yours," he says, laughing. "Mine."

On the wide streets near the city center, there are student demonstrations; my cousin says they're a response to a massacre of citizens by the military down south in Kwangju. After the riot troops clear the avenues, the air is laden with tear gas—"spicy," in the idiom. Whenever we're in a taxi, moving through there, I open the window and stick out my tongue, trying to taste the poison, the human repellent. My mother wonders what's wrong with me.

I don't know what's wrong. Or maybe I do. I'm bored. Maybe I'm craving a girl. I can't help staring at them, the ones clearing dishes in their parents' eateries, the uniformed schoolgirls walking hand in hand, the slim young women who work in the Lotte department store, smelling of fried kimchi* and L'Air du Temps. They're all stunning to me, even with their bad teeth. I let myself drift near them, hoping for the scantest touch.

But there's nothing. I'm too obviously desperate, utterly hopeless. Instead, it seems, I can eat. I've always liked food, but now I'm bent on trying everything. As it is, the days are made up of meals,

---

*kimchi: a salted, pickled, and fermented vegetable (often cabbage-based) presented as a basic side dish or condiment

formal and impromptu, meals between meals and within meals; the
streets are a continuous outdoor buffet of braised crabs, cold buck-
wheat noodles, shaved ice with sweet red beans on top. In Itaewon,
the district near the United States Army base, where you can get
anything you want, culinary or otherwise, we stop at a seafood stand
for dinner. Basically, it's a tent diner, a long bar with stools, a camp
stove and fish tank behind the proprietor, an elderly woman with a
low, hoarse voice. The roof is a stretch of blue poly-tarp. My father
is excited; it's like the old days. He wants raw fish, but my mother
shakes her head. I can see why: in plastic bins of speckled, bloody
ice sit semi-alive cockles, abalones, eels, conchs, sea cucumbers, por-
gies, shrimps. "Get something fried," she tells him, not caring what
the woman might think. "Get something cooked."

A young couple sitting at the end of the bar order live octopus.
The old woman nods and hooks one in the tank. It's fairly small, the
size of a hand. She lays it on a board and quickly slices off the head
with her cleaver. She chops the tentacles and gathers them up onto a
plate, dressing them with sesame oil and a spicy bean sauce. "You
have to be careful," my father whispers, "or one of the suction cups
can stick inside your throat. You could die." The lovers blithely feed
each other the sectioned tentacles, taking sips of *soju** in between.
My mother immediately orders a scallion-and-seafood pancake for
us, then a spicy cod-head stew; my father murmurs that he still
wants something live, fresh. I point to a bin and say that's what I
want—those split spiny spheres, like cracked-open meteorites, their
rusty centers layered with shiny crenellations.† I bend down and

---

* soju: a clear alcoholic beverage whose main ingredient is rice, almost always in
combination with other ingredients, such as wheat, barley, sweet potato, or tapioca
† crenellations: the distinctive pattern that frames the tops of the walls of many
medieval castles, most commonly taking the form of multiple, regular rectangular
spaces cut out of the top of the wall to allow defenders spaces from which to shoot
arrows, as well as spaces to hide behind

smell them, and my eyes almost water from the intense ocean tang. "They're sea urchins," the woman says to my father. "He won't like them." My mother is telling my father he's crazy, that I'll get sick from food poisoning, but he nods to the woman, and she picks up a half and cuts out the soft flesh.

What does it taste like? I'm not sure, because I've never had anything like it. All I know is that it tastes alive, something alive at the undragged bottom of the sea; it tastes the way flesh would taste if flesh were a mineral. And I'm half gagging, though still chewing; it's as if I had another tongue in my mouth, this blind, self-satisfied creature. That night I throw up, my mother scolding us, my father chuckling through his concern. The next day, my uncles joke that they'll take me out for some more, and the suggestion is enough to make me retch again.

But a week later I'm better, and I go back by myself. The woman is there, and so are the sea urchins, glistening in the hot sun. "I know what you want," she says. I sit, my mouth slick with anticipation and revulsion, not yet knowing why.

FROM *PERSEPOLIS: THE STORY OF A CHILDHOOD*

THE VEIL

Marjane Satrapi

"The Veil" is excerpted from Marjane Satrapi's bestselling Persepolis *series, a memoir about growing up in Tehran during the Iranian Revolution. The shah's drastic attempts to western- ize Iran and use of secret police led to widespread dissatisfac- tion, paving the way for the 1979 revolution that ended 2,500 years of monarchy and placed an exiled Islamic fundamental- ist cleric, the Ayatollah Khomeini, in charge. "The Veil" deals with one of the first changes instituted by the new Islamist regime—gender segregation in school and mandatory veils for women and girls. Islam challenged Zoroastrianism (Iran's an- cient religion concerned with the perpetual war between good and evil), and Satrapi's use of naive-style, black-and-white comic strips conveys the confusion of ten-year-old Marjane, who wants to be a prophet.*

Marjane Satrapi was born in 1969 in Rasht, Iran. The great-great-granddaughter of one of the last emperors, she grew up with intellectual relatives and family friends routinely be- ing jailed. When she was fourteen, her parents sent her abroad to escape Khomeini's regime. After studying illustration in

Strasbourg, she moved to Paris, where she lives today. While working in a studio with artists who introduced her to graphic novels, Satrapi decided to write Persepolis *(2000) to counter negative media images about Iran. The choice of* Persepolis *for the title—an ancient Greek name that means "city of Persians"—refers to Iran's long history prior to Arab and Muslim invasions. Satrapi currently works as a children's book author and newspaper and magazine illustrator.*

Though Persia (renamed Iran in 1935) has a rich, thousand-year literary tradition, women have been allowed only limited public expression. A nineteenth-century movement against the veil accompanied the rise of female writers; the 1960s saw the emergence of women writers concerned with sociopolitical issues and complex female portrayals. Satrapi joins a growing number of first- and second-generation exiled women who've adopted memoir as their genre. In France, however, she is one of the new stars of la BD *(bande dessinée, usually translated into English as either "cartoon strips" or "comic strips"). In the United States, these serious, adult comics are considered graphic novels, a genre popularized in 1986 with the appearance of Art Spiegelman's Holocaust-themed* Maus. *In addition to critiquing Iranian patriarchy,* Persepolis *considers the contradictions between public and private life, and the costs of political repression for individuals. You may wish to compare it to "The Women's Swimming Pool," Hanan al-Shaykh's story about an Arab Muslim girl negotiating the politics of something as simple as trying to find a place to swim.*

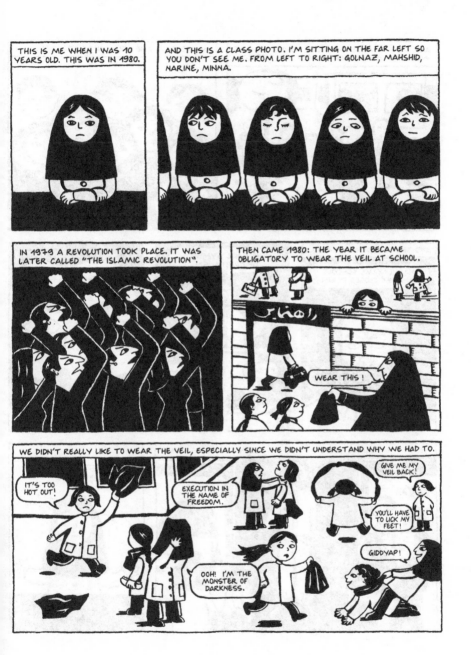

THE WOMEN'S SWIMMING POOL

Hanan al-Shaykh

TRANSLATED BY DENYS JOHNSON-DAVIES

"The Women's Swimming Pool" ("Hamman al-Niswan" in Arabic) comes from the 1982 untranslated collection Wardat 'I-Sahra *by Hanan al-Shaykh. In the story, a Lebanese village girl drags her grandmother to the capital in search of a female-only swimming pool. Her determination to gaze upon the sea for the first time is daring, even foolhardy, in light of the restrictions placed on women in public spaces. In cosmopolitan Beirut, she realizes how she and her grandmother—rural southerners in traditional dress—appear. Like al-Shaykh's family, the characters are Shi'ite (or Shi'a), a minority in Lebanon but the second-largest Muslim denomination worldwide.*

One of the leading writers in the Arab world, novelist, short-story writer, and playwright Hanan al-Shaykh burst onto the international literary scene with The Story of Zahra *(Hikayat Zahra, 1980), about a woman who finds personal liberation through the Lebanese civil war. The novel, deemed "a classic by any standards" by the* Village Voice, *was banned in most Arab countries for its frank treatment of sexuality. Born in Beirut in 1945, al-Shaykh started writing while a teenager as a reaction*

*against her father's and brother's control. After attending college
in Cairo, she became a successful journalist in Beirut, writing
for the prestigious newspaper* Al-Nahar, *among others. In 1976,
like many Lebanese, she fled the civil war, first to Saudi Arabia
and then to London, where she now lives with her family.*

*In addition to pioneering writing about sexual themes, al-
Shaykh is among the first group of Lebanese writers concerned
with the civil war (1975–90). In "The Women's Swimming
Pool," references to her primary themes—women's search for
agency and cross-cultural encounters—abound. Tradition is
symbolized by* salat *(the daily call to prayer) and* hijab *(literally "barrier," which has come to refer to the practice of women
covering all but their face and hands). Modernity can be seen
in the French-influenced café culture and public monuments.
Also evident is al-Shaykh's innovative fictional and psychological technique, which mixes tenses and discourses, using the
past, the present, narration, dialogue, and internal monologue
to indicate the young narrator's questioning and growing awareness of her world. You may wish to compare it to the excerpt
from* Persepolis, *Marjane Satrapi's memoir about being a
young girl in Iran when the Islamist regime instituted mandatory head scarves; "The Lost Child," Albert Bensoussan's story
about a boy forced to abandon his friendship with a prepubes-
cent Arab girl; and Juozas Aputis' "The Glade with Life-Giving
Water," also about a young girl leaving country life for the
strange new world of the city.*

I am in the tent for threading the tobacco amidst the mounds of
tobacco plants and the skewers. Cross-legged, I breathe in the
green odor, threading one leaf after another. I find myself dreaming

and growing thirsty and dreaming. I open the magazine: I devour the words and surreptitiously gaze at the pictures. Exasperated at being in the tent, my exasperation then turns to sadness.

Thirsty, I rise to my feet. I hear Abu Ghalib say, "Where are you off to, little lady?" I make my way to my grandmother, saying, "I'm thirsty." I go out. I make my way to the cistern, stumbling in the sandy ground. I see the greenish blue waters. I stretch out my hand to its still surface, hot from the harsh sun. I stretch out my hand and wipe it across my brow and face and neck, across my chest. Before being able to savor its relative coldness, I hear my name and see my grandmother standing in her black dress at the doorway of the tent. Aloud I express the wish that someone else had called to me. We have become like an orange and its navel: my grandmother has welded me so close to her that the village girls no longer dare to make friends with me, perhaps for fear of rupturing this close union.

I return to the tent, growing thirsty and dreaming, with the sea ever in my mind. What were its waters like? What color would they be now? If only this week would pass in a flash for I had at last persuaded my grandmother to go down to Beirut and the sea, after my friend Sumayya had sworn that the swimming pool she'd been to had been for women only.

My grandmother sat on the edge of a jagged slab of stone, leaning on my arm. Her hand was hot and rough. She sighed as she chased away a fly.

What is my grandmother gazing at? There was nothing in front of us but the asphalt road, which, despite the sun's rays, gave off no light, and the white marble tombs that stretched along the high mountainside, while the houses of Upper Nabatieh looked like deserted Crusader castles, their alleyways empty, their windows of iron. Our house likewise seemed to be groaning in its solitude, shaded by the fig tree. The washing line stirs with the wind above the tomb of my grandfather, the celebrated religious scholar, in the courtyard of the house. What is my grandmother staring at? Or does someone who is waiting not stare?

Turning her face toward me, she said, "Child, what will we do if the bus doesn't come?" Her face, engraved in my mind, seemed overcast, also her half-crossed eyes and the blue tattoo mark on her chin. I didn't answer her for fear I'd cry if I talked. This time I averted my gaze from the white tombs; moving my foot away from my grandmother's leg clothed in thick black stockings, I began to walk about, my gaze directed to the other side where lay the extensive fields of green tobacco, their leaves glinting under the sun, leaves that were imprinted on my brain, and with the marks of them still showing on my hands, towering and gently swaying.

My gaze reached out behind the thousands of plants, then beyond them, moving away till it arrived at the tent where the tobacco was threaded. I came up close to my grandmother, who was still sitting in her place, still gazing in front of her. As I drew close to her, I heard her give a sigh. A sprinkling of sweat lay on the pouches under her eyes. "Child, what do you want with the sea? Don't you know that the sea puts a spell on people?" I didn't answer her: I was so worried that the morning would pass, that noonday would pass and that I wouldn't see the green bus come to a stop by the stone my grandmother sat on and take us with it to the sea, to Beirut. Again I heard my grandmother mumbling, "That devil Sumayya . . ." I pleaded with her to stop, and my thoughts rose up and left the stone upon which my grandmother sat, the rough road, left everything. I went back to my dreams, to the sea.

The sea had remained my preoccupation ever since I had seen it for the first time inside a colored ball; with its blue color it was like a magic lantern, wide open, the surface of its water unrippled unless you tilted the piece of glass, with its small shells and white specks like snow. When I first became aware of things, it was this ball, which I had found in the parlor, that was the sole thing that animated and amused me. The more I gazed at it the more cold I could feel its waters, the more they invited me to bathe myself in them; they knew that I had been born amidst dust and mud and the stench of tobacco.

If only the green bus would come along—and I shifted my bag from one hand to the other. I heard my grandmother wail, "Child, bring up a stone and sit down. Put down the bag and don't worry." My distress increased and I was no longer able to stop it turning into tears that flowed freely down my face, veiling it from the road. I stretched up to wipe them with my sleeve: in this heat I still had to wear that dress with long sleeves, that head-covering over my plaits, despite the hot wind that set the tobacco plants and the sparse poplars swaying. Thank God I had resisted her and refused to wear my stockings. I gave a deep sigh as I heard the bus's horn from afar. Fearful and anxious, I shouted at my grandmother as I helped her to her feet, turning round to make sure that my bag was still in my hand and my grandmother's hand in the other. The bus came to a stop and the conductor helped my grandmother on. When I saw myself alongside her and the stone on its own, I tightened my grip on my bag, in which lay Sumayya's bathing costume, a sleeveless dress, and my money.

I noticed as the bus slowly made its way along the road that my anxiety was still there, that it was in fact increasing. Why didn't the bus pass by all these trees and fallow land like lightning? Why was it crawling along? My anxiety was still there and increased till it predominated over my other sensations, such as nausea and curiosity.

How would we find our way to the sea? Would we see it as soon as we arrived in Beirut? Was it at the other end of it? Would the bus stop in the district of Zeytouna,* at the door of the women's swimming

* *Zeytouna*: the Arabic word for olive tree

pool? Why, I wondered, was it called Zeytouna? Were there olive trees there? I leaned toward my grandmother with her silent face and long nose, which almost met up with her mouth. Thinking that I wanted a piece of cane sugar, she put her hand to her bosom to take out a small twist of cloth. Impatiently I asked her if she was sure that Maryam al-Taweela knew Zeytouna, to which she answered, her mouth sucking at the cane sugar and making a noise with her tongue, "God will look after everything." Then she broke the silence by saying, "All this trouble is that devil Sumayya's fault—it was she who told you she'd seen with her own eyes the swimming pool just for women and not for men."

"Yes, Grandma," I answered her.

She said, "Swear by your mother's grave."

I thought to myself absentmindedly, Why only my mother's grave? What about my father's? Or did she acknowledge only her daughter's death? "By my mother's grave, it's for women."

She inclined her head and still munching the cane sugar and making a noise with her tongue, she said, "If any man were to see you, you'd be done for, and so would your mother and father and your grandfather, the religious scholar—and I'd be done for more than anyone because it's I who agreed to you and helped you."

I would have liked to say to her, They've all gone, they've all died, so what do we have to be afraid of? But I knew what she meant: that she was frightened they wouldn't go to heaven.

I began to sweat and my heart again contracted as Beirut came into view with its lofty buildings, car horns, the bared arms of the women, the girls' hair, the tight trousers they were wearing. People were sitting on chairs in the middle of the pavement eating and drinking; the trams; the roasting chickens revolving on spits. Ah, these dresses for sale in the windows, would anyone be found actually to wear them? I see a Japanese man, the first ever member of the yellow races outside of books; the Martyrs' monument, Riad Solh

Square. I was wringing wet with sweat and my heart pounded—it was as though I regretted having come to Beirut, perhaps because I was accompanied by my grandmother. It was soon all too evident that we were outsiders to the capital. We began walking after my grandmother had asked the bus driver the whereabouts of the district of Khandak al-Ghamik where Maryam al-Taweela lived. Once again my body absorbed all the sweat and allowed my heart to flee its cage. I find myself treading on a pavement on which for long years I have dreamed of walking; I hear sounds that have been engraved on my imagination, and everything I see I have seen in daydreams at school or in the tobacco-threading tent. Perhaps I shouldn't say that I was regretting it, for after this I would never forget Beirut. We begin walking and losing our way in a Beirut that never ends, leads nowhere. We begin asking and walking and losing our way, and my going to the sea seems an impossibility; the sea is fleeing from me. My grandmother comes to a stop and leans against a lamppost, or against the litter bin attached to it, and against my shoulders, and puffs and blows. I have the feeling that we shall never find Maryam al-Taweela's house. A man we had stopped to ask the way walks with us. When we knock at the door and no one opens to us, I become convinced that my bathing in the sea is no longer possible. The sweat again pours off me, my throat contracts. A woman's voice brings me back to my senses as I drown in a lake of anxiety, sadness, and fear; then it drowns me once again. It was not Maryam al-Taweela but her neighbor who is asking us to wait at her place. We go down the steps to the neighbor's outdoor stone bench, and my grandmother sits down by the door but gets to her feet again when the woman entreats her to sit in the cane chair. Then she asks to be excused while she finishes washing down the steps. While she is cursing the heat of Beirut in the summer, I notice the tin containers lined up side by side containing red and green peppers. We have a long wait, and I begin to weep inwardly as I stare at the containers.

I wouldn't be seeing the sea today, perhaps not for years, but the thought of its waters would not leave me, would not be erased from my dreams. I must persuade my grandmother to come to Beirut with Sumayya. Perhaps I should not have mentioned the swimming pool in front of her. I wouldn't be seeing the sea today—and once again I sank back into a lake of doubt and fear and sadness. A woman's voice again brought me back to my senses: it was Maryam al-Taweela, who had stretched out her long neck and had kissed me, while she asked my grandmother, "She's the child of your late daughter, isn't she?"—and she swore by the Imam* that we must have lunch with her, doing so before we had protested, feeling perhaps that I would do so. When she stood up and took the Primus stove from under her bed and brought out potatoes and tomatoes and bits of meat, I had a feeling of nausea, then of frustration. I nudged my grandmother, who leaned over and whispered, "What is it, dear?" at which Maryam al-Taweela turned and asked, "What's your granddaughter want—to go to the bathroom?" My mouth went quite dry and my tears were all stored up waiting for a signal from my heartbeats to descend. My grandmother said with embarrassment. "She wants to go to the sea, to the women's swimming pool—that devil Sumayya put it into her head." To my amazement Maryam al-Taweela said loudly, "And why not? Right now Ali Mousa, our neighbor, will be coming and he'll take you, he's got a car"—and Maryam al-Taweela began peeling the potatoes at a low table in the middle of the room and my grandmother asked, "Where's Ali Mousa from? Where does he live?"

I can't wait, I shan't eat, I shan't drink. I want to go now, now. I remained seated, crying inwardly because I was born in the South, because there's no escape for me from the South, and I go on rubbing

* This refers to Ali ibu Abi Talib, cousin and son-in-law of the Prophet, and is an indication that the characters in the story are Shi'ite Muslims.

my fingers and gnawing at my nails. Again I begin to sweat: I shan't
eat, I shan't drink, I shan't reply to Maryam al-Taweela. It was as
though I were taking vengeance on my grandmother for some wrong
she did not know about. My patience vanished. I stood up and said to
my grandmother before I should burst out sobbing, "Come along,
Grandma, get up and let's go." I helped her to her feet and Maryam
al-Taweela asked in bewilderment what had suddenly come over me.
I went on dragging my grandmother out to the street so that I might
stop the first taxi.

Only moments passed before the driver shut off his engine and
said, "Zeytouna." I looked about me but saw no sea. As I gave him
a lira I asked him, "Where's the women's swimming pool?" He
shrugged his shoulders. We got out of the car with difficulty, as was
always the case with my grandmother. To my astonishment the
driver returned, stretching out his head in concern at us. "Jump in,"
he said, and we got in. He took us round and round, stopping once
at a petrol station and then by a newspaper seller, asking about the
women's swimming pool and nobody knowing where it was. Once
again he dropped us in the middle of Zeytouna Street.

Then, behind the hotels and the beautiful buildings and the date
palms, I saw the sea. It was like a blue line of quicksilver: it was as
though pieces of silver paper were resting on it. The sea that was in
front of me was more beautiful than it had been in the glass ball. I
didn't know how to get close to it, how to touch it. Cement lay between us. We began enquiring about the whereabouts of the swimming pool, but no one knew. The sea remains without waves, a blue
line. I feel frustrated. Perhaps this swimming pool is some secret
known only to the girls of the South. I began asking every person I
saw. I tried to choke back my tears; I let go of my grandmother's
hand as though wishing to reproach her, to punish her for having
insisted on accompanying me instead of Sumayya. Poor me. Poor
Grandma. Poor Beirut. Had my dreams come to an end in the middle

of the street? I clasp my bag and my grandmother's hand, with the sea in front of me, separating her from me. My stubbornness and vexation impel me to ask and go on asking. I approached a man leaning against a bus and to my surprise he pointed to an opening between two shops. I hurried back to my grandmother, who was supporting herself against a lamppost, to tell her I'd found it. When I saw with what difficulty she attempted to walk, I asked her to wait for me while I made sure. I went through the opening but didn't see the sea. All I saw was a fat woman with bare shoulders sitting behind a table. Hesitating, I stood and looked at her, not daring to step forward. My enthusiasm had vanished, taking with it my courage.

"Yes," said the woman.

I came forward and asked her, "Is the women's swimming pool here?"

She nodded her head and said, "The entrance fee is a lira."

I asked her if it was possible for my grandmother to wait for me here and she stared at me and said, "Of course." There was contempt in the way she looked at me—was it my southern accent or my long-sleeved dress? I had disregarded my grandmother and had taken off my headshawl and hidden it in my bag. I handed her a lira and could hear the sounds of women and children—and still I did not see the sea. At the end of the portico were steps that I was certain led to the roofed-in sea. The important thing was that I'd arrived, that I would be tasting the salty spray of its waters. I wouldn't be seeing the waves; never mind, I'd be bathing in its waters.

I found myself saying to the woman, or rather to myself because no sound issued from my throat, "I'll bring my grandmother." Going out through the opening and still clasping my bag to my chest, I saw my grandmother standing and looking up at the sky. I called to her but she was reciting to herself under her breath as she continued to look upwards: she was praying, right there in the street, praying on the pavement at the door of the swimming pool. She had spread out a paper bag and had stretched out her hands to the sky. I walked off in another direction and stopped looking at her. I would have liked to persuade myself that she had nothing to do with me, that I didn't know her. How, though? She's my grandmother, whom I've dragged with my entreaties from the tobacco-threading tent, from the jagged slab of stone, from the winds of the South; I have crammed her into the bus and been lost with her in the streets as we searched for Maryam al-Taweela's house. And now here were the two of us standing at the door of the swimming pool and she, having heard the call to prayers, had prostrated herself in prayer. She was destroying what lay in my bag, blocking the road between me and the sea. I felt sorry for her, for her knees that knelt on the cruelly hard pavement, for her tattooed hands that lay on the dirt. I looked at her again and saw the passersby staring at her. For the first time her black dress looked shabby to me. I felt how far removed we were from these passersby, from this street, this city, this sea. I approached her and she again put her weight on my hand.

Family

OF WHITE HAIRS AND CRICKET

Rohinton Mistry

The narrator of this story, bored and slightly repulsed by his Sunday task of tweezing out white hairs from his father's head, shrewdly observes his household's family dynamics. His grandmother, confined to the apartment by her weak spine, spins thread and cooks forbidden treats for her grandson that are too rich for his sensitive digestive system; his mother, increasingly depressed by the family's poverty, tries to be a practical counterbalance to her husband, a dreamer. Things don't seem to change for the narrator—except that they do, as represented by the father's increasingly thinning and graying hair and the mortal illness of his best friend's father.

Mistry's Parsi heritage forms the silent background for the story. The Parsis, marginalized by Hindu society because of their Zoroastrian faith and Persian heritage, were more open toward the British colonizers and the modern education that they brought to India. While Parsis enjoyed success in British-occupied India's industry and commerce, they suffered the stigma of trying to be too Western. After the end of British rule in India in 1947, their unpopularity influenced another diaspora, this time to the West. Mistry's sensibility reflects his position as part of a twice-displaced people. The narrator's terror at the end of "Of White Hairs and Cricket" may seem out of proportion to what has happened (not much); however, his sense that change inevitably brings loss, and his own sense of powerlessness in the face of this change, make this story a vivid account of dreams going up in the smoke of the Primus-stove fire.

"Of White Hairs and Cricket" forms part of a body of stories that all take place at Firozsha Baag, a decrepit apartment block in the Bombay of Rohinton Mistry's youth. They rely on Mistry's childhood memories and even become the "creation" of a former resident who has emigrated to Canada—Mistry himself, who came to Toronto from Bombay in 1975. After a few years in Canada, Mistry began to write stories, which achieved almost immediate success. His first novel, Such a Long Journey *(1991), won the Commonwealth Writers Prize; two later novels,* A Fine Balance *(1996) and* Family Matters *(2002), have been short-listed for the Booker Prize for Fiction.*

The "imaginary homeland" of Mistry's fiction inevitably leads to comparisons with Salman Rushdie, another Bombay author now living abroad; however, while Rushdie's fiction focuses on the Muslim middle classes, Mistry's fiction lays its claim to the Parsi community and the poor. While Rushdie employs magical realism (a technique through which magical elements appear in a reality setting), Mistry relies solely on the grittiness of realism.

The nostalgia for losses to come and for those suffered already as part of a historical past in "Of White Hairs and Cricket" can be compared to Juozas Aputis' "The Glade with Life-Giving Water" and to Colum McCann's "Everything in

This Country Must." The connections that Mistry's narrator has with his family and the objects of their affection and concern are similar to those in David Bezmozgis' "Tapka."

The white hair was trapped in the tweezers. I pulled it taut to see if it was gripped tightly, then plucked it.

"Aaah!" grimaced Daddy. "Careful, only one at a time." He continued to read the *Times of India*, spreading it on the table.

"It *is* only one," I said, holding out the tweezers, but my annoyance did not register. Engrossed in the classifieds, he barely looked my way. The naked bulb overhead glanced off the stainless steel tweezers, making a splotch of light dart across the Murphy Radio calendar. It danced over the cherubic features of the Murphy Baby, in step with the tweezers' progress on Daddy's scalp. He sighed, turned a page, and went on scrutinizing the columns.

Each Sunday, the elimination of white hairs took longer than the last time. I'm sure Daddy noticed it too, but joked bravely that laziness was slowing me down. Percy was always excused from this task. And if I pointed it out, the answer was: your brother's college studies are more important.

Daddy relied on my nimble fourteen-year-old fingers to uproot the signposts of mortality sprouting week after week. It was unappetizing work, combing through his hair greasy with day-old pomade, isolating the white ones, or the ones just beginning to turn—half black and half white, and somehow more repulsive. It was always difficult to decide whether to remove those or let them go till next Sunday, when the whiteness would have spread upward to their tips.

The Sunday edition of the *Times of India* came with a tabloid of comics: Mandrake the Magician, The Phantom, and Maggie and Jiggs in "Bringing Up Father." The drab yellow tablecloth looked festive with the vivid colours of the comics, as though specially decorated for Sunday. The plastic cloth smelled stale and musty. It was impossible to clean perfectly because of the floral design embossed upon its surface. The swirly grooves were ideal for trapping all kinds of dirt.

Daddy reached up to scratch a spot on his scalp. His aaah surprised me. He had taught me to be tough, always. One morning when we had come home after cricket, he told Mummy and *Mamaiji*,* "Today my son did a brave thing, as I would have done. A powerful shot was going to the boundary, like a cannonball, and he blocked it with his bare shin." Those were his exact words. The ball's shiny red fury, and the audible crack—at least, I think it was audible—had sent pain racing through me that nearly made my eyes overflow. Daddy had clapped and said, "Well-fielded, sir, well-fielded." So I waited to rub the agonized bone until attention was no longer upon me. I wish Percy had not lost interest in cricket, and had been there. My best friend, Viraf from A Block, was immensely impressed. But that was all a long time ago, many months ago, now Daddy did not take us for cricket on Sunday mornings.

I paused in my search. Daddy had found something in the classifieds and did not notice. By angling the tweezers I could aim the bulb's light upon various spots on the Murphy Radio calendar: the edges of the picture, worn and turned inward; the threadbare loop of braid sharing the colour of rust with the rusty nail it hung by; a corroded staple clutching twelve thin strips—the perforated residue of months ripped summarily over a decade ago when their days and weeks were played out. The baby's smile, posed with finger to chin, was all that had fully endured the years. Mummy and Daddy called it so innocent and joyous. That baby would now be the same age as me. The ragged perimeter of the patch of crumbled wall it tried to hide strayed outward from behind, forming a kind of dark and jagged halo

---

* *Mamaiji*: Gujarati for "grandmother"

around the baby. The picture grew less adequate, daily, as the wall kept losing plaster and the edges continued to curl and tatter.

Other calendars in the room performed similar enshroudings: the Cement Corporation skyscraper; the Lifebuoy Soap towel-wrapped woman with long black hair; the Parsi calendar, pictureless but show-ing the English and Parsi names for the months, and the *roje** in Gu-jarati† beside each date, which Mummy and *Mamaiji* consulted when reciting their prayers. All these hung well past their designated time span in the world of months and years, covering up the broken promises of the Firozsha Baag building management.

"Yes, this is it," said Daddy, tapping the paper, "get me the scissors."

Mamaiji came out and settled in her chair on the veranda. Seated, there was no trace of the infirmity that caused her to walk doubled over. Doctors said it was due to a weak spine that could not erect against the now inordinate weight of her stomach. From photographs of Mummy's childhood, I knew *Mamaiji* had been a big handsome woman, with a majestic countenance. She opened her bag of spin-ning things, although she had been told to rest her eyes after the re-cent cataract operation. Then she spied me with the tweezers.

"Sunday dawns and he makes the child do that *duleendar* thing again. It will only bring bad luck." She spoke under her breath, ar-ranging her spindle and wool; she was not looking for a direct con-frontation. "Plucking out hair as if it was a slaughtered chicken. An ill-omened thing, I'm warning you, Sunday after Sunday. But no one listens. Is this anything to make a child do, he should be out playing, or learning how to do *bajaar*, how to bargain with butcher and *bunya*." She mumbled softly, to allow Daddy to pretend he hadn't heard a thing.

I resented her speaking against Daddy and calling me a child.

* *roje*: Gujarati word meaning "celebration"
† Gujarati: the language of the center west part of India

She twirled the spindle, drawing fibres into thread from the scrap of wool in her left hand as the spindle descended. I watched, expecting—even wishing—the thread to break. Sometimes it did, and then it seemed to me that *Mamaiji* was overcome with disbelief, shocked and pained that it could have happened, and I would feel sorry and rush to pick it up for her. The spindle spun to the floor this time without mishap, hanging by a fine, brand new thread. She hauled it up, winding the thread around the extended thumb and little finger of her left hand by waggling the wrist in little clockwise and counter-clockwise half-turns, while the index and middle fingers clamped tight the source: the shred of wool resembling a lock of her own hair, snow white and slightly tangled.

Mamaiji spun enough thread to keep us all in *kustis*.* Since Grandpa's death, she spent more and more time spinning, so that now we each had a spare *kusti* as well. The *kustis* were woven by a professional, who always praised the fine quality of the thread; and even at the fire-temple,† where we untied and tied them during prayers, they earned the covetous glances of other Parsis.

I beheld the spindle and *Mamaiji*'s co-ordinated feats of dexterity with admiration. All spinning things entranced me. The descending spindle was like the bucket spinning down into the sacred Bhikha Behram Well to draw water for the ones like us who went there to pray on certain holy days after visiting the fire-temple. I imagined myself clinging to the base of the spindle, sinking into the dark well, confident that *Mamaiji* would pull me up with her waggling hand before I

---

* *kustis*: sacred-thread girdles with a string about the size of a thin lace, long enough to pass three times very loosely around the waist, and tied twice in a double knot, leaving the short ends hanging behind; it is composed of 72 very fine white threads

† fire-temple: the symbol of fire represents the energy of the creator in Zoroastrianism; Zoroastrians usually pray in front of some form of fire or any source of light as a focal point, much like the crucifix in Christianity

drowned, and praying that the thread would not break. I also liked to stare at records spinning on the old 78-rpm gramophone. There was one I was particularly fond of: its round label was the most ethereal blue I ever saw. The lettering was gold. I played this record over and over, just to watch its wonderfully soothing blue and gold rotation, and the concentric rings of the shiny black shellac, whose grooves created a spiral effect if the light was right. The gramophone cabinet's warm smell of wood and leather seemed to fly right out of this shellacked spiral, while I sat close, my cheek against it, to feel the hum and vibration of the turntable. It was so cosy and comforting. Like missing school because of a slight cold, staying in bed all day with a book, fussed over by Mummy, eating white rice and soup made specially for me.

Daddy finished cutting out and re-reading the classified advertisement. "Yes, this is a good one. Sounds very promising." He picked up the newspaper again, then remembered what *Mamaiji* had muttered, and said softly to me, "If it is so *duleendar* and will bring bad luck, how is it I found this? These old people—"and gave a sigh of mild exasperation. Then briskly: "Don't stop now, this week is very important." He continued, slapping the table merrily at each word: "Every-single-white-hair-out."

There was no real enmity between Daddy and *Mamaiji*, I think they even liked each other. He was just disinclined towards living with his mother-in-law. They often had disagreements over me, and it was always *Mamaiji* versus Mummy and Daddy. *Mamaiji* firmly believed that I was underfed. Housebound as she was, the only food accessible to her was the stuff sold by door-to-door vendors, which I adored but was strictly forbidden: *samosa,** *bhajia,†* *sevganthia,‡* or

---

* *samosa*: a common snack in India, generally consisting of a fried triangular-shaped pastry with a savory potato, onion, and pea stuffing
† *bhajia*: a side dish, usually of vegetables, served as an accompaniment to the main-course curry
‡ *sevganthia*: a crunchy fried snack made of chickpea flour

the dinners she cooked for herself, separately, because she said that Mummy's cooking was insipidity itself: "Tasteless as spit, refuses to go down my throat."

So I, her favourite, enjoyed from time to time, on the sly, hot searing curries and things she purchased at the door when Daddy was at work and Mummy in the kitchen. Percy shared, too, if he was around; actually, his iron-clad stomach was much better suited to those flaming snacks. But the clandestine repasts were invariably uncovered, and the price was paid in harsh and unpleasant words. *Mamaiji* was accused of trying to burn to a crisp my stomach and intestines with her fiery, ungodly curries, or of exposing me to dysentery and diphtheria: the cheap door-to-door foodstuff was allegedly cooked in filthy, rancid oil—even machine oil, unfit for human consumption, as was revealed recently by a government investigation. *Mamaiji* retorted that if they did their duty as parents she would not have to resort to secrecy and *chori-chhoopi*; as it was, she had no choice, she could not stand by and see the child starve.

All this bothered me much more than I let anyone know. When the arguments started I would say that all the shouting was giving me a headache, and stalk out to the steps of the compound. My guilty conscience, squirming uncontrollably, could not witness the quarrels. For though I was an eager partner in the conspiracy with *Mamaiji*, and acquiesced to the necessity for secrecy, very often I spilled the beans—quite literally—with diarrhoea and vomiting, which *Mamaiji* upheld as undeniable proof that lack of proper regular nourishment had enfeebled my bowels. In the throes of these bouts of effluence, I promised Mummy and Daddy never again to eat what *Mamaiji* offered, and confessed all my past sins. In *Mamaiji's* eyes I was a traitor, but sometimes it was also fun to listen to her scatalogical reproaches: "*Muà ugheeparoo!* Eating my food, then shitting and tattling all over the place. Next time I'll cork you up with a big *bootch* before feeding you."

Mummy came in from the kitchen with a plateful of toast fresh off the Criterion: unevenly browned, and charred in spots by the vagaries of its kerosene wick. She cleared the comics to one side and set the plate down.

"Listen to this," Daddy said to her, "just found it in the paper: "A Growing Concern Seeks Dynamic Young Account Executive, Self-Motivated. Four-Figure Salary and Provident Fund." I think it's perfect." He waited for Mummy's reaction. Then: "If I can get it, all our troubles will be over."

Mummy listened to such advertisements week after week: harbingers of hope that ended in disappointment and frustration. But she always allowed the initial wave of optimism to lift her, riding it with Daddy and me, higher and higher, making plans and dreaming, until it crashed and left us stranded, awaiting the next advertisement and the next wave. So her silence was surprising.

Daddy reached for a toast and dipped it in the tea, wrinkling his nose. "Smells of kerosene again. When I get this job, first thing will be a proper toaster. No more making burnt toast on top of the Criterion."

"I cannot smell kerosene," said Mummy.

"Smell this then," he said, thrusting the tea-soaked piece at her nose, "smell it and tell me," irritated by her ready contradiction. "It's these useless wicks. The original Criterion ones from England used to be so good. One trim and you had a fine flame for months." He bit queasily into the toast. "Well, when I get the job, a Bombay Gas Company stove and cylinder can replace it." He laughed. "Why not? The British left seventeen years ago, time for their stove to go as well."

He finished chewing and turned to me. "And one day, you must go, too, to America. No future here." His eyes fixed mine, urgently. "Somehow we'll get the money to send you. I'll find a way."

His face filled with love. I felt suddenly like hugging him, but we never did except on birthdays, and to get rid of the feeling I looked away and pretended to myself that he was saying it just to humour me, because he wanted me to finish pulling his white hairs. Fortunately, his jovial optimism returned.

"Maybe even a fridge is possible, then we will never have to go upstairs to that woman. No more obligations, no more favours. You won't have to kill any more rats for her." Daddy waited for us to join in. For his sake I hoped that Mummy would. I did not feel like mustering any enthusiasm.

But she said sharply, "All your *shaik-chullee* thoughts are flying again. Nothing happens when you plan too much. Leave it in the hands of God."

Daddy was taken aback. He said, summoning bitterness to retaliate, "You are thinking I will never get a better job? I'll show all of you." He threw his piece of toast onto the plate and sat back. But he recovered as quickly, and made it into a joke. He picked up the newspaper. "Well, I'll just have to surprise you one day when I throw out the kerosene stoves."

I liked the kerosene stoves and the formidable fifteen-gallon storage drum that replenished them. The Criterion had a little round glass window in one corner of its black base, and I would peer into the murky depths, watching the level rise as kerosene poured through the funnel; it was very dark and cool and mysterious in there, then the kerosene floated up and its surface shone under the light bulb. Looking inside was like lying on Chaupatty beach at night and gazing at the stars, in the hot season, while we stayed out after dinner till the breeze could rise and cool off the walls baking all day in the sun. When the stove was lit and the kitchen dark, the soft orange glow through its little mica door reminded me of the glow in the fire-temple *afargaan*, when there wasn't a blazing fire because hardly any sandalwood offerings had been left in the silver *thaali*; most people came only on the holy days. The Primus stove was fun, too, pumped up hot and roaring, the kerosene emerging under pressure and igniting into sharp blue flames. Daddy was the only one who lit it; every year, many women died in their kitchens because of explosions, and Daddy said that though many of them were not accidents, especially the dowry cases, it was still a dangerous stove if handled improperly.

Mummy went back to the kitchen. I did not mind the kerosene smell, and ate some toast, trying to imagine the kitchen without the stoves, with squat red gas cylinders sitting under the table instead. I had seen them in shop windows, and I thought they were ugly. We would get used to them, though, like everything else. At night, I stood on the veranda sometimes to look at the stars. But it was not the same as going to Chaupatty and lying on the sand, quietly, with only the sound of the waves in the dark. On Saturday nights, I would make sure that the stoves were filled, because Mummy made a very early breakfast for Daddy and me next morning. The milk and bread would be arriving in the pre-dawn darkness while the kettle was boiling and we got ready for cricket with the boys of Firozsha Baag.

We always left by seven o'clock. The rest of the building was just starting to wake up: Nariman Hansotia would be aligning, on the parapet of his ground floor veranda, his razor and shaving brush and mirror beside two steaming cups, one of boiling water and the other of tea, and we often wondered if he ever dipped the brush in the wrong cup; and the old spinster Tehmina, still waiting for her cataracts to ripen, would be saying her prayers facing the rising sun, with her duster-coat hoisted up and slung over the left shoulder, her yellowing petticoat revealed, to untie and tie her thick rope-like *kusti* around the waist; and the *kuchrawalli* would be sweeping the compound, making her rounds from door to door with broom and basket, collecting yesterday's garbage. If she happened to cross Tehmina's line of vision, all the boys were sure to have a fine time, because Tehmina, though blurry with cataracts, would recognize the *kuchrawalli* and let loose at her with a stream of curses fouler than any filth in the garbage basket, for committing the unspeakable crime of passing in front of her, thereby polluting her prayers and vitiating their efficacy.

Even Daddy laughed, but he hurried us along as we lingered to there to follow the ensuing dialogue. We picked our way through sleeping streets. The pavement dwellers would stretch, and look for a place to relieve themselves. Then they would fold up their cardboard pieces and roll away their plastics before the street sweepers arrived and the traffic got heavy. Sometimes, they would start a small fire if they had something to cook for breakfast, or else try to beg from people who came to the Irani restaurant for their morning *chai** and bun. Occasionally, Mummy would wrap up leftovers from the night before for Daddy and me to distribute to them along the way.

It had been such a long time since we last played cricket. Flying kites had also become a thing of the past. One by one, the things I held dear were leaving my life, I thought gloomily. And Francis. What about poor Francis? Where was he now, I wondered. I wished he was still working in the Baag. That awful thrashing he got in Tar Gully was the fault of Najamai and Tehmina, those stupid old women. And Najamai saying he stole eighty rupees was nonsense, in my opinion; the absent-minded cow must have forgotten where she left the money.

I put down the tweezers and reached for the comics. Daddy looked up. "Don't stop now, it should be perfect this week. There will be an interview or something."

Avoiding his eye, I said stolidly, "I'm going to read the comics," and walked out to the compound steps. When I turned at the doorway Daddy was still looking at me. His face was like *Mamaiji's* when the thread broke and slipped through her fingers and the spindle fell to the floor. But I kept walking, it was a matter of pride. You always did what you said you were going to do.

---

* *chai*: the Hindi word for "tea"

The comics did not take long. It used to be more fun when Daddy and I had a race to the door to grab the *Times*, and pretended to fight over who would read the comics first. I thought of the lines on Daddy's forehead, visible so clearly from my coign of vantage with the tweezers. His thinning hair barely gave off a dull lustre with its day-old pomade, and the Sunday morning stubble on his chin was flecked with grey and white.

Something—remorse, maybe just pity—stirred inside, but I quashed it without finding out. All my friends had fathers whose hair was greying. Surely they did not spend Sunday mornings doing what I did, or they would have said something. They were not like me, there was nothing that was too private and personal for them. They would talk about anything. Especially Pesi. He used to describe for us how his father passed gas, enhancing the narrative with authentic sound effects. Now he was in boarding-school. His father was dead.

From our C Block stone steps I could observe the entire length of the compound, up to A Block at the far end. Dr. Sidhwa's black Fiat turned in at the gate and trundled laboriously over the rough-hewn flagstones of Firozsha Baag. He waved as he went past. He looked so much like Pesi's father. He had the same crow's-feet at the corners of his eyes that Dr. Mody used to have, and even their old cars seemed identical, except that Dr. Mody healed animals and Dr. Sidhwa, humans. Most of us had been treated by him at one time or another. His house and dispensary were within walking distance of Firozsha Baag, even a sick person's walking distance; he was a steadfast Parsi, seen often at fire-temples; and he always drove over for his house-calls. What more could we want in a doctor?

The car stopped at the far end of the compound. Dr. Sidhwa heaved out, he was a portly man, and reached in for his bag. It must be an emergency in A Block, I decided, for someone to call him on Sunday. He slammed the door, then opened and slammed it again, harder now. The impact rocked the old car a little, but the door shut properly this time. Viraf emerged from the steps of A Block. I waved to him to let him know I was waiting.

Viraf was my best friend. Together we learned bicycling, on a rented contraption of bent spokes and patchwork tyres from Cecil Cycles of Tar Gully: Fifty Paise per Hour. Daddy used to take us to practise at Chaupatty on the wide pavements by the beach. They were deserted in the early morning—pavement dwellers preferred the narrow side streets—except for pigeons gathering in anticipation of the pigeon-man, who arrived when the streets stirred to life. We took turns, and Daddy ran behind, holding the seat to keep us steady. Daddy also taught the two of us to play cricket. Mummy had been angry when he brought home the bat and ball, asking where the money had come from. His specialty on his own school team had been bowling, and he taught us the leg break and off break, and told us about the legendary Jasu Patel, born with a defective wrist which turned out to be perfect for spin bowling, and how Jasu had mastered the dreaded curl spin which was eventually feared by all the great international batsmen.

Cricket on Sunday mornings became a regular event for the boys in Firozsha Baag. Between us we almost had a complete kit; all that was missing was a pair of bails, and wicket-keeping gloves. Daddy took anyone who wanted to play to the Marine Drive *maidaan*,* and organized us into teams, captaining one team himself. We went early, before the sun got too hot and the *maidaan* overcrowded. But then one Sunday, halfway through the game, Daddy said he was going to rest for a while. Sitting on the grass a little distance away, he seemed so much older than he did when he was batting, or bowling leg breaks. He watched us with a faraway expression on his face. Sadly, as if he had just realized something and wished he hadn't.

---

* *maidaan*: Urdu for a ground or field

There was no cricket at the *maidaan* after that day. Since we were not allowed to go alone, our games were now confined to the Firozsha Baag compound. Its flagstoned surface would not accept the points of stumps, and we chalked three white lines on the compound's black stone wall. But the compound was too cramped for cricket. Besides, the uneven ground made the ball bounce and rear erratically. After a few shattered panes of glass and several complaints from neighbours, the games ceased.

I waved again to Viraf and gave our private signal, "OO ooo OO ooo," which was like a yodel. He waved back, then took the doctor's bag and accompanied him into A Block. His polite demeanor made me smile. That Viraf. Shrewd fellow, he knew the things to do to make grownups approve of him, and was always welcome at all the homes in Firozsha Baag. He would be back soon.

I waited for at least half an hour. I cracked all my fingers and knuckles, even the thumbs. Then I went to the other end of the compound. After sitting on the steps there for a few minutes, I got impatient and climbed upstairs to find out why Viraf was buttering up the doctor.

But Dr. Sidhwa was on his way down, carrying his black bag. I said, "*Sahibji*, doctor," and he smiled at me as I raced up to the third floor. Viraf was standing at the balcony outside his flat. "What's all the *muskaa-paalis* for the doctor?"

He turned away without answering. He looked upset but I did not ask what the matter was. Words to show concern were always beyond me. I spoke again, in that easygoing debonair style which all of us tried to perfect, right arm akimbo and head tilted ever so slightly, "Come on *yaar*, what are your plans for today?"

He shrugged his shoulders, and I persisted, "Half the morning's over, man, don't be such a cry-baby."

"Fish off," he said, but his voice shook. His eyes were red, and he rubbed one as if there was something in it. I stood quietly for a while, looking out over the balcony. His third-floor balcony was my favourite spot, you could see the road beyond Firozsha Baag, and sometimes, on a sunny day, even a corner of Chaupatty beach with the sun gleaming on the waves. From my ground floor veranda the compound's black stone wall was all that was visible.

Hushed voices came from the flat, the door was open. I looked into the dining-room where some A Block neighbours had gathered around Viraf's mother. "How about Ludo or Snakes-and-Ladders?" I tried. If he shrugged again I planned to leave. What else could I do?

"Okay," he said, "but stay quiet. If *Mumma* sees us she'll send us out."

No one saw as we tiptoed inside, they were absorbed in whatever the discussion was about. "*Puppa* is very sick," whispered Viraf, as we passed the sickroom. I stopped and looked inside. It was dark. The smell of sickness and medicines made it stink like the waiting room of Dr. Sidhwa's dispensary. Viraf's father was in bed, lying on his back, with a tube through his nose. There was a long needle stuck into his right arm, and it glinted cruelly in a thin shaft of sunlight that had suddenly slunk inside the darkened room. I shivered. The needle was connected by a tube to a large bottle which hung upside down from a dark metal stand towering over the bed.

Viraf's mother was talking softly to the neighbours in the dining-room. ". . . in his chest got worse when he came home last night. So many times I've told him, three floors to climb is not easy at your age with your big body, climb one, take rest for a few minutes, then climb again. But he won't listen, does not want people to think it is too much for him. Now this is the result, and what I will do I don't know. Poor little Viraf, being so brave when the doctor . . ."

Supine, his rotundity had spread into a flatness denying the huge bulk. I remembered calling Viraf a cry-baby, and my face flushed with shame. I swore I would apologize. Daddy was slim and wiry, although there were the beginnings of a small pot, as Mummy called it.

He used to run and field with us at cricket. Viraf's father had sat on the grass the one time he took us. The breath came loud and rasping. His mouth was a bit open. It resembled a person snoring, but was uneven, and the sound suggested pain. I noticed the lines on his brow, like Daddy's, only Daddy's were less deep.

Over the rasp of his breath came the voice of Viraf's mother. ". . . to exchange with someone on the ground floor, but that also is no. Says I won't give up my third-floor paradise for all the smell and noise of a ground-floor flat. Which is true, up here even B.E.S.T. bus* rattle and rumble does not come. But what use of paradise if you are not alive in good health to enjoy it? Now doctor says intensive care but Parsi General Hospital has no place. Better to stay here than other hospitals, only . . ."

My eyes fixed on the stone-grey face of Viraf's father, I backed out of the sickroom, unseen. The hallway was empty. Viraf was waiting for me in the back room with the boards for Ludo and Snakes-and-Ladders. But I sneaked through the veranda and down the stairs without a word.

The compound was flooded in sunshine as I returned to the other end. On the way I passed the three white stumps we had once chalked on the compound wall's black stone. The lines were very faint, and could barely be seen, lost amongst more recent scribbles and abandoned games of noughts and crosses.

Mummy was in the kitchen, I could hear the roaring of the Primus stove. *Mamaiji*, sinister in her dark glasses, sat by the veranda window, sunlight reflecting off the thick, black lenses with leather blinders at the sides; after her cataract operation the doctor had told her to wear these for a few months.

---

*B.E.S.T. bus: Mumbai's bus company; its founders were the Brush Electrical Company of London, who were originally given the rights to run an electric tramway service in then-Bombay

Daddy was still reading the *Times* at the dining-table. Through the gloom of the light bulb I saw the Murphy Baby's innocent and joyous smile. I wondered what he looked like now. When I was two years old, there was a Murphy Baby Contest, and according to Mummy and Daddy my photograph, which had been entered, should have won. They said that in those days my smile had been just as, if not more, innocent and joyous.

The tweezers were lying on the table. I picked them up. They glinted pitilessly, like that long needle in Viraf's father. I dropped them with a shudder, and they clattered against the table.

Daddy looked up questioningly. His hair was dishevelled as I had left it, and I waited, hoping he would ask me to continue. To offer to do it was beyond me, but I wanted desperately that he should ask me now. I glanced at his face discreetly, from the corner of my eye. The lines on his forehead stood out all too clearly, and the stubble flecked with white, which by this hour should have disappeared down the drain with the shaving water. I swore to myself that never again would I begrudge him my help; I would get all the white hairs, one by one, if he would only ask me; I would concentrate on the tweezers as never before, I would do it as if all our lives were riding on the efficacy of the tweezers, yes, I would continue to do it Sunday after Sunday, no matter how long it took.

Daddy put down the newspaper and removed his glasses. He rubbed his eyes, then went to the bathroom. How tired he looked, and how his shoulders drooped; his gait lacked confidence, and I'd never noticed that before. He did not speak to me even though I was praying hard that he would. Something inside me grew very heavy, and I tried to swallow, to dissolve that heaviness in saliva, but swallowing wasn't easy either, the heaviness was blocking my throat.

I heard the sound of running water. Daddy was preparing to shave. I wanted to go and watch him, talk to him, laugh with him at the funny faces he made to get at all the tricky places with the razor, especially the cleft in his chin.

Instead, I threw myself on the bed. I felt like crying, and buried my face in the pillow. I wanted to cry for the way I had treated Viraf, and for his sick father with the long, cold needle in his arm and his rasping breath; for *Mamaiji* and her tired, darkened eyes spinning thread for our *kustis*, and for Mummy growing old in the dingy kitchen smelling of kerosene, where the Primus roared and her dreams were extinguished; I wanted to weep for myself, for not being able to hug Daddy when I wanted to, and for not ever saying thank you for cricket in the morning, and pigeons and bicycles and dreams; and for all the white hairs that I was powerless to stop.

SHADOWS ON THE WALL

Charles Mungoshi

Charles Mungoshi's short tale explores the psychology of a young, unnamed boy in an unnamed African village struggling with his father's brand of tough love. After a series of quarrels, one in which the father accuses the mother of coddling the boy ("He is a man and you want to turn him into a woman"), she returns to her village. The father then acquires a minor or secondary wife, who also runs home and has to be brought back. His insistence that the boy call the new wife mother causes the boy to retreat further into silence, responding only to the shadows on the wall.

Charles Mungoshi was born in 1947 on a farm near Chivu in central Zimbabwe (then Rhodesia). The eldest of eight, he spent his afternoons alone herding cattle. He published his first story while still attending mission school. Prior to independence, he worked for the Forestry Commission, in a bookshop, and as an editor; after independence he served as writer-in-residence at the University of Zimbabwe. Considered one of the most productive and multitalented writers in Zimbabwe—which has the highest literacy rate in Africa, with 90 percent of the population able to read and write—Mungoshi has published stories, novels, poetry, plays, and children's books in English and Shona. He is the recipient of a Commonwealth Writers Prize, two PEN Awards, and a Noma Award for outstanding work published in Africa.

Mungoshi's first collection of stories, The Coming of a Dry Season *(1972), in which "Shadows on the Wall" appears, was banned by authorities for its depiction of the daily and psychological impact of colonization. It was written after the white minority government declared independence from Britain and implemented a system similar to apartheid in neighboring South Africa, but before black rule was won and the country became Zimbabwe. As such, the father's pressure on the boy to forget his real mother can be read as symbolic in terms of indigenous struggle, as can the wild birds with which the boy is preoccupied. You may wish to compare the story to Ben Okri's "In the Shadow of War," also from the viewpoint of an African village boy unable to communicate with his father, and the excerpt from* Baby No-Eyes, *Patricia Grace's tale of the tragedy resulting from a young Maori girl losing her spirit.*

Father is sitting just inside the hut near the door and I am sitting far across the hut near the opposite wall, playing with the shadows on the wall. Bright sunlight comes in through the doorway now and father, who blocks most of it, is reproduced in caricature on the floor and half-way up the wall. The wall and floor are bare, so he looks like a black scarecrow in a deserted field after the harvest.

Outside, the sun drops lower and other shadows start creeping into the hut. Father's shadow grows vaguer and climbs further up the wall like a ghost going up to heaven. His shadow moves behind sharper wriggling shadows like the presence of a tired old woman in a room full of young people, or like that creepy nameless feeling in a house of mourning.

He has tried five times to talk to me but I don't know what he wants. Now he talks about his other wife. He wants me to call her "mother" but I can't because something in me cries each time I say it. She isn't my mother and my real mother is not dead. This other woman has run away. It is now the fourth time she has run away and tomorrow he is going to cycle fifty miles to her home to collect her. This will be the fourth time he has had to cycle after her. He is talking. I am not listening. He gives up.

Now the sun shines brilliantly before going down. The shadows of bushes and grass at the edge of the yard look as if they are on fire and father's features are cut more sharply and exaggerated. His nose becomes longer each time he nods because now he is sleeping while sitting, tired of the silence.

Father dozes, wakes up; dozes, wakes up and the sun goes down. His shadow expands and fades. Now it seems all over the wall, behind the other shadows, moving silently like a cold wind in a bare field. I look at him. There is still enough light for me to see the grey stubble sticking up untidily all over his face. His stubble, I know, is as stiff as a porcupine's, but as the light wanes now, it looks fleecy and soft like the down on a dove's nestling.

I was in the bush, long ago, and I came upon two dove nestlings. They were still clumsy and blind, with soft pink vulnerable flesh planted with short scattered grey feathers, their mouths open, waiting for their mother. I wished I had corn to give them. As it was, I consoled myself with the thought that their mother was somewhere nearby, coming home through the bush in the falling dark with food in her mouth for her children.

Next day I found the nestlings dead in their nest. Somewhere out in the bush or in the yellow ripe unharvested fields, someone had shot their mother in mid-flight home.

Not long after that, I was on my father's shoulders coming home from the fields at dusk. Mother was still with us then, and father carried me because she had asked him to. I had a sore foot and couldn't walk and mother couldn't carry me because she was carrying a basket of mealies for our supper on her head and pieces of firewood in her arms. At first father grumbled. He didn't like to carry me and he didn't like receiving orders from mother: she was there to listen to him always, he said. He carried me all the same although he didn't like to, and worse, I didn't like him to carry me. His hands were hard and pinchy and his arms felt as rough and barky as logs. I preferred mother's soft warm back. He knew, too, that I didn't want him to carry me because I made my body stiff and didn't relax when he rubbed his hard chin against my cheek. His breath was harsh and foul. He wore his battered hat and stank of dirt, sweat and soil. He was trying to talk to me but I was not listening to him. That was when I noticed that his stubble looked as vulnerable as the unprotected feathers on a dove's nestling. Tears filled my eyes then and I tried to respond to his teasing, but I gave it up because he immediately began picking on mother and made her tense and tight and this tension I could feel in me also.

After this he always wanted me to be near him and he made me ignore mother. He taught me to avoid mother. It was hard for me but he had a terrible way of making mother look despicable and mean. She noticed this and fought hard to make me cheerful, but I always saw father's threatening shadow hunched hawkishly over me. Instead of talking to either of them I became silent. I was no longer happy in either's presence. And this was when I began to notice the shallows on the wall of our hut.

One day the eternal quarrel between mother and father flared up to an unbelievable blaze. Mother went away to her people. After an unsuccessful night full of nightmares with father in the hut, he had to follow her. There had been a hailstorm in the night and everything looked sad in the dripping chill of the next day. The small mealie plants in the yard had been destroyed by the storm; all the leaves torn off except the small hard piths which now stood about in the puddles like nails in a skull. Father went away without a word and I was alone.

I lay under the blankets for a long time with the door of the hut open. One by one, our chickens began to come in out of the cold.

There is something in a cold chicken's voice that asks for something you don't know how to give, something more than corn.

I watched them come into the hut and I felt sorry for them. Their feathers were still wet and they looked smaller and sicker than normal. I couldn't shoo them out. They came and crowded by the fire, their little bird voices scarcely rising above the merest whisper. My eyes left them and wandered up and down the walls.

At first I couldn't see them but when one chicken made a slight move I noticed that there were shadows on the wall.

These shadows fascinated me. There were hundreds of them. I spent the whole day trying to separate them, to isolate them, but they were as elusive and liquid as water in a jar. After a long time looking at them, I felt that they were talking to me. I held my breath and heard their words distinctly, a lullaby in harmony: sleep, sleep, you are all alone, sleep and don't wake up, ever again.

I must have fallen asleep because I remember seeing later on that the sky had turned all dark and a thin chilly drizzle was falling. The chickens, which must have gone out feeling hungry, were coming in again, wet, their forlorn voices hardly audible above the sound of the rain. I knew by the multitude of shadows on the wall that night was falling. I felt too weak to wake up and for a long time watched the shadows multiply and fade, multiply, mingle and fade, and listened to their talk. Again I must have fallen asleep because when I woke up

I was well tucked in and warm. The shadows were now brilliant and clear on the wall because there was a fire on the hearth.

Mother and father had come in and they were silent. Seeing them, I felt as if I were coming from a long journey in a strange country. Mother noticed that I was awake and said,

"How do you feel?"

"He's just lazy," father said.

"He is ill," mother said. "His body is all on fire." She felt me.

"Lies. He is a man and you want to turn him into a woman."

After this I realized how ill I was. I couldn't eat anything: there was no appetite and I wasn't hungry.

I don't know how many days I was in bed. There seemed to be nothing. No light, no sun, to show it was day or darkness to show it was night. Mother was constantly in but I couldn't recognize her as a person. There were only shadows, the voices of the shadows, the lonely cries of the dripping wet fowls shaking the cold out of their feathers by the hearth, and the vague warm shadow that must have been mother. She spoke to me often but I don't remember if I answered anything. I was afraid to answer because I was alone on a solitary plain with the dark crashing of thunder and lightning always in my ears, and there was a big frightening shadow hovering above me so that I couldn't answer her without its hearing me. That must have been father.

They might have had quarrels—I am sure they had lots of them—but I didn't hear them. Everything had been flattened to a dim depthless grey landscape and the only movement on it was of the singing shadows. I could see the shadows and hear them speak to me, so I wasn't dead. If mother talked to me at all, her voice got lost is the vast expanse of emptiness between me and the shadows. Later, when I was beginning to be aware of the change of night into day, her voice was the soft pink intrusion like cream on the hard darkness of the wall. This turned later into a clear urgent sound like the lapping of water against boulders in the morning before sunrise. I noticed too that she was often alone with me. Father was away and must have been coming in late after I had fallen asleep.

The day I saw father, a chill set in the hut.

There was another hailstorm and a big quarrel that night. It was the last quarrel.

When I could wake up again mother was gone and a strange woman had taken her place in the house.

This woman had a shrill strident voice like a cicada's that jarred my nerves. She did all the talking and father became silent and morose. Instead of the frightful silences and sudden bursts of anger I used to know, he now tried to talk softly to me. He preferred to talk to me rather than to his new life.

But he was too late. He had taught me silence and in that long journey between mother's time and this other woman's, I had given myself to the shadows.

So today he sits just inside the hut with the sun playing with him: cartooning him on the bare cold floor and the bare dark walls of the hut, and me watching and listening to the images on the wall. He cannot talk to me because I don't know how to answer him, his language is too difficult for me. All I can think of, the nearest I can come to him, is when I see that his tough grey stubble looks like the soft unprotected feathers on a dove's nestling; and when I remember that the next morning the nestlings were dead in their nest because somebody had unknowingly killed their mother in the bush on her way home, I feel the tears in my eyes.

It is all—all that I feel for my father; but I cannot talk to him. I don't know how I should talk to him. He has denied me the gift of language.

BLACK MEN

Faith Adiele

Faith Adiele's firsthand account of being the only black member in her Nordic American family revolves around three generations of Finnish men. In the absence of her Nigerian father, these stoically tragic misfits become the "black men" in her world. As she unravels family secrets illuminating the immigrant and Americanization experience, Adiele is particularly drawn to her dashing young uncle, who suffers a physical disfigurement she sees as similar to her biracial identity.

Memoirist and travel writer Faith Adiele was born in 1963 and raised by her mother on her grandparents' farm in Washington state. As an adult she traveled to Nigeria to find her father and siblings. This experience inspired the PBS documentary My Journey Home *and the memoir-in-progress from which "Black Men," short-listed for* Best American Essays 2005 *and winner of the John Guyon Prize from* Crab Orchard Review, *is excerpted. A graduate of Harvard University and the University of Iowa, she has worked as a community activist and educator, and is currently a professor at the University of*

Pittsburgh in Pennsylvania. Her first memoir, Meeting Faith *(2004), won a PEN Award.*

Though set in the United States, Adiele's memoir inhabits a psychic space stretching back to the Finland of the late 1800s and early 1900s, when poor farming conditions, coupled with newspaper accounts of America as the land of freedom and equality, spurred substantial immigration to such Finnish American settlements as Ashtabula Harbor, Ohio. Recalling chain immigration (the practice of families immigrating one member at a time) and the Underground Railroad, "Black Men" uncovers American history as well, debunking the tragic mulatta stereotype. A standard feature of northern antebellum literature, beginning with Lydia Maria Child's "The Quadroons" (1842) and popularized by Danish/African American author Nella Larsen, the beautiful mulatta is doomed to suffer because of her mixed heritage. By retelling different versions of her family's story, always subverting reader expectations of black and white, Adiele critiques the limitations of language to express identity and emotional reality.

You may wish to compare "Black Men" to the excerpt from Aminatta Forna's The Devil That Danced on the Water, *also by a biracial woman raised by her white mother in the absence of her African father, and to the excerpt from Alexandra Fuller's* Don't Let's Go to the Dogs Tonight, *by an Anglo-African girl confused about her identity; to David Malouf's "Closer," a similar attempt to define a more humane notion of truth through language; and to Victor Perera's "Kindergarten," another struggle to make sense of oneself in an environment both familiar and alien.*

Falling

When I was five years old, I tripped on a throw rug in my babysitter's house and hurtled face forward onto the coffee table, an immense slab of petrified California redwood. Quick as it happened, each arc of my fall segmented itself, colors separating in a kaleidoscope, and crystallized in my memory: the rug sucking at my ankles, the giddy lurch across the floor, the crest through the air, weightless, my jangling heart, disbelief as I spied the waiting block—soild, glistening.

I was already screaming when my nose smacked the table. Over the noise, I heard a crack like the cut that severs the tree, saw the brown spine of a Douglas fir submitting to my grandfather's ax.

The babysitter, who'd been in the kitchen coating slices of Wonder Bread with thick swirls of margarine and dousing them with sugar (an after-school snack I adored, much to my mother's horror), came tearing down the hall.

"What happened?" she shouted, the sugar shaker still clutched in her fist.

I couldn't respond. Pain vibrated through cartilage into the roots of my teeth. I crumpled to the floor, clutching my face against my skull.

She yanked my quivering hands away to check for fracture, her fingers leaving a gritty trail of sugar across my cheeks. Then, though not a particularly demonstrative woman, she lifted me into the large recliner and locked her arms around me.

"Go 'way!" I shrieked at the other children who, wide-eyed and solemn, ringed the recliner, some wailing helpfully, others tugging the babysitter's apron, wanting to know, "Why she crying?"

I howled and howled. More than the pain itself, I remember the taste of sugar mixed with tears leaking into my mouth, salt and sweet, the flavor of amazement, amazement to learn that yes, life was this too. I don't remember the trip to the ER, the arrival of my mother, the painkillers, the days and nights of ice packs.

By some miracle, my nose wasn't broken. "I fell," I announced proudly to strangers, and in 1968, people believed me, could still believe in children, especially brown ones, falling. Over the next few days, a thick root of blood spread out beneath the golden surface of my cheeks, staining them the color of bruised plums. The bridge of my nose puffed and held. For nearly six months I resembled a raccoon—curious, slightly anxious, with crusty, purple skin ringing my eyes.

One of my favorite photographs was taken a few months later. Michael-Vaino, a.k.a. Uncle Mike, and a friend are dancing in my grandparents' living room in cowboy hats. Uncle Mike, his pale Finn eyes droopy, snaps the fingers of one hand, wobbles a bottle of gin in the other. His friend, a Swede like Old Pappa, my lumberman grandfather, balances me on his hip, beaming at my bruised face.

My mother had been playing Nigerian Highlife LPs on the stereo, and Uncle Mike's friend, drawn by the hypnotic twang of the talking drum speaking to the guitar like someone calling your name under-water, popped his head into the room. "Hey, what's this music?"

"Yeah, cool." Uncle Mike followed behind, drawing the string of his flat-brimmed hat tight. Ever since childhood, he'd dressed like a cowboy in an old black-and-white movie.

My mother stared pointedly at his hand and shook her head.

"I know, I know." He gave the bottle a fluid twist of the wrist, a cowboy spinning his pistols before re-holstering. "It's only for a second. We're on our way out."

The Highlife swelled, spurred by the singer's admonition that *Everybody dey party*, and my uncle's friend swept me into his arms, saying, "Hear that? Everybody party, something-something."

My mother hesitated a moment, then smiled. Extending her arms before her like a hula dancer, crooked at the elbows, she swiveled her hips to the slower under-beat, the way my Nigerian father had taught her before he left. Like a grass skirt, her brown ponytail swayed from side to side.

Uncle Mike snapped his fingers, shuffled his feet across the carpet, sang "something-something" in my ear, and despite the fact that it was his friend holding me, his friend who told me how pretty I was (something Uncle Mike had never said, either before or after my raccoon rings), my uncle was the one I loved.

My mother ended it.

"Look goofy!" she called, framing us in the lens of her Brownie camera. "In other words, just be yourselves." The flash bleached the room, breaking the spell.

Uncle Mike checked his watch and jerked his head toward the door. Outside, the crunch of gravel signaled that the others were assembling in the driveway. Whenever his pack of loud, good-natured friends came by in their well-ironed jeans, they left their bottles outside in fast cars with deep bucket seats and carried me on their shoulders, recounting their latest motorbike triumphs.

The friend spun me one last time and released. "Thank you, madam." He bowed.

"Don't go," I begged.

Uncle Mike doffed his hat and flattened it onto my head with two pats. "'Night, cowpoke." Then he was gone. I listened hard in his wake: gravel flying, welcome shouts, car doors opening to blasts of squealing electric guitar and shuddering bass, metallic slams and revved motors. The music of my disappeared-to-Africa father couldn't compete.

Most nights Uncle Mike came home after I was in bed. Most days he slept past noon. Awake, he was often grumpy. His jovial moments were brief, always halfway out the door.

Baby Vaino, the One Left Behind

I come from a long line of unlucky men, men who disappeared to unsettled countries, to civil-war-torn countries, to mental institutions, to the barn with a bottle of vodka. Men in our family couldn't quite manage to stay home. They wandered—restless, driven by gold, war, emotion—and rarely returned, despite the best intentions. Growing up in their wake on the family farm, I inherited the understanding that men were fragile, prone to leaving us behind.

Who's to blame? Let's start with country—Finland, with its brooding soundtrack by Sibelius and tight-lipped, hard-drinking citizens. A Finnish friend once told me that she had never really heard her father speak. Occasionally he would grunt if asked a direct question. When, in his late seventies, he retired from the fields, she and her sisters were amazed to find that he had plenty to say. The family sat together at the kitchen table, drinking tiny cups of Finnish *kahvi* and peeling potatoes for *kalavuoka*, the women's mouths ajar as their father chatted about God, the annual moose hunt, the mid-summer strawberry harvest. That was the odd thing—not the seventy-year silence—but the decision finally to speak.

I blame the flat, icy landscape with its meager sunlight and long winter days. I blame history—Sweden and Russia leaning like the long shadow of death, recurring conquests interspersed with ill-fated stoic resistance. Or shall I blame hunger and displacement, the generic lot of the immigrant?

But why is it each generation assumed that history and landscape were things only women could survive? For that I blame twin legacies—names and lies: All the men in the family are named after Baby Vaino, the One Left Behind. His abandonment was the original lie.

———

In 1889 my great-grandfather the Cursed was born in Finland, the second of three sons. When he was still young, his father snatched him and his older brother out of the shade of Russia and fled to the United States. His mother remained behind with Vaino the baby. Father and sons settled in Ashtabula, Ohio, a bustling port city on Lake Erie, where the father found work as a carpenter.

When I was nine and much enamored of slave narratives, I thrilled to learn that, fifty years before my ancestor's arrival, the Ashtabula River had been a stop on the Underground Railroad for slaves fleeing to Canada. I studied how runaways walked for miles in the dark, running their blistered hands up the sides of trees to feel where the north-facing moss was growing, how conductors placed burning candles in station windows, much like the ones we lit in December for the *tonttu*, farm sprites. My heart throbbed with justice and injustice. Despite a Nigerian and Nordic heritage, I longed to claim Black Americans like John Park, who ferried hundreds of fellow slaves across the Ohio River.

I had to settle for the Hubbards, a white family who owned a successful lumberyard and belonged to Ashtabula's antislavery society. William Hubbard built a large, white-pillared house near the lake, where nearly every night passengers slipped into cubbyholes in the cellar and hayloft, their last stop before freedom. The white man who likely employed my Finnish ancestors was as close as I came to slave resistance.

I imagined my great-grandfather the Cursed, in his dark woolens and heavy boots, clomping in late from Hubbard's lumberyard, unaware of the legacy of black slaves above his head, beneath his feet.

When his mother and Baby Vaino, the One Left Behind, died back in Finland, his father remarried and fathered three more children.

Handicaps

Michael-Vaino, a.k.a. Uncle Mike, is handicapped.

I am six, and we have moved to my grandparents' farm. This means two things: one, my mother and Old Pappa have reconciled, and two, my interest in family gossip is born. The sound of dropping voices, as my mother and Mummi start to whisper, is my sign to creep into hiding.

Handicapped! I freeze in the hallway. It sounds bad, like being retarded. Like giant Mark Kludas two doors down, who smells and weeps like an angry baby whenever the neighborhood kids rile him. Uncle Mike, who wears tight jeans and races motocross, is nothing like Mark.

Nonetheless, Handicapped is why he isn't able to go to Vietnam. This is also confusing. I've been in more protests than I can count, bearded graduate students passing me from shoulder to shoulder and singing folksongs Mom taught me on her Autoharp, so that he and his friends don't have to go. Uncle Mike will be the one who didn't disappear. Why, then, should he be disappointed?

"*Shhh,*" my grandmother warns my mother. Uncle Mike is self-conscious about his handicap.

When Uncle Mike finally awakens at three, I am stationed outside his door, trying not to stare. He grunts and staggers to the bathroom. Hearing the door, Mummi darts into his bedroom with a stack of freshly ironed clothes and grabs as many things as she can carry off the floor.

When Uncle Mike emerges in his white terrycloth robe, the bathroom mirror steamed up and his shaggy blond hair combed wet over his ears, I am waiting. He gives me a puzzled glance. I tilt my chin and pretend to study the embroidered hanging above the laundry hamper. Shaking his head, he saunters to the kitchen. I follow, close on his heels.

When he lifts me onto a stool, I scan his face, searching for handicap. I see Uncle Mike: Round ruddy face. My mother's blue, hounddog eyes. Dashing blond mustache that droops a bit on the left beneath a slightly flattened nose.

Disappointed at the handicap's reluctance to show itself, I frown and demand to know what he's making.

He ignores me, his head burrowed in the refrigerator. Seconds later he emerges, arms loaded. Movements smooth and sure, no evidence of handicap, he builds a giant sandwich out of leftovers, cottage cheese, fried eggs, and catsup.

"What next?" I ask of every step, trembling with horror.

He snorts an occasional answer: Meatloaf. Pickles. He loads the finished sandwich onto a baking sheet and shoves it into the oven. My stomach recoils.

"You know," he says, looking up from sawing at the bubbling sandwich, suddenly talkative. "I heard that President Nixon puts catsup on his cottage cheese." He grins. "He must be the only other person besides me!"

And though I know we aren't supposed to like President Nixon, I giggle.

Great-Grandpa the Cursed

Sometime in the immigrant wave of the 1890s, my great-great-grandfather and his two elder sons came to Ohio. As was customary in chain immigration, his wife and newborn remained in Finland. When they died, my great-great-grandfather remarried and fathered three more children.

"Actually," my grandmother confesses, "they didn't die. My grandmother and Baby Vaino lived on in Finland for years."

Stunned, I watch her hands smelling of yeast and rye as she kneads the *limpa*. At ten I'm obsessed with family stories and photos. I can't imagine what compelled a father to tell his sons that their mother and brother had died. Was it his plan from the start to abandon his wife and construct a new life on the blank page of America?

Mummi shakes her head, working the brown dough with strong fingers. She doesn't know. Her father, my cursed great-grandfather, died of stomach ulcers when she was a baby. The story came second-hand to her.

I wonder if the two brothers knew what their father had done. In my experience, Finnish men are hardly forthcoming. Did they believe his terse story?

I imagine that this event—the loss of his mother and baby brother, his father's lie—is the moment my great-grandfather became cursed. I know how he feels. We two are alike, caught in between, with one foot, one parent in the New World, one still in the Old. Two years after my birth, without ever having seen me, my father disappeared to deepest, darkest Africa, never to be seen again. Like so many of those who invented America, my great-grandfather emerged from the dream of migration only partly intact. Half of himself he carried never waking, forever out of reach.

I study Mummi's face, her nose like a soft, drooping beak, and try to imagine her cursed father as a boy. I see a sleepwalker. A dark boy with light eyes, he stumbles though a house with hidden rooms beneath the stairs, behind the fireplace, blind to his American stepmother and new siblings. He tries to recall his mother's face, tries to imagine Baby Vaino, the One Left Behind, now grown to a boy. He lies awake nights, troubled by the voices of former slaves praying beneath the floorboards. Like them, he will rest in this place only momentarily. He wonders if he'll ever see his mother and brother again, fears they await a summons that will never come.

Bad Habits

Michael-Vaino, a.k.a. Uncle Mike, is in trouble.

From my hiding place in the hall linen closet, I hear Mummi stirring her tea, teaspoon tinkling. She says she fears he may take after Great-Uncle Vaino-Johan, her brother, and begins to cry.

"No, Mom," my mother says. "He just has Bad Habits."

Like not taking out the trash? Or watching too much TV, which rots your noodle?

Uncle Mike didn't come home last night. Wherever he was, Old Pappa wanted him to stay there overnight "to learn his lesson." So of course Tati Rauha's husband went to get him out, "just to spite Old Pappa."

My mother chuckles. "Dinner tonight should be fun." A metal chair leg scrapes across the linoleum. "Let me call the Funks to see if Faith can eat there."

Foiled, I steam in the closet. I am the only child among adults. If I am six, Uncle Mike is twenty-two, the family member closest to me in age.

I insist on taking my naps in his room. Except for the same heavy Scandinavian furniture that looks as if it's been shellacked in honey, his bedroom differs from the rest of the house. His shelves are crammed with tall, sparkly racing trophies. Two doors in the bed's golden headboard slide back to reveal tiny packets of tissue-thin paper called *zigzag* and tall glass tubes of stinky water. I am convinced these have something to do with Uncle Mike's Bad Habits. Back issues of *Playboy* and *Penthouse* rise in the closet. Fending off sleep, I read voraciously, dazed by mounds of breasts like the pale mountains surrounding our valley home.

Rivers

In the 1890s, one adult male and two male children, all named Hautajoki, left Finland for America. My great-great-grandmother nodded grimly from the misty banks of the Hauta River, their namesake (*joki* means river). The newborn balanced on her hip, she watched her husband and sons go. This was their agreement. He would take the two elder sons; she would remain behind with Baby Vaino. The Lutheran church banned divorce but couldn't control for the vicissitudes of immigration.

Father and sons settled in Ashtabula, where there was carpentry work and a thriving Finnish community. After some time, Great-Great-Grandpa Hautajoki took a wife. The Hautajoki thus cleaved in two, one stream on the motherland, the other a tributary transplanted to America. In time it split again. The branch from which I am descended turned out to be perpetually sickly, as if we never quite recovered from the wound.

On November 11, 1908, the cursed middle son left his father's house to marry another Finnish immigrant. He was nineteen. Like his father, he became a carpenter and fathered three children: Tati Rauha, the eldest; my grandmother, the baby; and a son. He named the son Vaino-Johan, after his younger and older brothers.

Even as a child, I knew that he had erred in naming. For a time, however, things were good. Husband and wife lived in a comfortable house that he built, and food was plentiful.

There is only one photograph of my great-grandfather the Cursed. In 1911 the family sat for a formal studio portrait: Husband, wife, and the two elder children; my grandmother was not yet born.

Tati Rauha, large bow atop her pale curls, stands on a table, her hand pressed for leverage to her mother's breast. Holding her bottom lip between her teeth, she clutches her brother's hand.

Great-Grandpa the Cursed, well groomed in a dark suit, also holds Vaino-Johan. The two of them, with their wide, angular jaws and olive skin, couldn't be more different from the women.

An odd distortion breaks the sharp sepia images, a smear or blur in the upper right-hand corner throwing Great-Grandpa's head out of focus. Already, three or four years before his death at age twenty-six to stomach ulcers, he is receding from his family, becoming indistinct.

As if she senses this, Tati Rauha clenches her brother's hand, seemingly determined to wrest Vaino-Johan from their cursed father's grasp and keep him safe in the world with her—a role she and my grandmother played, with only limited success, all his life.

Gifts

Presents from Michael-Vaino, a.k.a. Uncle Mike, are always worth the wait. Despite this, as each birthday and *Joulu* approach, I see my mother watching him, worried, wondering if he will make it on time, or even remember.

There is the Frosty the Snowman Snowcone Maker, which though it requires hours of hard scraping to make a single snow cone, is exactly like the one I admired on television. There is a battery-powered pottery wheel that sprays mud everywhere.

One *Joulu* he builds a three-story dollhouse from my mother's design with real tile and Formica floors from factory remnants at work. He is so exhausted from all the late nights that he snores through Christmas dinner.

The *Joulu* I enter junior high, he hands me a heavy tan-and-brown envelope. Having recently discovered clothes, I instantly recognize the logo for Nordstrom's, a department store in Seattle, and do a little prayer, *Please let it be a lot, like twenty-five dollars,* before ripping it open.

A certificate for fifty dollars—more money than I have ever seen—slips into my trembling fingers. After he drags my arms from around his neck, I spend the rest of the evening glowing and shy.

"Half that amount would've been generous," my mother marvels later as they sit in the darkened living room sipping *glögi*. From my perch in the laundry room, I can see the colored lights blinking on the tree.

Uncle Mike chuckles. "Well, in fact, I only intended to spend twenty-five, but . . ." His voice drops, conspiratorial. "The guy in front of me spent forty dollars, and the saleswoman was uh, you know, pretty foxy."

My mother laughs. "Praise God for the male ego!"

I slump against the cold washing machine, careful not to make any noise. Junior high will be full of moments like this, the adult in me recognizing humor and the child wanting to cry. For one entire evening, I'd thought that his love finally matched mine. That I was worth twice as much.

Three decades after her father's death, sometime between the end of World War II and 1958, when she started keeping a diary, my grandmother discovered that her father the Cursed had not died of stomach ulcers in 1915. In fact, he had not died at all.

She tells me the story when I'm eleven, sitting on my kitchen stool watching the *limpa* turn dark brown through the little yellowed window in the oven door.

One day, by some miracle of mail forwarding, a letter arrived all the way from Ohio from the director of a sanitarium who regretted to inform the Hautajoki family that he had just expired.

Like milk left on the shelf too long.

Mummi pulls the *limpa* from the oven, heavy and dark. An acrid wave of rye floods the kitchen. Thirty years later, her dead father had died again, his life flickering across her cornea for only an instant.

I'm full of questions. How did her mother carry so many secrets to her grave? That her husband had been alive all this time, insane, institutionalized for more than half his life. That all this time, his children had been carrying this gene unawares. What, who, where?

When Mummi learned the truth she was in her thirties, the only one of her siblings to have children, approximately the age her mother had been when she surrendered her husband to the State.

She cuts the *limpa*, holding the sharp knife in soft hands, her voice low. She doesn't say how it felt to learn the news about her father once it was too late to do anything. I imagine she simply transferred those dark buds of emotion to her brother, Great-Uncle Vaino-Johan, who was becoming increasingly antisocial. I know she worried about her son, Michael-Vaino, a.k.a. Uncle Mike.

Whatever her feelings, she does not voice them, does not commit them to her diary, does not change the family register at the back of the album. Great-Grandpa the Cursed remains dead at age twenty-six of stomach ulcers. This is an oral story, passed from her to my mother and me.

Rivers

After my great-grandfather the Cursed's institutionalization, the family was always poor. For the next ten years, wife and three children lived like nomads, moving from state to state on the immigrant circuit, chasing rumors of work. There is no family account of what happened to the other Hautajoki men, father and older brother to the Cursed. Supposedly the new American stepmother discouraged close relations. There is no explanation for the older brother's disappearance, another split in the river.

Bad Genes

Later I lug the encyclopedia up to the roof and pore over entries on schizophrenia and depression, studying them as carefully as photos in the family album. I'm convinced that I too am insane. I wonder how to break the news to my mother. I am prone to fits of disordered thinking. Extreme sadness. Exaggerated gaiety. Blame Finland.

Looking out on fields of mint, I weep a bit for Great-Grandpa the Cursed, my oft-abandoned, lied-to and lied-about forebear. First taken from his childhood home, and then replaced by an American step-mother and three half-siblings until, haunted by the voices beneath his bed, he was finally abandoned in the middle of a strange and unfriendly country by his young wife.

Then I mist for his wife, left like my mother to raise her children alone. How in the world had she, who never learned to speak English, negotiated the American mental health system of 1915? Now I understand why she fled Ohio, taking her children west. And once the family got as far west as you can go, enter my mother, disowned at nineteen by Old Pappa for "going black," then abandoned for Africa, now trying to be both (white) mother and (black) father to the American child.

"More stories!" I demand, and my grandmother explains that Uncle Mike's mustache droops to hide the white veins where his face is sewn together, where there used to be an open cavity.

I follow her lead, punching the puffy *limpa*, watching it collapse.

Born with a cleft palate, ruptured left eardrum, and fused nasal cavity, Michael-Vaino, a.k.a. Uncle Mike, spent his babyhood in hospitals, arms sheathed in cardboard restraints. Mummi holds up her arms, articulating them stiffly at the elbows. So he couldn't pick at his face.

By the time he got out of the hospital, he was timid and cross.

He hated speech therapy. He hated change. Every winter he cried at having to wear long sleeves, and then when summer rolled around, he cried to see his short-sleeved shirts again. Even now he refuses a hearing aid, despite my mother's claim that he can't hear "half of what's said." He would rather appear stuck-up than weak.

Mummi works the dough methodically, sniffling because *limpa* makes her cry.

"She blames herself," my mother explains later as we cut paper dolls at kitchen table. "She blames herself for Bad Genes."

My mother arranges a fan of American Revolution costumes across the sunny Formica. "And she's never forgiven herself for leaving him alone in the hospital. The doctors made her go home, but Mike was terrified. He sobbed all night. By morning the restraints were shredded."

Over the years, a series of operations were performed on Uncle Mike's face and ear. Every time he screamed, my grandmother screamed too. One, when he was an adult, entailed systematically shattering his nose and then reconstructing it like an ancient artifact, shard by shard. The procedure was so excruciating that he could only endure it partway and refused to return for the second installment. The left half of his nose remains smashed.

Great-Uncle Vaino-Johan the Depressed

During the Great Depression, the family split for the first time since their father the Cursed's disappearance. Over his sister's objections, Great-Uncle Vaino-Johan headed to Alaska. By 1934 he had panned enough gold to buy his mother and sisters a house in Portland, Oregon. He then embarked on a series of business ventures with his brothers-in-law and, for the next two decades, lived with or near the two couples. When my grandparents bought their farm, they built a bunkhouse especially for him, and when, in 1945, my perpetually stoned Uncle Mike was born, a sickly, scarred creature who required a series of violent operations to repair a cleft palate and punctured eardrum, they named him Michael-Vaino, yet another ill-advised naming decision.

Soon after the truth about Great-Grandpa the Cursed was revealed, his legacy began to manifest itself in Vaino-Johan, his son.

When my mother was a teenager, her uncle Vaino-Johan began to disappear for days at a time. The only hint a "spell" was coming was that he spoke even less than usual—if such a thing were possible. Though she knew her uncle's drinking binges involved hard liquor, she never saw him pick up anything harder than beer and never witnessed him drunk.

"What was he like?" I once asked.

She furrowed her brow, cocked her head, and finally shrugged. "I don't know."

"What do you mean you don't know? He lived with you your entire life!"

"I know." Her pouty lips rippled with concentration. "He was quiet. Very sweet. He would smile at you, but he never really talked."

She shrugged again, like my Finnish friend before her father's seventy-year-old decision to speak. "I don't know what he was like."

According to Mummi's diaries, Great-Uncle Vaino-Johan the Depressed was industrious and easygoing. He worked around the house and farm, babysat my mother and Uncle Mike, built and fixed and painted things for both sisters. In turn, his sisters fed him, washed his plastic bachelor's dishes when he wasn't living with them, and drove him to jobs and to each other's houses in their pale, large-fender cars.

On the weekends he fished and hunted with my grandfather; in the evenings he worked puzzles and word games with my grandmother. One day in 1960, he and my grandmother spent seven hours driving to farms looking for harvest work.

As far as I can tell from Mummi's restrained wording, Vaino-Johan had a breakdown in 1958, the year she began keeping a diary. Like the family album, her diary maintains the official fiction of their father's death. And though she faithfully records driving Vaino-Johan to the doctor week after week, my mother along for company, she neglects to mention that the doctor is administering electroshock therapy.

According to my encyclopedia, shock therapy is exactly what it sounds like: currents of electricity zapping through the patient's head until he loses consciousness or convulses. It was, in 1958, a common treatment for depression.

My grandmother's diary reads like a catalogue of Vaino-Johan's disappearances, hospital sessions, more disappearances. Her February 26, 1959, entry stuns me: *Thursday, after having my regular argument with Vaino about keeping on going to the Dr., he left for his appt.* Amusing as it is to try to imagine either of my soft-spoken relatives arguing with anyone—let alone each other, regularly—it hurts to know that Vaino-Johan resisted. That same night, after the argument and treatment, he drank himself into oblivion.

Five years later, in February 1962, he and a friend went gold prospecting in California. There was no warning in the diary of the intended trip, and after his departure, he virtually disappears from its pages. As far as I can tell, he never returned.

Handicaps

Occasionally my mother and Michael-Vaino, a.k.a. Uncle Mike, slip into the comfort of childhood. These moments she is once again his sister, not The One Who Got Herself Knocked Up By A Black African, and he is just her brother, not The One Who Is At Best An Unreliable And At Worst A Bad Influence on her child.

One evening she follows him into the bathroom and perches on the edge of the bathtub. She's been prattling about Borlaug winning the Nobel Peace Prize—*Yay for farmers!*—but falls silent, watching him shave.

He laughs uneasily. "It's hard to get it even," he apologizes, "with the deformity."

"What're you talking about?"

He shrugs, the blade flashing up the tender flesh of his neck.

She joins him at the mirror, standing on tiptoe, tan cowlicks sprouting like weeds over the hill of his shoulder. "Describe yourself!"

"Go away," he says, resting his elbow atop her head. "You're short, and I'm late."

"I may be short, but I'm tougher than you." She ducks and jabs his ribs. When he doubles over, she grabs his ears. "There." She turns him back to the mirror. "Tell me what you see."

He describes a face split like a mask, a huge, jagged scar and flattened, misshapen nose cleaving the landscape in two. Under the spell of his words, he transforms into an ogre straight out of Norse mythology, the goddess Hel who haunts me too. In my grandmother's tales, Hel appears vertically split, half white, half black, the black half a putrefying corpse. Though not perhaps the healthiest biracial model for me, she is satisfyingly literal.

My mother gasps. "Sweetie, are you crazy?"

Years later she will find me weeping before a mirror after my first junior-high dance—*Big Lips*, the only black girl in school, left to hold up the gymnasium walls for two excruciating hours—and ask the same of me.

It seems that leaving the house is a dangerous proposition. Difference announces itself out there, worms its way in. Strangers for whom familiarity doesn't hide handicap see clearly, instantly, who is half-rebuilt and who is half-black. *Hey man, why is your moustache so weird? What are you, deaf? Hey little girl, that white lady can't be your mom; where's your real mom? And why are your lips so big?*

In the unforgiving fluorescence of the bathroom, my mother tries to explain to her brother that his scar and nose are virtually unnoticeable, much as she will try to convince me after the dance that *Black is Beautiful, fuck junior high.* She speaks desperately, her hands, her cowlicks waving, but it is years too late.

"Yeah, whatever," he says, slapping on Brut cologne like punishment, slipping a flask of something clear into his rear jeans pocket.

Genes

I am pilfering again. Searching for someone who looks like me. Anyone.

Wedging myself into the back of my grandparents' closet, among board games and jigsaw puzzles, I sift through shoeboxes of photographs: Monochrome snapshots of white relatives in black clothes. Hand-tinted portraits with my grandmother's whimsical colors. These are the ones that didn't make the cut; I've already looted the official family album.

It takes a while, the trick of comparing color to black-and-white distracting me, but I finally see the connection. Michael-Vaino, a.k.a. Uncle Mike, looks like his uncle, Vaino-Johan the Depressed, only paler. And Great-Uncle Vaino-Johan looks like his father, Great-Grandpa the Cursed. Only Baby Vaino, the One Left Behind, who started it all, is missing.

The few times Great-Uncle Vaino-Johan eyes the camera directly, he still seems somehow at a distance, the forehead beneath his dark, slicked-back hair perpetually wrinkled from squinting. His broad, swarthy face with cleft chin and hooked nose (the only trait shared with the rest of the family) evokes the unknown origins of the Finns. In his face lies the possibility of Turkey and Hungary. He looks more Inuit than Nordic, and when he laughs, the dark slits of his eyes disappear completely.

In he goes to the box beneath my bed. He doesn't look like me, but at least he is different and dark.

Now I'm back for more. Snapshots soar through the air, piling up on the closet floor.

The aroma of *limpa* blooms at the mouth of the hallway, persistently faint as the cancer eating away at Mummi's insides, but at twelve I'm pushing my way out of childhood, wondering what I will become. After this golden skin and dark eyes my mother rhapsodizes over, these curls my grandmother twists around her fingers, this round nose my grandfather tugs before hanging me upside down, then what?

Gifts

My mother always knew the truth about her grandfather, Great-Grandpa the Cursed, but can't recall what her mother did upon learning the news. What was the name of the Ohio sanitarium? How had it located the family after so many moves west? What was his official diagnosis? What happened to the letter? The body?

The details are forgotten, and who can tell whether it was Finnish closed-mouthedness, immigrant confusion, or newly acquired middle-class shame that allowed Great-Grandpa the Cursed to be lost in America yet again?

This is the crossroads between the official family history that exists on paper, a more authentic history that was passed orally, and a third, more potent history that couldn't be spoken and is fading.

After Mummi's death, I combed her journal for clues, convinced that Great-Uncle Vaino-Johan the Depressed held the key to his father's mysterious madness. I remember once getting a birthday card from Great-Uncle Vaino-Johan as a very young child. Inside was an entire five-dollar bill. Perhaps because of this, or perhaps because I grew up hearing my grandmother missing him, I missed him too, just as I missed the African father I had never seen. Like my scarred, stoned Uncle Mike, like me, Great-Uncle Vaino-Johan was half in, half out. I imagined him as the key to all the family men who disappeared.

No Tragic Mulattoes in our tree, only tragic Finns.

I question medicine. Michael-Vaino's, a.k.a. Uncle Mike's, ear and nose surgery. Great-Uncle Vaino-Johan's electroshock treatments. Great-Grandpa the Cursed's institutionalization.

I'm adult, at the kitchen table with my mother, wondering how necessary shock treatments were for a man who disappeared quietly, sweetly, to the barn with a bottle of vodka. Certainly Vaino-Johan's benders wouldn't have caused alarm back in Finland. And what of his cursed father, institutionalized three decades?

My mother jokes. "They're Finns, for God's sake," she says. "How on earth did anyone even notice there was anything wrong?"

We imagine that Great-Grandpa the Cursed was like his son, Great-Uncle Vaino-Johan—quiet, prone to depression, at worst a drunk. Was it any more than standard Finnish dourness? Besides, what did 1915 America know about the mental health of a non-English-speaking immigrant who'd been ripped from mother and home?

Surely he couldn't have been violent, destructive, threatening. Not if his son is any indication. "Perhaps he just stopped functioning," my mother suggests. One day he didn't leave his room, content instead to listen to the faint voices in the walls, pleas from home.

Despite our shared genes, I pray that he was completely mad, better off forgotten by the few who knew where he was, hidden from those who might have saved him in more enlightened times. I pray that, at age twenty-six, his was an illness more profound than what afflicted his morose son Vaino-Johan, that it was something able to weather the vast medical improvements from 1915 to 1945. I pray to God there was no mistake.

Falling

After Mummi's death, my mother and I move to town. Michael-Vaino, a.k.a. Uncle Mike, who still lives at home, visits late in the evenings. I creep out in my nightgown to sit on his lap.

One night, when I am full in the throes of adolescence, he points to the floor.

I look down.

He runs his finger up my chest and flicks my bottom lip. My lip, loose and jutting out, bobs up and down. An old trick, a child's trick.

"Got-cha!" he crows. He roars with laughter, much more so than the trick seems to warrant.

Smiling weakly, I look to my mother for direction.

She is staring at Uncle Mike, her mouth tight, eyes slitted. None of the usual gentle pity or wary tolerance.

I know he can't be drunk or high, or she wouldn't have let him in. Those are the rules. So this is something else.

Each time my half-built uncle looks at me, he bursts into renewed, helpless gales.

Years later I recall the incident, the pain as sharp and stunning as the lesson of the coffee table against my nose when I was five, its taste as salty-sweet. I am grown before I finally realize, my stomach falling in disbelief the way it had that night, what he had been reacting to—the fullness of my lip. My difference, not ours.

IN HEAVEN

Guadalupe Dueñas

TRANSLATED BY JOHN BENSON

*While at first these memory fragments may seem like insub-
stantial shards from the shadows of a past life, a closer look
will yield something more. You will see how Guadalupe
Dueñas captures moments that have deepened her adolescence,
making it both magical and torturous.*

*"In Heaven" relies on the visual and olfactory senses to pro-
duce a magical interlude in an otherwise solitary and impover-
ished life. Cosmetic samples, specifically perfumes, face creams,
and powder, transform the narrator's world into a paradise of ex-
otica and luxury that suggest a European presence. These samples
become the narrator's conduit to another identity, even to another
class where women are celebrities capable of eliciting jealousy and
an emotional intensity bordering on hysteria. But the samples
hide a desperate loneliness as well as "much-mended stockings."*

*"Shoes for the Rest of My Life" displays the confluence of
father/daughter ingenuity. When the narrator's father resolves
to provide shoes in perpetuity for his family once his shoe-
manufacturing business goes bankrupt, the narrator responds
by systematically attempting to eliminate every pair: wearing*

them out, leaving the odd shoe at a friend's, giving them as presents, giving them to beggars, involving them in traffic accidents. But no matter what she does, there seem to be more shoes, enough for "seven lives." The shoes, outdated and ugly, embarrassing and smelly, become part of her.

Dueñas is the mistress of the metaphor. In each unique piece, she creates comparisons between symbolic objects and a persona that the narrator wishes to acquire or takes for granted. The tiny, exquisite vials, bottles, and stoppers of "In Heaven" evoke the narrator's escape to a foreign fantasy and glamour not accessible in her world. The endless pairs of "crypts for desperate feet" describe the narrator's relationship with her father— his relentless love that will not allow her to dispense with him, no matter how hard she tries.

Guadalupe Dueñas, who died in 2003, was born in Guadalajara, Mexico, in 1920. In addition to her successful career as a fiction writer, Dueñas wrote a series of Mexican soap operas and a TV series adapted from Daphne du Maurier's novel Rebecca *that achieved a high degree of popularity. Her short stories have been widely anthologized in Spanish, English, and German.*

These memory pieces can be compared most effectively to Chang-rae Lee's "Sea Urchin." Both Dueñas and Lee yearn for a world where they can fit in but on their own terms, and while Lee makes himself ill to achieve his goal of belonging to his desired adult world, Dueñas uses metaphoric objects to draw closer to or move away from hers.

The only bright spot in my youth was the abundance of perfumes, soaps and cosmetics teeming in the basement of our house. I spent my adolescence bathed in the effluvia of their exotic exhalations as sister after sister appeared each year—seven in all.

I was allowed one perfume each day of the week. Monday it was "Heliotrope," Tuesday, "Rumor," the day after, "Scandal," then "Arpège," "Intimate Hour," "Intermezzo" and on Sunday, "La nuit bleue." Each morning I would pick a different flower from the fantasy garden: it was like having the rainbow at my command. I was steeped in colognes and perfumes and I don't think there's a single one I haven't tried. I covered myself ankle to thigh in costly wrinkle creams; their softness still lingers.

When it was time for the powder, I covered myself from head to toe until I practically looked like a ghost. Even after I was dressed it would shower off me like pollen off wheat.

This magic garden compensated for many disappointments. I spent long hours eyeing the encased vials, absorbed in the diademed bottles and in exotic stoppers in the form of African princesses with jeweled necklaces. There were cut glass stoppers bigger than the bottles themselves, others shaped like prisms or tears, and a fascinating one encrusted with rubies and little silver cloverleaves with striped bubbles in the melted opal inside.

Essences of twilight! Avidly eyeing them, greedily unstoppering them! Mysterious, magical, debutantes in line.

There were perfumes that inexplicably hemorrhaged from untouched vials, stealing away like life itself. The unopened bottles yielded up their essence in short order and the prospect of their leaving chilled me, terrified me.

Our perfumes were popular throughout the region. Though this bothered some in the family, I was proud of it.

I was something of a celebrity at home—my friends were jealous. They were amazed that I had four different soaps: "Hiel de Toro" for my hair, "Grass of Pravia" from the neck to the waist, real "Lavender" from there to the ankles (I never put it on my feet) and, finally, "Rose" for my face and hands. It was the living end when, like some eccentric millionaire, I showed off the lotions I used every day, impressing them while I gave away a bunch of expensive perfume samples—I had such a good time I almost forgot the cheap, much-mended stockings I had on.

When some nice girl exclaimed, "You must be very rich!" I would hide my tacky shoes and coyly answer: "Oh, not really . . ." There were also mean ones who tried to upset me, calling me "Miss Heavenly" and pretending to gag and vomit when my implacable vapors overtook them: they swore it gave them headaches.

But aside from those unpleasant moments, I was happy in the forest of fragrances that was all mine, like my tresses and my tears.

Luckily my parents never worried about what became of those samples. If they ever gave some away to a friend, they had to put up with my disconsolate and hysterical crying because I felt that they were mine.

They never realized how important that colorful paradise was for me, to my soul lost in the solitary rapture of that enchanted basement.

SHOES FOR THE REST OF MY LIFE
Guadalupe Dueñas

TRANSLATED BY JOHN BENSON

E verything went sour the day my father went bankrupt in the shoe manufacturing business.

We could have gotten along fine somehow except for his brilliant idea of sorting out all the shoes by sizes and figuring out how many pair everyone in the family would need up till their dying day. Let's see, if I wore a size 19 when I was twelve, I would need 23's at twenty, and, after all was said and done, I would have enough shoes to last me forever.

The shoes for the rest of my life were boxed up in the corners of my room, piles of little coffins reaching up to the sky. I had plenty of time at night to feast my eyes on the bonds that would forever imprison my hapless feet.

Randomly I picked out a box, trying to avoid the collapse of my tower of Babel. And you can imagine my despair when I saw the curious sandals, hard as iron, invariably looking like women's shoes on a man and indubitably like men's shoes on women. Their abominable, iridescent color was the last straw. In another box I found some boots that might have aspired to goatskin but were actually made from canvas with rows of buttons on the sides, white with occasional black spots and miles of ribbon. There wasn't a single reasonable-looking pair—they were combat boots, iron-soled crypts for desperate feet.

I envied Indians and barefoot children, and dreamed of getting run over by a truck just so my father would have to atone for his sins. Luckily my feet weren't growing any and so I walked gingerly to make my red moccasins last.

Finishing off the pointy yellow shoes, all the sandals and funny little boots, tearing off the silk ribbons and ruining the finish in dirty water, mutilating straps and slippers, taking no hostages, leaving nary a pair to strangle my feet—this was the overriding obsession that dominated my life.

To carry out my plan I supplied myself with the right tools for the job: scissors, knives, sandpaper, a pumice stone and a couple of good spikes.

I went without sleep so I could continue wearing them out on both hands and feet in the hallways and the cobbled yard. I debuted a new pair twice a week. My friends were the beneficiaries of my largesse on their saint's day as well as on birthdays. I shod the local beggars. I often tried leaving one behind when visiting, but it didn't work: people kept returning the orphan shoe and I was punished for it. It was better just to forget about the newest ones that fit the children in the house.

I was so upset with the backstitched ones that a large number of them perished under the wheels of streetcars. I also collected bits of chewing gum from desks everywhere: it's very effective on satin and glossy finishes.

But it's getting to me. Sometimes I'll walk for miles harassing the tough, charmed leather that neither yields nor changes, suffering immutably under my corns and blisters. I have come up with new steps that wear them out twice as fast, but it's killing me. Their malignant tongues and fiery soles mock me. There's no end of it. I try

on six new pair a day and still only a few of the stacks have disappeared. The white boxes seem to band together as I writhe in agony.

It's hard sanding them down, hard jumping up and down trying
to break them. I crack my nails and bloody my fingers in this un-
equal combat. The smell of cowhide precedes me wherever I go; I
don't normally sweat much, but these instruments of torture could
wring it out of anyone. Every day they get more and more out of
date, it's embarassing. It would take seven lives to get through them
all. There's just no end to it.

Permissions